COMMUNITY
AND
NEIGHBOUR MEDIATION

Cavendish
Publishing
Limited

London • Sydney

COMMUNITY AND NEIGHBOUR MEDIATION

Edited by Marian Liebmann

Gavin R Beckett
May Curtis
Jim Dignan
John C Patrick
Marion Wells

Cavendish
Publishing
Limited

London • Sydney

First published in Great Britain 1998 by Cavendish Publishing Limited,
The Glass House, Wharton Street, London WC1X 9PX.
Telephone: 0171-278 8000 Facsimile: 0171-278 8080
e-mail: info@cavendishpublishing.com
Visit our Home Page on http://www.cavendishpublishing.com

Community and neighbour mediation
1. Dispute resolution (Law) – Great Britain
I. Liebmann, Marian II. McFarlane, Julie
344.1'079

1 85941 156 8

Printed and bound in Great Britain by
. Biddles Ltd, Guildford and King's Lynn

This book is dedicated to all mediators and especially the increasing company of volunteer mediators in the UK and worldwide

ACKNOWLEDGMENTS

We would like to acknowledge the help of MEDIATION UK staff and all those members and member services who have provided us with information and suggestions.

In addition we would like to acknowledge the support and help of the following individuals: Paul Clifford, Mike Coldham, Jeremy Hibbert, Jill Patrick, Vicky Preece and Angela Sorsby.

The contributors would like to thank Marian Liebmann for her efforts as editor and initiator of this project. She has played a major role in making this a coherent book. They also thank Gavin Beckett for his computer expertise in formatting the final manuscript.

CONTENTS

Contents

LIST OF FIGURES

CHAPTER ONE

INTRODUCTION

Marian Liebmann

This book is written from the UK perspective but most of the material will also be relevant elsewhere. Many of the ideas and practices grew from contact with American and Australian mediation services, were amended to suit UK circumstances, and are now being adopted and adapted by several European countries.

The writing of this book has been very much a team effort. It is not the usual edited volume in which the editor commissions related but separate pieces of work loosely bound together by a common theme. Rather it is a systematic and, we hope, coherent account of community and neighbour mediation in the UK. The main reason for including a team of writers is that all of us are too busy to complete such a large undertaking on our own; yet it has been crying out to be written for some years, as there is very little literature on the subject, despite the advanced state of much practice. The writing has benefited from the involvement of a group of people, as we have been able to allocate chapters to those with strengths and experience in particular areas.

The group of contributors came together through their membership of MEDIATION UK, the umbrella organisation for almost all community mediation services in the UK. Together they include experience of mediating neighbour disputes, training in mediation skills, management issues, research, standards and accreditation, and a national overview.[1]

To ensure the coherence of the whole book, we have held two meetings of the contributors. The first meeting laid out the scope of the book, the structure and the chapter titles. It also allocated chapter titles to group members. Then each chapter was also allocated a mentor, who acted as a reader and consultant to the author. This helped to ensure consistency and also helped those who, while extremely experienced in mediation matters, were less experienced in writing about it. Each writer also undertook to liaise with the author of the chapter before and the chapter after, to minimise overlaps and gaps. Finally, we agreed to circulate all our second drafts (after mentor comments on first drafts) to all members of the group for comments. This too highlighted overlaps and helped ensure coherence. This means that everyone has been involved in some way in every chapter, to the benefit of the whole project and of course the readers. Authors naturally retain their own styles of expression, and we hope this will add to the interest of the book.

---

1   See Appendix 1 for a list of community mediation services in the UK and Appendix 2 for information about MEDIATION UK.

This introductory chapter contains some basic definitions and an outline of legal remedies for neighbour disputes, with a few examples. It describes how a dispute can escalate, and looks at the different outcomes of legal remedies and mediation. The limitations of mediation are indicated, and the conflict resolution principles lying behind mediation are listed. The chapter finishes with an overview of the rest of the book.

SOME DEFINITIONS[2]

It may be helpful to include some definitions, as there is sometimes confusion over different terms.

Negotiation is a general term for the process of disputants working out an agreement between themselves.

Mediation is a process by which an impartial third party helps two (or more) disputants work out how to resolve a conflict. The disputants, not the mediators, decide the terms of any agreement reached. Mediation usually focuses on future rather than past behaviour.

Arbitration is a process in which an impartial third party makes a final, usually binding decision. The discussion and decision, whilst structured, may not be as regulated by formal procedures and rules of evidence as is courtroom procedure.

Litigation is the process of settling a dispute in court according to legal statutes, with advocates presenting evidence on behalf of the parties. Litigation is an adversarial process, in which a judge (or jury) adjudicates in favour of one party after hearing both sides.

In general these processes range from the least intervention (negotiation) to the most intervention (litigation). At either end are two other forms of dealing with conflict: avoidance as the very least interventionist and aggression as the most interventionist.[3]

---

2   These definitions are taken from the MEDIATION UK *Training Manual in Community Mediation Skills*, which in turn are based on other definitions in common usage in the field.

3   Moore, C, *The Mediation Process: Practical Strategies for Resolving Conflict*, 1986, San Francisco: Jossey Bass.

Least interventionist

Avoidance

Negotiation

Mediation

Arbitration

Litigation

Aggression

Most interventionist

Thus mediation is the least formal of the dispute resolution methods which involve a third party, and the intervention by the third party is limited, as the decision-making remains with the parties themselves.

Community/neighbour mediation

When people talk about community and neighbour mediation, for the most part this concerns disputes between neighbours, but it can also include other disputes such as wider community matters, or disputes between groups and organisations. It does not usually include commercial disputes or family disputes concerning divorce and separation of couples and the ensuing problems surrounding children, property and money. However, family disputes outside the divorce/separation arena may well come to community mediation services as the only 'generalist' mediation service; these may be family disputes such as those concerning parents and teenagers, or estrangement of family members after a particular incident.

LEGAL REMEDIES FOR NEIGHBOUR DISPUTES

Although this book concentrates on mediation, it is worth looking briefly at the legal remedies which are available, as they form the framework of adversarial options to which mediation provides an alternative.

Noise problems

These are mostly covered by the Environmental Protection Act 1990, as amended by the Noise and Statutory Nuisance Act 1993 and the Noise Act 1996 (England and Wales; similar legislation exists for Scotland and Northern Ireland). Under this legislation, statutory nuisance proceedings can be taken to deal with any matters which affect physical health or are a nuisance, in particular noise problems. The local council environmental health department has a statutory duty to investigate complaints about noise made to it, although the way it does this varies from area to area. The environmental health department determines whether the noise is a 'statutory nuisance' under the law; if so it can serve an 'abatement notice' on the neighbour, saying how the noise must be reduced. If the neighbour does not comply, the department can take proceedings in the magistrates' court (sheriff court in Scotland).

Neighbours themselves can complain directly to the magistrates' court (sheriff court in Scotland). To do this, they need to produce evidence, including a written record of dates, times and how long the noise lasted. Evidence from other neighbours can also be included. The magistrates' court will issue a summons to the noise maker with a date for a court hearing, to be attended by both parties. Neighbours can act for themselves or employ solicitors, but legal aid is not available. Free initial advice may be available for those on low incomes.

The magistrates' court can make an order for the noise to stop, and fine the noise maker up to £5,000, but usually the fine is much less. If the case is proved, then costs will also be awarded. Equipment can be seized in extreme cases. If the noise makers do not comply, they can eventually be sent to prison.

Alternatively, civil action can be taken to the county court, which can grant an injunction to stop the noise (an interdict in the sheriff court in Scotland). Neighbours have to pay their own costs in the county court, and things may take a long time.

If the noise from neighbours is a nuisance or a breach of the peace (noise that affects a whole neighbourhood) neighbours can contact the police.

The law covering noise nuisance is contained in s 82 of the Environmental Protection Act 1990 (England, Wales and Northern Ireland), s 59 of the Control of Pollution Act 1974 (Scotland), the Noise and Statutory Nuisance Act 1993 (England, Scotland and Wales) and the Noise Act 1996 (England, Wales and Northern Ireland).

Boundary and property disputes

Many problems involving boundaries and properties can be very difficult to solve, because there is little statutory law covering these issues. It is necessary to look at the title deeds of the property, and sometimes at local byelaws, and often neither of these have enough detail to settle a dispute.

If the position is not clear from the title deeds, the best way of solving the problem is through mediation.

The other avenue is to look at the title deeds, and contact the solicitor who did the original conveyancing, to clarify what is written in the deeds, the land certificate or replies to enquiries. A surveyor can sometimes help if the documents are not clear.

If all else fails, neighbours can take action through the county court, as described above. This may be expensive, take a long time and lead to worse relationships.

Overhanging trees

If a neighbour's tree or bush overhangs into the next garden, the law allows that neighbour to prune it back to the boundary. However, the branches still belong to the neighbour whose tree it is, so they should be offered back to them. Before taking any action, it is necessary to check with the local council, just in case there is a tree preservation order. It is also sensible to consult with neighbours first and try to reach an agreement before taking any action, whatever the legal position is.

Neighbours' extensions

If planning permission is not needed, then there are no legal provisions. If planning permission is needed, then the planning department of the local authority will be involved. Before granting planning permission, a local authority (or Department of the Environment inspector) must take into account neighbours' views, and those of a parish council where one exists. Among issues considered are the obstruction of light, and safety of vehicle access and parking.

Pets

Neighbours are expected to keep reasonable control over their pets. If a dog is dangerous, and a neighbour does not take reasonable steps to control it, a magistrates' court can (under the Dangerous Dogs Act 1991) order the dog to be kept on a lead, neutered or put down. The dog owner can be fined up to £2,000 and be disqualified from having a dog for a certain length of time. The local council dog warden is usually found in the Environmental Health Department, which also deals with issues of noise and smells of pets generally.

If a neighbour's pet damages someone else's property, and the neighbour refuses to pay for the damage, the neighbour can be sued for damages under the trespass laws.

Harassment or verbal abuse

If the harassment or verbal abuse is severe or threatening, the police can be involved. Many forms of harassment are criminal offences, such as assault, including pushing or throwing stones. The Public Order Act 1986 also made abusive or insulting behaviour a criminal offence, so that people can be arrested if they continue after a warning has been given. Sometimes such behaviour can also be judged a breach of the peace and offenders can be bound over to keep the peace for a specified length of time.

If the police decide not to act, a neighbour can take out a private prosecution in the magistrates' court; however, legal aid is not available and cases may be difficult to prove.

The housing department, under the Housing Act 1985, can evict council tenants who are causing nuisance to their neighbours. This is called a possession action by the housing department. The powers of local authority housing officers have been considerably strengthened as a result of the Housing Act 1996.[4]

Another way of dealing with this situation, in the case of local authority or housing association tenants, is by writing conditions into tenancy agreements. These conditions can forbid certain types of behaviour, and if these conditions are breached, then possession can be sought.

Racial harassment

This is illegal, and can be prosecuted by the police. The Race Relations Act 1976 empowers police and housing departments to take action, and both have been using these powers more in recent years. Some cases are also handled by local racial equality councils.

Many housing departments and social landlords are reluctant to bring prosecution actions for eviction for several reasons:

- There may be budgetary constraints on legal sections of local authorities.
- There may be a lack of legal expertise in smaller housing associations.
- The publicity from an unsuccessful case can be damaging.
- It is often difficult to prove the nuisance in a formal manner.
- Some district judges are unsympathetic to possession actions.
- Fear of reprisals may result in witnesses being unwilling to give evidence.
- Witnesses may need help in getting to court.

---

4   See Dignan, J, Sorsby, A and Hibbert, J, *Neighbour Disputes: Comparing the Cost-effectiveness of Mediation and Alternative Approaches*, 1996, Sheffield: University of Sheffield, pp 17–19.

- Many courts award suspended possession orders, which are less effective.
- Often the problem is merely pushed to another address.

Some local authorities are trying out injunctions, which prohibit a particular activity and empower someone to take action, for example to avoid a nuisance being caused. Some housing organisations have started to use injunctions to tackle noise, harassment, abuse, threatening behaviour, violence and vandalism. Failure to comply with an injunction is contempt of court, and this can be punished by a fine or a prison sentence.

Injunctions are useful for housing management staff because they can be obtained quickly (within 24 hours if need be). The aim of an injunction is to change behaviour, and if this is successful, there is no need to go on to a possession action.[5]

SOME EXAMPLES

Legal remedies have become very expensive in both time and money,[6] and there are many stories of neighbour disputes which have cost thousands of pounds. These cases often reach the newspapers, and the following cases are a selection from the last year.[7]

One case led to legal costs of £50,000 as two neighbours had rows over the height of trees in one of the gardens.[8]

In another case a 73-year-old woman was evicted from her flat which she had occupied for nearly 40 years, because of debts of over one million pounds incurred through legal action she had taken against residents of other flats in the house.[9]

A case which ran on for 12 years started in 1984, when the miners strike led to two previously friendly neighbours, a miner and a policeman, falling out. The dispute escalated into a series of claims and counterclaims which eventually reached the local county court. Most of the claims were dismissed by the judge, who awarded each party £75 against the other. However, the costs of the case ran to a five-figure sum – and these were met by the public purse since both parties were on legal aid.[10]

---

5   Karn, V, Lickiss, R, Hughes, D and Crawley, J, *Neighbour Disputes – Responses by Social Landlords*, 1993, Coventry: Institute of Housing.
6   See Dignan *et al*, *op cit*.
7   Further examples are given in Dignan *et al*, *op cit*, Chapter 5.
8   'Mediators cut cost of conciliation', *Sunday Times*, 25 February 1996.
9   *Guardian*, 8 May 1996 and 'Love thy neighbours', *HomeStyle*, November 1996.
10   *The Times*, 4 June 1996.

Councils say the average cost of transferring a tenant is £823 and of evicting one is £3,907; mediation is much cheaper than this,[11] usually £250 to £300.[12]

Several people have even died from neighbour disputes, as the next two examples illustrate. An argument over a barking dog led to a neighbour killing the dog's owner with a crowbar. He was jailed for life.[13] After two years of feuding over late-night parties, a man committed suicide as he 'couldn't stand it any longer'.[14]

Although many of these disputes were obviously particularly intractable, all of them must have started in a small way at some point, and some of them may well have been sorted out better through mediation.

HOW A DISPUTE ESCALATES

A typical neighbour dispute might arise over the issue of noise. The neighbour might start by contacting the other party to complain about the sound of their CD system. If that does not solve the problem, they will then contact their landlord. If the landlord does nothing, the neighbour might then try the Environmental Health Department, the police, the council, the Citizens' Advice Bureau and anyone else they can think of who might be able to help. Often the Environmental Health Department suggests keeping a 'noise diary', which means listening out for any sounds over a period of some weeks – a process which can further polarise matters through encouraging people actively to look for faults. Even after this it may turn out that the noise is below a level which can be prosecuted, or the Environmental Health Department cannot catch the 'offenders' while they are committing the alleged nuisance.

When all these avenues have been exhausted without result, the neighbour might decide to take the matter to court. By this time, the dispute will probably have been going on for many months (in some cases, years), and what started out as a disagreement over noise may well have mushroomed into a conflict including a catalogue of incidents, allegations, frustrations and grievances on both sides. Both parties will by now have probably lost sight of the original problem, and only see each other as the problem in a personal vendetta.

When the neighbour takes the case to court, they will be armed with diaries and records documenting the disturbance, and an injunction may be

---

11 'A friendly chat stops a rowdy neighbour', *Daily Telegraph*, 3 December 1996.
12 Dignan *et al*, *op cit*, p 76.
13 *The Times*, 20 March 1996.
14 'Turn it down', *Saturday Telegraph*, 20 January 1996.

granted ordering the second party to stop playing their music. However, this does not necessarily mean that the neighbour will stop. They might feel aggrieved by the decision and now choose to play their music louder or later at night. They may even take the matter into their own hands and resort to violence.

Many people think that going to court is the only option available to them to get what they want, and they can be very disappointed with the outcome.

MEDIATION AND LEGAL REMEDIES

Legal remedies may be useful for persistent and identified offenders, where there seems to be a general consensus that the behaviour of one neighbour is at fault. Where the dispute has two sides to it, legal remedies may actually make matters worse, in further polarising and escalating the dispute. It may be worth trying mediation even when legal remedies are in process, as there is some evidence that, when people realise how onerous the legal process is, they may be prepared to think again.[15]

The court process is an adversarial one, so that even when a neighbour wins a court case against another neighbour, the resentment built up does nothing for neighbourly relations, and in many cases makes things worse. Sometimes disputes have gone to court, neighbours have been fined or put in prison, and still the dispute carries on. Mediation has been able to help in some of these disputes.

WHY DOES MEDIATION WORK?

- Instead of polarising parties into two enemy camps, it encourages them to focus on the problem between them rather than on each other. Instead of taking up positions, parties are encouraged to look at their needs and feelings in a particular situation. Mediators do not have to spend time looking at flaws in the argument of the other side but instead focus on common ground between the disputants and the way forward. It gives both parties an opportunity to tell their version of events fully and to hear what the other party has to say. There are always two sides to the story and both sides may have legitimate concerns and grievances.

- People are more likely to change their actions if they hear how their behaviour is affecting the other person than if they are told not to do something.

---

15 Faulkes, W, *Mediation as a Crime Prevention Strategy*, conference paper, 1991, Bristol: MEDIATION UK.

- People are more likely to keep to a solution they have been involved in than one imposed by an outside person. A solution imposed by the court generally makes one party a winner and the other party a loser. Mediators believe in the idea that both sides can win – that there is likely to be a solution that will meet most of the needs of both sides involved.

- People are able to reach agreements appropriate to their particular situation; their needs might be quite different from the requirements of others with a similar type of dispute.

- Mediators ask people what they want. In many cases they simply want an apology from the other person for the distress they have caused, but once they have taken the matter to a solicitor they find themselves on a rollercoaster ride they cannot stop.

- Mediation is a confidential process – this enables people to say whatever they want without the fear that it will be taken down and used in evidence against them. The Court of Appeal decided that admissions or conciliatory gestures made during mediation are not admissible if the mediation is unsuccessful and comes to court, except in the rare case where someone indicated that he had caused, or was likely the cause of, severe harm to a child (*Re D (Minors)*, Court of Appeal, 11 February 1993).[16] This confidentiality allows people to express their emotions and also provides a safe place for people to vent their anger.

- Mediation is more likely to get to the root of the problem, particularly in neighbour disputes – quite often one incident may have been the cause of a long-running neighbour dispute. The resolution of the conflict often depends on finding out the real cause, which may be lost in the involved legal history of the case. Cases which have been thrown out of court, when it was deemed that the dispute was caused by 'six of one and half a dozen of the other', have then successfully been solved by mediation.

- Disputes have many strands or aspects to them – however the courts can only deal with matters of law, which means in many cases they cannot deal with the whole picture.

- Although mediation looks at the past, its focus is on the future – how do the parties want the situation to be from now on? This is important because usually, after neighbours have taken each other to court, they have to go back home to carry on living next door to each other.

---

16 *Re D (Minors)* [1993] TLR 12 February.

LIMITATIONS OF MEDIATION

It is important to know when mediation is appropriate and when it is not. There are several indications which may help to determine this.[17]

Mediation can help when:
- The law is not clear.
- Both parties want to keep on good terms with each other.
- It is in both parties' interests to sort things out.
- Both parties are tired of the dispute.
- There is goodwill on both sides.

Mediation is not appropriate if:
- Either party is unwilling.
- It is not really in one party's interest to settle.
- There are threats or fear of violence, and police action may be indicated.
- The dispute needs a public judgment.

This is dealt with in more detail in Chapter 8.

CONFLICT RESOLUTION PRINCIPLES

Implicit in mediation work are a set of ideas and values, which emphasise such concepts as:[18]
- listening to others, for feelings as well as facts;
- co-operation with others, valuing their contributions;
- looking for common ground rather than for differences;
- affirmation of self and others as a necessary basis for resolving conflict;
- speaking for oneself rather than accusing others;
- separating the problem from the people;
- trying to understand other people's points of view;
- using a creative problem-solving approach to work on conflicts;
- looking at what people want for the future rather than allocating blame for the past;

---

17 Liebmann, M, *Neighbours' Quarrels*, 1994, London: Channel 4 Television, and Acland, A, *Resolving Disputes Without Going to Court*, 1995, London: Century.

18 Cornelius, C and Faire, S, *Everyone Can Win*, 1989, New York and Sydney: Simon and Schuster, also Liebmann, *op cit*, 1994 and Liebmann, M, *Arts Approaches to Conflict*, 1996, London: Jessica Kingsley Publishers.

- looking at all the options before selecting one to try;
- looking for a 'win/win' solution, where everyone's interests are satisfied, rather than the adversarial 'win/lose' approach where one person wins and the other person loses.

OVERVIEW OF CHAPTERS

This section gives an overview of the themes dealt with by each chapter.

Chapter 2 – The history of community mediation in the UK (Marian Liebmann)

This chapter looks at the early beginnings of mediation in the UK in the early 1980s, especially the early community mediation services. Two philosophies of community mediation emerge – the 'grass-roots' community-based and the more agency-led outcome-focused practice – and these continue to inform later developments. The national organisation MEDIATION UK was formed, acting as a catalyst for a rapid expansion of community mediation. Other factors leading to this expansion are also explored. There is a brief account of the parallel developments of other kinds of mediation in the UK – industrial, family, schools, victim/offender, commercial, medical, environmental, elder and organisational mediation.

Chapter 3 – The mediation process (John Patrick)

This chapter looks at the mediation process in seven stages:

(1) Initial contact with the first party.
(2) Initial contact with the second party.
(3) Preparing to work on the dispute.
(4) Setting the scene – hearing the issues.
(5) Exploring the issues.
(6) Building agreements.
(7) Closure and follow-up.

The chapter also looks at the issues of co-mediating, shuttle mediation, the use of caucuses, multi-party disputes, the attendance of non-disputants and other influences on the parties.

Chapter 4 – Models for delivering mediation (Marian Liebmann)

This chapter looks at different models for delivering mediation, under six headings:

(1) Different organisational structures:
  (a) training existing staff to be specialists in mediation;
  (b) using freelance mediators;
  (c) in-house mediation service;
  (d) independent community mediation service (including how to set one up);
  (e) community mediation service as a base to develop further services.

(2) How a community mediation service is funded.

(3) Use of paid staff/volunteers and their roles.

(4) Referrals, cases and record-keeping.

(5) Geographical situation.

(6) Philosophy and ethos.

An appendix gives a questionnaire which attempts to gather a nationwide picture of community mediation, with a look at the issue of how to measure 'success'.

Chapter 5 – Growth and development of a service (Marion Wells)

This chapter charts the growth and development of a community mediation service based in a large city. It describes the beginnings from a small group of people to a steering committee to achievement of funding and establishment of the mediation service. It then goes on to give an outline of the service five years on (winter 1996/97), with 50 volunteer mediators and six paid staff, covering schools as well as neighbour mediation, and providing training to many other groups as well as its own volunteer mediators. There is a description of a day in the life of the intake worker and a mediation story. It also includes notes on staff and volunteer issues, management committee roles, communication (internal and external), policy making, funding, and monitoring and evaluation – all from the point of view of this particular service.

Chapter 6 – Mediators: recruitment, selection, training and support (Gavin Beckett and Marion Wells)

This chapter looks at the whole process of working with volunteer mediators, from recruitment to selection, then training and ongoing support. It includes an outline of the core content of a typical mediation skills training course, with examples of exercises; and notes on training methods, style, expectations and objectives. It ends with a section on the support and supervision of mediators, including an overview of different models for supervision.

Chapter 7 – Dispute analysis (Gavin Beckett)

This chapter looks at the causes and characteristics of neighbour disputes, and at a way of mapping conflicts, based on an analytical framework developed by Paul Wehr. This includes conflict history, conflict context, primary and secondary parties to the conflict, different kinds of conflict issues (based on facts, values, interests or relationships), dynamics of a conflict (precipitating events, stage of intervention, polarisation, spiralling, stereotyping) and alternative routes to solutions. Awareness of the structural and psychological aspects of conflict can help mediation services to select disputes more effectively.

Chapter 8 – Selecting disputes (John Patrick)

This chapter looks at the way community mediation services 'select out' those cases which are not suitable for mediation. As the selection process continues throughout the work with each case, the chapter looks at the decision-making at the different stages of the mediation process, concentrating on how the service should proceed, and drawing out general principles. The chapter covers referrals, work with referrers, the assessment process, limiting factors and assessing suitability for mediation. The latter considers three interlinking areas: (i) the attitude of each party; (ii) the relationship between the parties; (iii) the nature of the conflict. Work with one party is considered briefly. Selection and effectiveness are discussed with reference to six categories of dispute.

Chapter 9 – Case studies (compiled by Marian Liebmann from contributions from five of the authors and elsewhere)

This chapter consists of case studies from a wide range of community mediation services, structured in order of the mediation process:

- Cases where mediation was not tried, but where it might have been useful.
- Cases where mediation was tried but no way forward was found.
- Cases where the parties resolved the matter without mediators.
- Cases involving shuttle mediation.
- Cases involving face-to-face meetings between parties.
- Cases involving multi-party mediations.

Chapter 10 – Equal opportunities and anti-discriminatory practice (John Patrick)

This chapter starts by emphasising the importance of this topic for community mediation services, both to comply with legislation and to recognise the multicultural nature of British society. It covers accessibility to the whole community (eg premises; use of interpreters), recruitment of volunteers and staff, awareness of bias and stereotyping, and the nature and effects of oppression. It also looks at the role of power in the mediation process, and the need to balance power in mediation, and finishes with comments on mediation and culture.

Chapter 11 – Standards and accreditation (May Curtis)

This chapter first emphasises the importance of finding ways of ensuring high standards of mediation, and outlines MEDIATION UK's development of practice standards and creation of an ongoing accreditation committee with six key principles to guide it. There are four elements requiring accreditation:

(1) services;

(2) mediators;

(3) training programmes;

(4) mediation trainers.

The established MEDIATION UK accreditation scheme for community mediation services in the UK is described. Accreditation of mediators is discussed, with reference to National Vocational Qualifications. The next section focuses on the endorsement and accreditation of training programmes in mediation skills, including reference to the MEDIATION UK *Handbook for the Training Programme in Community Mediation Skills* and its endorsement by the National Open College Network. The last section discusses the steps MEDIATION UK is taking to work towards accrediting trainers. The chapter finishes with quotations from services for and against accreditation in the field of community mediation.

Chapter 12 – Evaluating community and neighbour mediation (Jim Dignan)

This chapter starts with a definition of evaluation research and three possible types: programme effectiveness analysis; comparative impact analysis; and cost-benefit analysis. It gives the history of evaluation research in the field of community mediation, and then describes the aims and approach of the Neighbour Dispute project, a research project which compared the cost-effectiveness of mediation and alternative measures. An evaluative framework is outlined and the findings of the project examined in terms of four sets of criteria:

(1) access to justice issues;

(2) quality of process issues;

(3) quality of outcome issues;

(4) value-for-money issues.

The chapter concludes by summarising what evaluation research can offer in the field of community and neighbour mediation.

Chapter 13 – Theory and ethics in community mediation (Gavin Beckett)

This chapter looks at the values, assumptions and beliefs that lie behind the practice of mediation. It looks at recent work by Robert Baruch Bush and Joseph Folger on the tension between achieving settlements and helping parties achieve understanding. It examines some criticisms of ADR by Joseph Scimecca in the USA. It goes on to discuss contingency (the idea that the method of intervention depends on the circumstances of the conflict) and complementarity (the idea that several different methods may be needed for different aspects of a conflict) in social conflicts. The chapter concludes by looking at the positive values which guide mediators in their practice.

Chapter 14 – Looking forward (Marian Liebmann)

This chapter looks at current developments in community mediation in the UK and Europe, and some of the discussions and debates which may shape the future of community mediation.

CHAPTER TWO

THE HISTORY OF COMMUNITY MEDIATION IN THE UK

Marian Liebmann

EARLY BEGINNINGS

Although mediation is a traditional method of resolving conflict and practised widely in Asia and Africa, the influences on mediation in the UK came mainly from North America and Australia. In the early 1980s, several well-known leaders in mediation and conflict resolution from the USA and Australia came to the UK and spoke to a variety of audiences.

Wendy Faulkes came from Australia in 1983 to gather ideas, and brought news of the Community Justice Centres in New South Wales, which pioneered a legislative basis for community mediation. David Forrest came from the Institute for Mediation and Conflict Resolution (IMCR) in New York, and Dean Peachey from Community Justice Initiatives, Kitchener, Ontario. American Quakers came from the Community Dispute Settlement Program started in 1976 by the Friends Suburban Project, Philadelphia – my initiation into mediation was one of their courses in London in 1984. For several years, their *Mediator's Handbook – Peacemaking in your Neighborhood* was the only training manual available in the UK.[1]

These meetings and contacts spread information about what was happening, and at the same time brought together those in the UK who were interested in pursuing mediation, both in the community/neighbour context, and with victims and offenders in the criminal justice context.

Many of the early meetings were held at the City University, London, in the Department of Systems Science, in conjunction with the Conflict Research Society, which wanted to collaborate in setting up a university-based Conflict Conciliation and Mediation Service. One of the prime movers of this venture and mediation in general was Dr Chris Mitchell, now Cumbie Professor of Conflict Resolution on the Teaching Faculty of the Institute for Conflict Analysis and Resolution (ICAR) at George Mason University, Fairfax, Virginia, USA.[2] In 1982 he wrote: 'One aim for CCAMS should be to *prepare for its own obsolescence* by establishing trained and active personnel for grass-roots, local and regional mediation.'[3]

---

1   MEDIATION UK, 'Mediation takes a FIRM hold: The first ten years of MEDIATION UK' (1995), Bristol: MEDIATION UK. The *Mediator's Handbook* has been updated in 1997 and is available from New Society Publishers in the USA and Jon Carpenter Publishing in the UK.

2   ICAR leaflet 1997.

3   MEDIATION UK, 'Mediation takes a FIRM hold', *op cit.*

The first main interest in the UK was in victim/offender mediation and reparation, in which victims and offenders meet to discuss the crime and to work out how the offender can make amends. This interest led indirectly to the first victim support group, when members of BACRO (Bristol Association for the Care and Resettlement of Offenders) considered victim/offender mediation in 1972 – and then realised they knew nothing about victims of crime and their perspective. They therefore started a pilot victim support group in Bristol, which raised awareness of victims' needs and led to many other similar schemes and the formation of the National Association of Victims Support Schemes in 1979.[4]

The National Association of Victims Support Schemes (NAVSS, now called Victim Support) was approached by many enquirers (from agencies interested in starting mediation or reparation projects) who confused victim/offender mediation with victim support. To save time in passing on information, NAVSS set up a working party in 1980 and produced 'A First Survey of British Developments in Reparation and Mediation' in 1981.[5] In the same year, NAVSS also held a conference on reparation, and in 1982 it published a leaflet 'Establishing a Local Mediation Centre'.[6] From 1981, meetings were arranged at six-monthly intervals for all those interested. These informal meetings led to the establishment of the Forum for Initiatives in Reparation and Mediation (FIRM) in 1984.[7]

NAVSS decided to distance itself from the mediation and reparation movement, in order to prevent confusion, safeguard the identity of Victim Support and to establish a service for victims of crime in their own right. Nevertheless, it offered its Brixton base as a venue for FIRM committee meetings for several years to come.

A victim/offender mediation project was established in South Yorkshire in 1983, and four services were funded and researched by the Home Office between 1985 and 1987.[8] The Home Office took a great interest in the growing number of mediation schemes in the early 1980s, mainly with a view to diverting offenders from prison, which was beginning to be seen as an expensive and ineffective response to crime. As part of this interest, a senior Home Office researcher, Tony Marshall, undertook to update the NAVSS survey. This survey, published in 1984,[9] showed that 25 schemes were active:

---

4   Victim Support, 'Victim Support, the first ten years' (1982), London: Victim Support.

5   Reeves, H, 'Mediation from a Victim Support Perspective' (1987), London: Victim Support.

6   Victim Support, 'Establishing a Local Mediation Centre' (1982), London: Victim Support.

7   Reeves, *op cit*.

8   Marshall, T, and Merry, S, *Crime and Accountability*, 1990, London: HMSO.

9   Marshall, T, *Reparation, Conciliation and Mediation*, Home Office Research and Planning Unit, Paper 27, 1984, London: HMSO.

- two community mediation;
- five police-based reparation;
- three court-based reparation;
- nine victim-assistance repair schemes;
- four fundraising schemes (eg offenders making things to sell in aid of victims);
- two encounter groups (groups of victims and offenders meeting, not based on the same crime).

This list shows that 23 out of 25 schemes were concerned with reparation by offenders or victim/offender issues. Only two were community mediation schemes, Newham Conflict and Change Project and Edgware Mediation Service. At that time, mediation was virtually synonymous with victim/offender mediation.

Things were changing so fast that the list of projects became out of date very quickly, and the Home Office published a new version only a year later.[10] In 1985, the balance had changed slightly and there were seven community mediation services out of a total of 38 mediation schemes, in the following areas:

- Newham Conflict and Change Project, London;
- Stoke Newington Reconciliation Unit, London;
- Sandwell Mediation and Reparation Scheme, West Midlands (undertaking both community and victim/offender mediation);
- Bromley Dispute Settlement Centre, Kent;
- Southwark Mediation Centre, London;
- Extern Reparation Scheme, Northern Ireland (undertaking both community and victim/offender mediation);
- Reading Mediation Centre.

These surveys and their publication performed a very valuable service in spreading ideas and information – so that, for instance, when I was undertaking the background research needed to set up a community mediation service in Bristol in 1987, I was able to contact and visit five out of the seven schemes above.

---

10 Marshall, T, and Walpole, M, *Bringing People Together: Mediation and Reparation Projects in Great Britain*, Home Office Research and Planning Unit, Paper 33, 1985, London: HMSO.

EARLY COMMUNITY MEDIATION SERVICES

Most of the early mediation services were largely dependent on visions of particular people or groups, including professionals from probation and psychology, and religious groups such as Anglican clergy and Quaker meetings.

Newham Conflict and Change Project

The first community mediation service was Newham Conflict and Change Project. It was initiated by two ministers with parishes in Newham, arising out of their concern at the level of conflict they witnessed, particularly interracial tension. They had heard of community mediation growing in the USA, in particular the work of the IMCR in New York, and saw possibilities for similar work in Newham. However, they felt that American models could not necessarily be imported directly into a very different cultural context. They approached the Tavistock Institute of Human Relations, London, for advice and support in establishing the project, and two consultants worked with them. One of the main aims established was an educational one: to explore and understand the nature of conflict and change as experienced by residents in Newham. The conciliation service for actual disputes was seen as secondary to the main aim of understanding conflict.[11]

The main training for the volunteers in the conciliation service, and for the members of the project in general, was based on the Tavistock Group Relations Programme, consisting of an intensive residential event aimed at helping participants to reflect on their own experiences of conflict in that setting. Volunteers then took these reflections with them into their work helping to sort out community disputes. As time went on, support groups were organised for the volunteers to discuss cases and difficulties as they arose. It was not felt relevant to carry out structured skills training.

The Newham Project developed three strands to its work. The first was its general educational role, which included the annual residential event, and also outreach into many parts of the community – schools, police, women's groups, faith groups and so on. The second part was the conciliation work between neighbours in dispute, already mentioned. The third part was consultancy work with other organisations experiencing difficulties.[12]

As part of its educational role in helping the local community to understand conflict and societal changes, the project worked hard at attracting as members and volunteers a representative cross-section of the people of

---

11 OPUS, *Newham Conflict & Change Project, Evaluation Report*, 1989, London: OPUS (An Organisation for Promoting Understanding in Society).

12 *Ibid.*

Newham, to achieve a multiracial and multicultural ethos. This was not without its tensions, but the project has gained much respect over the years for its pioneering work in this direction.

Southwark Mediation Centre

The original impetus for the Southwark Mediation Centre arose from a conference in January 1984 at City University, addressed by members of the IMCR, New York. Two of the participants were an Anglican clergyman and a police committee member, both very concerned about the community in Southwark, where they worked. They saw the potential for mediation and called a meeting of interested local people in Southwark. An interim management committee came together and applied for a grant from the Greater London Council. They received a grant in March 1985 and appointed a co-ordinator in August 1985.[13]

The management committee wanted to establish a clearly defined base, and after many visits by the co-ordinator, a particular area was chosen for the initial focus. From an early stage, a commitment to face-to-face mediation emerged, drawing on the work of the IMCR in New York, and also the Family Conciliation Bureau in Bromley. In 1986, 11 volunteers started a structured training course of 10 evening sessions and one Saturday session. In 1987 the Centre expanded its catchment area to include the whole of Southwark and during the three years to December 1989, it received 583 enquiries.

Evaluation reports on Newham and Southwark

One source of funding for both these innovative projects was the City Parochial Foundation. In 1987, as a condition of making its grants, it requested (and funded) an evaluation of both projects. The Newham study was carried out by OPUS (an Organisation for Promoting Understanding in Society) and the Southwark study was carried out by the Grubb Institute.[14]

The studies were very different, in keeping with the different nature of the projects. The Newham study focused on the way the three aspects of the projects work interlinked, whereas the Southwark study focused more directly on the outcomes of the mediations, and the way they were organised.

One of the obvious measures of success for a project committed to face-to-face mediation was the number of agreements reached. Of 25 face-to-face mediations, 23 reached agreements, of which 18 were kept, either wholly (10)

---

13 Quine, C, Hutton, J and Reed, B, *Community Mediation of Disputes between Neighbours* (Report of an Evaluation Study on the work of Southwark Mediation Centre 1987–89), 1990, London: The Grubb Institute.

14 These have already been referred to in footnotes 11 and 13.

or in part (eight). Another way of measuring success was to look at how far relationships changed for the better. Out of the 25 mediations, 15 (60%) led to a transformation of the dispute with improved relationships, three resulted in an agreement but no change in relationships, and in seven cases neither happened.[15]

Despite the very different ethos of the two projects, there were many similarities between the schemes, concerning the nature of the disputes handled, the issues concerning volunteers, and the progression of cases. Both contributed greatly to the early stages of the community mediation movement, and have continued to do so.

Sandwell Mediation and Reparation Scheme

This is one of the early mediation services, and started in early 1985 after a successful application for Urban Aid funding by the West Midlands Probation Service and NACRO (National Association for the Care and Resettlement of Offenders). From the beginning it had two aspects:

1   mediating neighbour disputes; and

2   facilitating mediation and reparation between victims and offenders, with greater emphasis on the community aspect.

This emphasis was the reason for the West Midlands Probation Service's withdrawal in 1988 at the end of the funding period and pilot study.[16]

After an open meeting, a multi-agency committee was formed and a successful application made to the local authority for funding. Sandwell Mediation Scheme (now Sandwell Mediation Service) worked under the umbrella of Sandwell Council for Voluntary Service for two years before becoming an independent registered charity.[17]

During its pilot phase, Sandwell Mediation Scheme was also mentioned in one of the few pieces of research on neighbour disputes.[18] This report noted the success of the Sandwell scheme, in receiving 26 referrals during its first three months, of which nine resulted in an agreement, and recommended its approach as one of the main ways forward. Interestingly, even at that stage, the report suggested a strong community base, using trained volunteers, and independence from the housing department, to engender trust and preserve confidentiality.

---

15   Quine, Hutton and Reed, *op cit*.

16   Marshall and Walpole, *op cit* and Sandwell Mediation Service, 'Sandwell Mediation Service – The History' (1996), Sandwell: Sandwell Mediation Service.

17   Sandwell Mediation Service, *op cit*.

18   Tebay, S, Cumberbatch, G and Graham, N, 'Disputes between Neighbours' (1986), Birmingham: Aston University.

In 1990 Sandwell Mediation Scheme moved into joint accommodation with Sandwell Victim Support Scheme and developed close co-operation. In 1992 the West Midlands Probation Service seconded a probation officer to help develop victim/ offender mediation once more.

Although initially Sandwell Mediation Scheme trained volunteer mediators in the same way as the other schemes, for much of the service's existence most of the mediation has been carried out by the co-ordinator and, more recently, paid sessional mediators. Sandwell Mediation Scheme also managed to attract substantial local authority funding at an early stage, and this has contributed to its stability.

Mediation schemes which did not survive

Some early mediation schemes did not survive. Edgware Mediation Service, started by members of the Society of Friends, trained several volunteers over a whole year, using materials from American Quaker mediation projects.[19] However, they did not manage to attract enough referrals or funding to provide a public service, and so did not feature in the list of projects in 1985.[20]

Stoke Newington Reconciliation Unit began in January 1985, initiated by a Methodist minister, and aimed to facilitate 'reconciliation' of disputes and general conflict in the community, especially in terms of race relations.[21] It never acquired enough funds to survive.

The Extern Scheme in Northern Ireland never developed into the intended fully fledged community and victim/offender mediation service, as funding difficulties in 1985 changed the situation and many projects had to be shelved.[22] Meanwhile the Mediation Network for Northern Ireland started in 1986 as a 'network for people engaged in mediation/conflict resolution work', and this organisation later began to provide mediation.[23]

However, given the lack of awareness about mediation, a surprising number of the early community mediation services remained in existence (even if they experienced 'low' patches) and are still in operation. Among these are Bromley Dispute Settlement Centre (based on the local Citizens Advice Bureau) and Reading Mediation Centre (another group initiated by local Quakers), which both started in 1986.

---

19   Marshall, *op cit.*

20   Marshall and Walpole, *op cit.*

21   *Ibid.*

22   Conversation with Nigel Trainer, Extern, 17 April 1997.

23   MEDIATION UK, *Directory of Mediation & Conflict Resolution Services*, 1994 and 1996, Bristol: MEDIATION UK.

Philosophies of community mediation

From the early days, there were two strands of thinking which informed the community mediation movement. The first of these was the 'grass-roots' aim of providing self-help schemes for people to sort out their own problems rather than have them escalate into the hands of the law. This philosophy emphasises informality, volunteer help, benefits to the community as a whole, and community-based independent management of mediation services.

The second strand is more 'agency-led', a response by local authorities, Citizens Advice Bureaux and other statutory organisations to the ineffectiveness and expense of legal solutions to neighbour and community disputes. Moreover, if they provide the funding for the local mediation service, they want to see a degree of effectiveness in their terms. This philosophy emphasises clear procedures, a degree of formality and measurable outcomes.

These two strands are still present in the discussions and dilemmas facing mediation services today. They will be considered further in Chapter 4.

Other kinds of mediation

Parallel to these developments were similar initiatives in other fields of mediation, such as family mediation, with similar networks of mediation services and experienced people; 20 local services came together to form the National Family Conciliation Council in 1981. In addition, the Advisory, Conciliation and Arbitration Service (ACAS) had been set up by the government in 1974 to help resolve conflict between employers and employees. ACAS had become well-known for its pioneering work, and was involved in discussions with many of the new initiatives in the field of family and community mediation. The first conflict resolution work in schools started in 1981. Commercial mediation, medical mediation and environmental mediation started a few years later, in the late 1980s or 1990. These are described in a little more detail later in this chapter.

THE CREATION OF A NATIONAL ORGANISATION

From 1983, NAVSS held meetings of the Reparation Forum, an informal group of probation officers, academics and victim support workers. The name Forum for Initiatives in Reparation and Mediation (FIRM) was adopted.

At about the same time, Tony Marshall of the Home Office Research and Planning Unit undertook two surveys of projects, including both victim/offender and community mediation projects resulting in the directories *Reparation, Conciliation and Mediation* (1984) and *Bringing People*

Together (1985),[24] including both victim/offender and community mediation projects. A magazine/newsletter was started, edited by Yvonne Craig, who remained the editor until 1992.

Initial discussions centred around whether the group should cover mediation, reparation, or both. By 1986, its constitutional aims included providing a focal point for mediation initiatives, and also promoting the provision of new services. After considerable fundraising efforts from charities (mainly large Quaker charitable trusts with an interest in peace-making activities), a national office was started in Beaconsfield. Tony Marshall was seconded for two years from 1988–90 from the Home Office as the first director. Further fundraising led to the organisation financing its own director in 1990.[25]

Although the roots of FIRM were in victim/offender work, there was growing interest in neighbour mediation, and this found its expression in the increasing number of community mediation services.[26] Tony Marshall updated the list of services in 1989, as a FIRM publication.[27] This directory showed the following:

Fifteen victim/offender mediation services (14 operational, 1 planned).

Fifteen community mediation services (8 operational, 7 planned).

Eight schools conflict resolution services.

One commercial mediation service.

Six other services (youth work, racism, cross-cultural, etc).

This shows the balance of interest beginning to shift towards community mediation, with schools work also attracting more attention.

In 1991 FIRM changed its name to MEDIATION UK, to describe itself more simply and to reflect its purpose more clearly.

MEDIATION UK's aims are:[28]

- bringing conflict resolution skills to every individual as part of his or her basic education for citizenship in democracy;

- helping individuals and organisations of all kinds to identify methods for working through conflicts towards beneficial change and progress;

- identifying and promoting policies that will create a climate in which successful conflict resolution can be practised;

- building up resources to provide skilled third party intervention in current and potential conflicts.

24 See footnotes 9 and 10.

25 MEDIATION UK (1995), *op cit.*

26 *Ibid.*

27 Forum for Initiatives in Reparation and Mediation (FIRM), *Directory of Mediation Projects and Conflict Resolution Services*, 1989, Beaconsfield: FIRM.

28 MEDIATION UK information leaflet.

MEDIATION UK activities include the following:[29]

- putting people in touch with others who are interested in mediation;
- helping people find out if there is anyone else in their area interested in setting up a community mediation service;
- putting people in touch with experienced trainers and mediators;
- helping people with general queries about neighbour problems;
- assisting with setting up new services;
- providing support and access to documents for research;
- keeping people in touch with training and development opportunities and news from the field through *MEDIATION* and *MEDNews* – MEDIATION UK's regular publications for members;
- helping promote and build the image of mediation across the UK and internationally, by providing information to be used by the media, giving talks and writing articles;
- helping to achieve high standards in any field of work associated with conflict resolution.

MEDIATION UK's work also includes:

- organising events including an annual national conference, and briefings for MPs, the press etc;
- liaising with government departments and local authorities on developing policies and procedures associated with conflict resolution in practice;
- developing working groups to take forward particular aspects of mediation, and create effective strategies for the future;
- facilitating the development of regional and interest-based networks from within the mediation field and also with organisations outside it.

From 1991, the number of mediation services began to increase more rapidly:[30]

1991 – 59
1992 – 64
1993 – 77
1994 – 81
1995 – 94
1996 – 110
1997 – 135

---

29 *Ibid.*
30 These figures are compiled from MEDIATION UK Annual Reports 1991–92, 1992–93, 1993–94, 1994–95 and 1995–96, and involve a degree of estimation.

MEDIATION UK currently[31] has a membership of 489, of which 178 are organisations and 311 are individual members. One hundred and thirty-five of the organisations are mediation services:

Community/neighbour mediation   – 97

Victim/offender mediation   – 30

Conflict resolution work and mediation in schools.   – 25

(This adds up to more than 135 because some services do more than one kind of work.)

One of the largest areas of work for MEDIATION UK is helping new services, especially community mediation services. It does this by providing information, especially the *Guide to Starting a Community Mediation Service*[32] (collated from existing best practice), and by giving them advice and putting them in touch with the nearest similar mediation service. MEDIATION UK also tries to help with advice on fundraising (but cannot itself provide funding), and on training. It often provides speakers for exploratory discussions and public meetings.

MEDIATION UK's most useful publications for community mediation services are *Practice Standards* (1989 and being updated for 1997), *The Need for Community Mediation Services* (1990), *Guide to Starting a Community Mediation Service* (1993 and updated in 1996), the *Directory of Mediation and Conflict Resolution Services* (1994 and updated in 1996), the recently published *Training Manual in Community Mediation Skills* (1995), the *Handbook for the MEDIATION UK Training Programme in Mediation Skills* (1996), the *Community Mediation Video* (1996) and the *Accreditation Pack* (1996).[33]

To accomplish this work, MEDIATION UK has a small staff based in a national office (two full-time, five part-time, plus several volunteers) and an executive committee of 15 drawn from different projects throughout the UK. Recent developments are regional and interest networking groups, of which the community mediation network is one of the newest. This network meets twice yearly to bring together all those involved in community mediation, to discuss their work and develop good practice.

---

31   As at July 1997.

32   MEDIATION UK, *Guide to Starting a Community Mediation Service*, 1993, updated 1996, Bristol: MEDIATION UK.

33   All these publications are available from MEDIATION UK, Alexander House, Telephone Avenue, Bristol BS1 4BS, telephone: 0117 904 6661, fax: 0117 904 3331, e-mail: mediationuk@cix.compulink.co.uk.

EXPANSION OF COMMUNITY MEDIATION

Over the past two years, there has been a substantial expansion of community mediation. This has in part been a response to the growing incidence of neighbour nuisance. Local authority environmental health services are becoming deluged with neighbour noise complaints. In 1992–93 there were 3,317 domestic noise reports per million of the population,[34] a 20% increase over the previous year. The trend shows a sharp increase, with nearly double the number of complaints being received compared with five years before, in 1985–86.[35]

A research paper on disputes between neighbours reported in 1986 that Birmingham City Council received over 8,200 cases of neighbour nuisance each year. This meant that nine new cases were received every month, and housing assistants spent several hours every week dealing with neighbour disputes. They had experienced a steep increase in the number of cases over recent years, and also predicted that things were going to get worse.[36] This report also highlighted the inadequacy of traditional approaches to neighbour nuisance, and suggested that more use should be made of mediation, with its potential for changing the complainant-offender relationship. It quoted encouraging results from the first two mediation services in the UK, in Newham (London) and Sandwell (West Midlands).

Another more recent report[37] confirmed this picture, and suggested that the focus be shifted away from trying to determine what constitutes anti-social behaviour or who is a problem tenant, towards trying to respond to complaints which are made about that behaviour. A further handbook published at about the same time by the Institute of Housing[38] also surveyed complaining behaviour, and both books evaluate the possible responses from social landlords which can help, including mediation.

The increasing number of complaints shows a perception on many people's part that neighbour disputes are on the increase. There are many reasons which may account for this:[39]

1 Lifestyle clashes, especially between generations, or between elderly people and families with children, are more common as different generations often have different values and needs.

---

34 Institute of Environmental Health Officers (IEHO), *Environmental Health Statistics 1992–93*, 1994, London: IEHO.

35 Hughes, D, *Environmental Law*, 1992, London: Butterworths.

36 Tebay, Cumberbatch and Graham, *op cit*.

37 Farrant, S *et al*, *Managing Neighbour Complaints in Social Housing: a Handbook for Practitioners*, 1993, Aldbourne: Aldbourne Associates.

38 Karn, V, Lickiss, R, Hughes, D and Crawley, J, *Neighbour Disputes: Responses by social landlords*, 1993, Coventry: Institute of Housing.

39 See Farrant *et al* and Karn *et al*, *op cit*.

2   The shortage of housing means that different generations are more frequently housed side by side or above one another.

3   The 'right to buy' council houses means that many areas have a much more mixed population, with different views.

4   The 'care in the community' policy for mental health means that there are many more vulnerable people in the community, often inadequately supported. Some of them are more likely to get into disputes, or to have perceptions which differ significantly from their neighbours.

5   Over the past few years it has become more difficult to move house in the UK, whether as a tenant or as an owner-occupier, either because of a shortage of housing or because the housing market is very static.

6   More people are spending more time at home, due to unemployment, sickness, early retirement or part-time work, so that neighbour problems affect them more than if they were out at work all day.

7   The increased number of noise disputes is due partly to the availability of much louder noise-making equipment, together with poorer building standards and thinner walls. Older houses are converted into smaller living units with inadequate sound insulation, and new dwellings are often built without regard to noise pollution.

8   The increase in general stress, poverty and social dislocation makes difficulties with neighbours seem like the last straw.

Local authorities are interested in mediation for a variety of reasons:

- the failure of legal remedies to deal with neighbour conflict;
- a desire to provide an alternative to existing methods of resolving disputes;
- a belief that mediation is more appropriate for certain types of disputes;
- the realisation that mediation has a real potential for rebuilding communities;
- a sense that mediation may be more cost-effective and take less time than traditional methods.

Local authorities, especially housing and environmental health departments, have come to see community mediation services as cost-effective ways of dealing with neighbour nuisance. This means that they are often willing to fund or part-fund (either by grant or contract) mediation services, so that they can be enabled to do this work and relieve local authorities of an increasing burden which they feel they do not have the time or expertise to undertake. This process has encouraged the Department of Environment which produced (in conjunction with MEDIATION UK) a booklet *Mediation: Benefits and Practice* (1994),[40] which encourages local authorities to look seriously at the

---

40   Department of the Environment, *Mediation: Benefits and Practice*, 1994, London: DoE.

possibility of providing funds to help initiate and maintain local mediation services.

Whereas the first community mediation services were almost all to be found in very urban areas, some of the newer ones are based in small towns and rural areas. It is acknowledged that some of the rise in neighbour disputes is due to the stress of urban living, however there are also many neighbour disputes which are found in all sections of the community, eg boundary disputes, some noise disputes, and a whole range of other issues. For instance, in some rural districts, the issue of 'travellers' can cause serious disputes. In more remote areas, there may be friction between long-standing residents and incomers.

Some community mediation services are also bases for other kinds of mediation, such as elder mediation, which concentrates on disputes likely to be suffered by older people, particularly in institutions but also in the community. Medical mediation, environmental mediation, organisational mediation, public services mediation – these are all areas which are beginning to grow, and many of them form links with or are developed from existing community mediation services.

Neighbour disputes can escalate into violence, and may surface in victim/offender mediation services, in the areas where these are available. These cases are better resolved using mediation rather than criminal court procedures. Several community mediation services in the UK have been funded by the Home Office Safer Cities Scheme, in the hope that mediation might prevent crime by offering intervention in the early stages of a dispute. The existence of community mediation services can also help reduce fear of crime, especially on high-crime housing estates.

PARALLEL DEVELOPMENTS

While community mediation has been growing in so many different ways, other kinds of mediation have been doing the same. In this section, the main developments in each area are charted over the same period, to provide a context for viewing community mediation initiatives and progress. Several have had important links with community mediation and these will be mentioned below.

Industrial mediation

In the employment field, the development of conciliation/mediation services was associated with laws designed to safeguard individual employment rights. There were several Acts of Parliament over the years 1963 to 1974 (Contracts of Employment Act 1963, amended in 1972; Redundancy Payments

Act 1965; Industrial Relations Act 1971; Trade Union and Labour Relations Act 1974), leading to the provision of five services: collective conciliation, individual conciliation, arbitration, advisory work and longer term enquiries. These were all under way by the early 1970s.

However, there were worries, especially from trade unions, that these services might be affected by government incomes policy, and doubts also arose concerning the independence of the services from government influence or even control.[41]

The new (Labour) government which took office in February 1974 introduced the Trade Union and Labour Relations Act 1974, and then set up an independent Conciliation and Arbitration Service, which started on 2 September 1974, with a London headquarters and offices in Scotland, Wales and six English regional centres. In January 1975, the title was changed to the Advisory, Conciliation and Arbitration Service (ACAS), and on 1 January 1976 ACAS became a statutory body under the Employment Protection Act 1975. Its independence was enshrined in Schedule 1 (paragraph 11) of this Act:

> The functions of the Service and of its officers and servants shall be performed on behalf of the Crown, but the Service shall not be subject to directions of any kind from any minister of the Crown as to the matter in which it is to exercise any of its functions under any enactment.

Although ACAS is best known (especially in its early days) for resolving high-profile industrial disputes, it also does considerable work behind the scenes, preventing disputes escalating, promoting good industrial relations, and dealing with individual cases of employee and employer.[42] Its mission is 'to improve the performance and effectiveness of organisations by providing an independent and impartial service to prevent and resolve disputes and to build harmonious relationships at work'. To achieve this, ACAS seeks to:[43]

- prevent and resolve employment disputes;
- conciliate in actual or potential complaints to industrial tribunals;
- provide information and advice;
- promote good practice.

It is worth noting that ACAS uses the terms 'conciliation' and 'mediation' in a slightly different way from most other organisations. 'Conciliation' is used for the process which is elsewhere known as mediation, that is, a voluntary process in which a conciliator tries to facilitate two disputing parties to work out their own agreement. 'Mediation' is used for a process similar to arbitration, where the mediator hears the evidence and arguments of both

---

41   Advisory, Conciliation and Arbitration Service (ACAS), 'How ACAS started', undated, London: ACAS.

42   ACAS, '20 years of improving industrial relations', ACAS leaflet, 1996, London: ACAS.

43   ACAS, 'The role of ACAS', ACAS leaflet, 1996, London: ACAS.

sides, and then makes a decision. Whereas arbitration is binding, ACAS mediation makes formal but non-binding recommendations intended to provide a basis for settlement of the dispute.[44]

Most ACAS conciliators come to ACAS from other government posts in the field of employment and industry, and attend in-service training courses at appropriate intervals. They are usually full-time permanent employees.

There have been many links between ACAS and community mediation. At a local level, in the early days of community mediation, ACAS staff (as experienced practitioners of mediation skills) were often asked to join panels for information days on mediation. At a national level, there have been seminars and training sessions where ACAS staff provided relevant skills, and in the latter years where MEDIATION UK did the same for ACAS.

Family mediation

The roots of family mediation also go back to the 1970s. In 1973 the Finer Committee examined the situation of the growing number of one-parent families, and proposed a family court with a conciliation service attached to it, to tackle the issues arising from separation and divorce, which often led to poverty. The issues needing attention were children, finance and property. However, the government did not respond to these recommendations, and professionals dealing with these problems became increasingly frustrated.[45]

Two voluntary initiatives in the late 1970s attempted to address these problems. Senior court welfare officers in Surrey and south-east London set up a system of volunteer conciliators as an alternative to the ordering of welfare reports by the courts. In 1978 the first independent family conciliation service was set up as a pilot project in Bristol, to help separating or divorcing parents agree arrangements for their children.

More initiatives followed suit, and in 1981 they came together to form the National Family Conciliation Council (NFCC), with about 20 local services, of which 10 took referrals directly from the public. Although initially the word 'conciliation' was used (perhaps because of the ACAS usage), as time went on, the word 'mediation' began to be used more often, and both words described the same process. In recognition of this, NFCC changed its name in 1992 to the National Association of Family Mediation and Conciliation Services. This rather long title was abbreviated to National Family Mediation for most informal purposes.

Local family mediation services are funded from a variety of sources, such as the probation service, social services, charities, commerce and client fees.

---

44   ACAS, 'Preventing and resolving disputes', ACAS leaflet, 1995, London: ACAS.

45   Fisher, T, 'The History of Family Mediation Services', 1993, London: National Family Mediation.

The Solicitors Family Law Association (SFLA) was formed in 1982 to encourage a settlement-seeking approach in matrimonial proceedings, and many members of the SFLA were involved in their local family conciliation services.[46]

Family mediators were initially qualified social workers or trained Relate (formerly Marriage Guidance) counsellors, although more recently these criteria have become slightly more flexible to include a wider range of people. Most mediators are paid sessionally and undertake their training partly with their local service and partly at the annual national training course.

Most local family mediation services only mediated in cases where a separating couple had children, and dealt with issues around children, but not property or finance. The Family Mediators Association was launched in 1988[47] by Lisa Parkinson (the original founder of the first Family Conciliation Service in Bristol) and a management board, to provide mediation in respect of property and finance issues, which were often stumbling blocks preventing agreement concerning the children. The FMA offers the help of two mediators who work together as a team – one is an experienced family solicitor, the other a qualified professional with experience in marital and family work, both with mediation training.[48] It is a fee-paying service for any couple with or without children; however, the need to make this service pay for itself means that these fees are out of reach for many people.

The 1989 *Report of the Conciliation Project Unit on the Costs and Effectiveness of Conciliation in England and Wales* recommended that family mediation should not be restricted to issues directly connected with arrangements for children. In response, National Family Mediation developed pilot projects in five areas which already had family mediation services. These pilot projects were evaluated between 1990 and 1993. The report published in 1994 showed that users of 'all-issues mediation' gained greater benefit by sorting out all the issues, and saw mediation as a cost-effective alternative to the traditional legal process.[49]

There are now 70 family mediation services affiliated to NFM, of which 17 offer all-issues mediation. They are grouped into seven regions, covering England, Wales and Northern Ireland (list of affiliated services August 1996). There is a separate organisation, Family Mediation Scotland, which covers Scotland. On 1 January 1996, the three main family mediation bodies (National Family Mediation, Family Mediators Association and Family

---

46 Parkinson, L, 'Some landmarks in the history of family mediation', Appendix H in Parkinson, L, *Family Mediation*, forthcoming, London: Sweet and Maxwell.

47 *Ibid.*

48 Family Mediators Association leaflet.

49 Joseph Rowntree Foundation, 'The longer-term impact of family mediation', *Findings*, Social Policy Research 103, September 1996, York: Joseph Rowntree Foundation.

Mediation Scotland) jointly founded the UK College of Family Mediators, to promote family mediation, establish recognised standards of training and make available details of registered mediators. The College will establish standards of training, professional practice and service delivery in the field of family mediation.[50] These developments concerning quality assurance and accreditation are paralleled by similar ones for community mediation (see Chapter 11).

The Family Law Act 1996 introduced no-fault divorce proceedings and a staged process for divorcing couples to follow. The first step will be an information meeting to ensure that there is a full understanding of what divorce involves. This meeting also gives information on the availability and advantages of mediation, to encourage the use of mediation rather than litigation, where possible. Legal aid will be available for mediation in the same way as for legal representation.[51] Mediation will be available from National Family Mediation, the Family Mediators Association, Family Mediation Scotland and an increasing number of solicitors who have trained in family mediation, encouraged by the recently formed British Association of Lawyer Mediators (BALM). The SFLA offered its first training course for its members in all-issues mediation in June 1996.[52]

Some members of the public have been confused by the label 'family mediation', as they expect such a service to deal with all disputes within a family. However, only a few family mediation services take on family disputes outside separation and divorce. Although social and health services may help with very entrenched family conflict, using family counselling or therapy, there are few specialist services for families with the occasional dispute, such as intergenerational disagreements. In fact, community mediation services find themselves dealing with quite a few family disputes where they are outside the remit of family mediation.

One other important and pioneering application of family mediation (in its wider sense) is in the context of domestic violence, being undertaken by Plymouth Mediation, a combined community and victim/offender mediation service. Although this has hitherto been regarded as a taboo area for mediation, because of the coercion of violence or threats of violence, Plymouth Mediation has set up a successful service for victims of domestic violence, in conjunction with the local probation service.

There have been many links between family mediation and community mediation over the years. Again, many family mediators were involved in the early days of community mediation, as resources for new community

---

50 UK College of Family Mediators, leaflet, 1996.

51 National Family Mediation, 'The Family Law Bill: The Importance for Mediators' (1996), London: National Family Mediation.

52 Parkinson, L, *op cit.*

mediation services, and this is still true for a few of the recent community mediation services (see Chapter 4). Some of the MEDIATION UK regional groups have involved family mediation service staff alongside community and victim/offender mediation members. At a national level, there have been good informal links between MEDIATION UK and all the family mediation organisations, and MEDIATION UK is now represented on the Advisory Board of the new UK College of Family Mediators.

Schools conflict resolution and mediation

Conflict resolution in schools also started in the early 1980s, with the Kingston Friends Workshop Group, which developed methods of teaching children how to resolve conflict peacefully. The group came into being in 1981 as a result of a visit of the Quaker Peace Action Caravan, a project which took conflict resolution activities to Quaker Meetings around the UK. Members of the group offered a sixth form conference to local schools, entitled 'Can we make peace?' and went on to develop a programme of workshops on 'Problem Solving in Personal Relationships'. These workshops were taken up enthusiastically by teachers, social workers and managers in business and the community, as the group developed and discovered materials suitable for the task. A visit in 1982 from the 'Children's Creative Response to Conflict Programme' in the USA gave the group many new training methods and materials, including mediation skills.[53]

The materials were compiled into the manual *Ways and Means* in 1986 and sold out immediately; several editions have been produced since. As the group became known, it was necessary to employ a salaried co-ordinator. The work has expanded to include mediation skills and prevention of bullying, and in 1989 family workshops were started to help families where children were suffering from aggression and abuse at school or in the community. The group also offers some help with neighbour disputes.

Several other Quaker groups followed this example, and two workers from Quaker Peace & Service, based at Friends House, London, gave support to such initiatives. One of the ways they did this was by hosting twice-yearly meetings for all those (not just Quakers) interested in conflict resolution in schools. They also helped to form the European Network in Conflict Resolution in Education (ENCORE) in 1990, when a group of interested educationalists met in Brussels. ENCORE has held yearly conferences in a different place in Europe since then. In 1991 the group formulated its aims and produced a leaflet in four languages (English, French, Russian and Spanish). Its aims are to:

---

53   Rawlings, A, *Ways and Means Today*, 1996, Kingston: Kingston Friends Workshop Group.

- encourage and support the development of conflict resolution and mediation skills in schools and colleges throughout Europe;
- provide information about available resources and develop new resources;
- encourage education authorities, governments and international agencies to support this work and to implement the recommendations contained in the Council of Europe report 'Violence and Conflict Resolution in Schools';
- hold international summer schools for the training of trainers;
- maintain links with similar networks in Europe and on other continents.

There has never been a formal membership list, simply an address list, and the conferences have been organised by local groups who have offered to do so the previous year. Conferences have so far taken place in Belgium, Northern Ireland, Germany and Hungary.[54]

Schools work has grown gradually in the UK as interest in these ideas has grown. Several independent schools projects have been set up, and quite a few schools have incorporated conflict resolution practices into their framework, either 'piecemeal' or, better, as a whole-school policy.

As the community mediation movement grew, many services felt that the logical extension of their work was to take it into schools, and teach the next generation how to resolve conflict, as a preventative life skill. So there are now a considerable number of community mediation services which have a 'schools group' and, in fortunate cases, a funded schools worker to develop this work. Schools work may also be part of a 'crime prevention package' for intensive work on high-crime housing estates.

For the first few years, most of the schools work concentrated on teaching children, mostly in primary schools, about conflict resolution. More recently this work has developed to include schools-based peer mediation training and schemes, in which children are trained to mediate in playground disputes. Peer mediation has also begun to move into secondary schools, and a National Organisation of Peer Mediators for young people had its launch meeting in February 1997.

The links between schools mediation and community mediation are clear, and the existence of MEDIATION UK as the umbrella organisation for both kinds of mediation helps practitioners keep in touch with each other. There have also been instances where disputes in the community originated in school, and school disputes had their roots in family feuds: only a combined approach was able to sort things out.

---

54 European Network for Conflict Resolution in Education (ENCORE) leaflet; and Bentley, M, 'ENCORE: The European Network for Conflict Resolution in Education' (1997), London: Quaker Peace & Service.

Victim/offender mediation

The picture concerning victim/offender mediation has changed the least over the past 10 years. Some of the services in existence have ceased, due to financial cutbacks, and a few others have started. Three out of the four services originally funded by the Home Office in 1985–87 have gone from strength to strength. Three large county areas have supported victim/offender mediation in a big way, mostly funded by the probation service. There has been great interest, but the total number of services has remained static until recently, because of general cutbacks and because recent government criminal justice policy has emphasised punishment rather than rehabilitation.

Despite this, the services themselves have developed their work. Research on the 1985–87 phase showed a bias towards offenders, and since then most services have altered their practice to be more victim-friendly, so that now victims, offenders and courts alike find the service very helpful.

Over the past year there has been a surge of interest in victim/offender mediation, with several new services starting, mostly funded by some of the larger voluntary agencies for young offenders. The growing emphasis on helping victims has led many offender agencies to re-examine their practices, and it may be that this will lead to a rapid expansion of victim/offender mediation, similar to the recent expansion of community mediation.

Commercial mediation

The initial idea for a commercial Alternative Dispute Resolution (ADR) centre came to several prominent London lawyers in the late 1980s. They had heard of mediation being used in commercial disputes in the USA, and wanted to bring these benefits to the UK. A chance meeting between Eileen Carroll, with 10 years' experience in international commercial disputes, and Karl Mackie, at the American Bar Association conference in Hawaii, led to the idea of a centre in the UK. With the backing of the Confederation of British Industry (CBI) and several leading law firms in London, the Centre for Dispute Resolution (CEDR) was launched in November 1990.[55]

CEDR handles cases where two (or more) firms are in dispute and would otherwise go to court. Mediation can save substantial costs and also save considerable time, especially if several parties are involved. The same principles apply as for other kinds of mediation. CEDR carries out its own training and accredits its own mediators.

There are several other organisations offering commercial mediation, such as the ADR Group, which started in 1991 as a network of 12 firms of solicitors

---

55 Telephone conversation October 1996 with Katia O'Toole of Centre for Dispute Resolution (CEDR), and profile of Eileen Carroll in *Resolutions*, 15 November 1996, London: CEDR.

(there are now many more) called ADR Net. The ADR Group headquarters staff provide training and act as a referral agency, either mediating commercial cases themselves or referring them to a member of their network who is geographically nearer the client.

The Academy of Experts, likewise, developed its own training and literature, and provides its own training and accreditation for neutrals from a wide variety of disciplines. It also deals with personal, consumer and commercial disputes. The National Mediation Centre started much more recently (1996) to provide training and a mediation service in the areas of commercial and family mediation. It also provides advice on dispute and conflict management, and in-house training if required.[56] There are also many firms of solicitors who have recently undertaken training in mediation, with a view to adding mediation to their repertoire of skills.

Medical mediation

Many Family Health Service Authorities (FHSAs) have been offering informal conciliation/mediation services to patients who make complaints about their doctors. For example, the Leicester FHSA informal conciliation service was set up in 1991. When patients contacted the FHSA with a complaint, they were advised to contact their GP if they had not already done so. If the complaint could not be resolved locally, the patient was sent the options for pursuing the complaint, including conciliation as well as the more conventional formal complaints procedure. If the patient opted for informal conciliation, the FHSA staff wrote to the doctor asking if he or she was willing to participate. A meeting was arranged with a conciliator, and the process explained to both parties before they met. If the complaint was not successfully resolved at the meeting, the patient could take the complaint to the formal service committee, where it was treated as a completely new complaint, without any feedback from the conciliation session. However, many complaints were resolved by conciliation, especially where they were based on misunderstandings, incomplete information, third party perceptions and so on.[57]

In 1993 the Secretary of State set up a review of complaints procedures to ensure these were thorough, prompt and accessible – reducing waiting times and addressing the problems as close to the point of service delivery as possible. In 1996 the NHS Executive issued guidance packs for general practitioners in medicine and dentistry. These stated that the aim of the new complaints procedure was to resolve most complaints at practice level, and

---

56 MEDIATION UK, *Directory of Mediation & Conflict Resolution Services*, 1996, Bristol: MEDIATION UK.

57 Carmichael, R, 'First Report of Leicestershire FHSA on Informal Complaints: Helping Patients and Doctors to listen to each other' (1993), Leicester: Leicestershire FHSA.

provided guidance for medical and dental practices to develop their own procedures. However, if independent conciliation could be helpful, this would be available through the health authority. All health authorities have been asked to ensure that conciliation services are available to both parties to a complaint.[58]

Although there are no direct links between medical and community mediation, several community mediation trainers and mediators have been involved in setting up medical conciliation services, and acting as conciliators.

Environmental mediation

Environmental mediation has been used for many years in North America, to help resolve disputes concerning environmental and planning issues. It has been pioneered in the UK by a few individual practitioners and by Environmental Resolve, which started in 1992 when several like-minded people came together. It is an undertaking of the Environment Council, an independent charity which brings together many groups caring and campaigning for the environment. Environmental Resolve is a professional service providing consensus-building consultancy and training, and has a network of mediators and facilitators who can help organisations and groups of organisations to resolve environmental disputes and make the best decisions for all involved.[59]

One of the features of environmental mediation is that it usually involves many 'stakeholders' – often it is part of the process to decide who should be at the meetings. Building consensus between all the stakeholders can take several months, so it can be a slow process – but the decisions made are usually better than those decided by just one party, possibly followed by massive protests and a public inquiry. A further aim is to use the process to *prevent* conflict and make better decisions in the first place, thus contributing to improving the democratic process.[60]

There has been considerable informal liaison between community and environmental mediation, concerning training and conferences. There are also overlaps in that community mediation deals with many conflicts over noise problems – part of the remit of the Department of the Environment. Community mediation services also carry out large multi-party mediations from time to time – whole streets, for example – which require similar techniques to environmental mediation (or *vice versa*).

---

58 NHS Executive, 'Complaints Guidance Pack for General Medical/Dental Practitioners' (1996), London: NHS Executive.

59 Baines, J and Ingram, H, *Beyond Compromise: Building Consensus in Environmental Planning and Decision-making*, 1995, London: The Environment Council.

60 Telephone conversation with Hally Ingram, 20 February 1997.

Elder mediation

The Elder Mediation Project was founded in 1991 by Yvonne Craig after attending a conference and undertaking a fact-finding tour in the USA. Yvonne Craig had been a founder member of MEDIATION UK and had trained as a mediator with one of the London community mediation services. The need for EMP had been demonstrated by the rising numbers of old people living longer and becoming involved in increasing conflicts, in families, in institutions and in communities. There has been a firm focus on gathering a multicultural group of older volunteers to steer the project.[61]

Funding for the work was achieved in 1994 and 1995, and EMP embarked on a two-year pilot scheme, running many workshops on 'Coping with later life conflict', making presentations to groups of professionals, writing articles and liaising with many other organisations. During the past two years it has also undertaken 50 mediation cases referred to it by a variety of organisations.

The Elder Mediation Project has many links with community mediation, having gathered its practitioners largely from community mediation services, and also offers its workshops and training opportunities to those in community mediation.

Organisational mediation

There has been considerable interest in this area for a number of years, and many organisational consultants have seen conflict resolution as part of their general remit in helping organisations move forward, especially as very often unresolved conflict plays a part in organisations becoming 'stuck'. More recently consultants have been undertaking mediation skills training to enhance their ability to resolve conflict, and mediators have been offering their services to organisations as well as to individuals.

In 1995 the National Council of Voluntary Organisations (NCVO) launched its Dispute Resolution Service for Charities and Voluntary Organisations (now called the Voluntary Sector Dispute Resolution Service), offering mediation for disputes involving staff, volunteers or committee members of these organisations. NCVO recruited mediators from a wide background, including those with commercial and those with community mediation experience, and held a training day for this team.[62] Another similar service started in 1996, promoted by the Association of Chief Executives of Voluntary Organisations (ACENVO) and CEDR (see above), concentrating on disputes involving chief executives and their organisations.[63]

---

61   Elder Mediation Project leaflet.
62   NCVO Dispute Resolution Service for Charities and Voluntary Organisations leaflet.
63   CEDR/ACENVO Scheme leaflet.

Through this involvement, community mediation has had some influence on this area, along with others from different mediation backgrounds. At a local level, many community mediation services have been asked to mediate between and within other organisations in their area – work which they have taken in their stride as part of working in the community.

CONCLUSION

The early beginnings of modern mediation came from contact with America and Australia, and began to gain ground in the UK in the 1980s, with an initial emphasis on victim/offender mediation. The early community mediation services grew out of the visions of a small number of people, and developed according to different philosophies: the grass-roots community-based ideal or the more agency-led formal structure. The national organisation MEDIATION UK came into being to bring together all those interested in this field, started a magazine and newsletter, and produced much-needed publications.

By 1990 the number of community mediation services equalled the number of victim/offender mediation services, and the mid-1990s saw a rapid expansion of community mediation services. This is due to several causes: the increased awareness of mediation, through the work of MEDIATION UK; the escalation of neighbour disputes, especially noise disputes; the search by local authorities for a more effective way of dealing with such disputes; and the discovery by local authorities that mediation can replace some of the more traditional methods of dealing with disputes.

The development of community mediation in the UK has been part of the general development of all kinds of mediation – industrial mediation, family mediation, schools conflict resolution and mediation, victim/offender mediation, commercial mediation, medical mediation, environmental mediation, elder mediation and organisational mediation – and has both influenced and been influenced by these.

Many of the developments touched on in this chapter will be developed in more detail in the ensuing chapters. This expansion in turn has given rise to further initiatives, which will be described in Chapter 14.

CHAPTER THREE

THE MEDIATION PROCESS

John C Patrick

INTRODUCTION

It is important that any mediation works to a structure which allows the mediators to control the process while giving the parties the control of the content of any agreement reached. This structure is a series of stages through which the process is moved. The pace will vary according to the needs of the individual case. The structure can be described in a number of ways but this chapter will use the structure from the MEDIATION UK *Training Manual in Community Mediation Skills*.[1]

The staged structure can be seen to have a six-fold purpose:

1   It ensures that the process is controlled and offers a safe environment for the parties.

2   By giving structure it offers alternative ways to violence and aggression, and thus offers ritualised control of the parties' behaviour.

3   The structure ensures the neutrality of the mediators.

4   It offers a means of balancing any disparity in power between the parties.

5   The stages offer a step-by-step approach towards reaching an agreement.

6   It ensures that any agreement reached is owned by the participants, rather than being seen by them as an imposed solution.

The structure does require a good deal of flexibility and the service can be delivered in a number of ways within the framework in order to answer individual needs and differing situations. While the aim in most cases is to bring the parties together for a face-to-face meeting, alternative means of reaching an agreement are often explored. This is particularly relevant in cases where either of the parties is reluctant to meet or there appear to be other reasons for not meeting, such as power imbalances or risk of aggressive behaviour. The use of shuttle mediation, where the mediators move between the parties to try to reach an agreement without the parties meeting, will be discussed later in this chapter. Throughout the main body of this chapter the process will be described in terms of two parties' involvement for simplicity and consistency; some issues regarding multi-party disputes will be looked at later.

---

1   MEDIATION UK, *Training Manual in Community Mediation Skills*, 1995, Bristol: MEDIATION UK.

HOW A COMMUNITY MEDIATION SERVICE OPERATES

Before looking at the stages of community mediation in detail it is useful to look briefly at how the service operates from the receipt of a referral to the completion of the case. The process may vary from case to case and from service to service, but the following diagram represents the common flow of a case.

Figure 3.1: How a community mediation service operates.

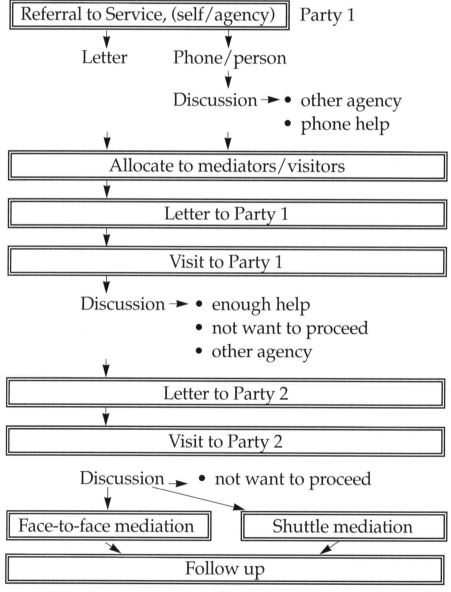

THE STAGES OF THE PROCESS

The process outlined is a seven-stage one, in which the stages will normally run chronologically, although there may be overlap between stages, and within a face-to-face meeting there can be movement between the stages in both directions. Any particular case may terminate at any point along the way, either because of a decision by one of the parties not to proceed or because an agreement has been reached or is likely to be reached by other means, for example, by the parties meeting privately without the mediators.

The seven stages are as follows:

(1) Initial contact with the first party.

(2) Initial contact with the second party.

(3) Preparing to work on the dispute.

(4) Setting the scene – hearing the issues.

(5) Exploring the issues.

(6) Building agreements.

(7) Closure and follow-up.

Throughout this chapter each stage will be illustrated by reference to a fictitious case used in the training video produced by MEDIATION UK.[2] This case resulted from a complaint by David and Rose McBride about Herman Jacobs and Leonie Paris who live in a flat above them.

STAGE ONE – INITIAL CONTACT WITH THE FIRST PARTY

The process usually starts with one party contacting the service either in person or by telephone and this can be a vital part of the process, where an early identification of the presenting problem and its suitability for mediation is made. This is dealt with in more detail in other chapters but usually results in mediators being selected and asked to undertake a home visit. A home visit enables the mediators to see the situation at first hand as well as establishing contact on the party's own ground. It is often important to see the layout and proximity of the housing and at times see or experience the cause of the original complaint.

Mediators are trained in the skills of active listening and rapport building, and use these to establish a working relationship with the party and get a full story of the dispute and its history. It is often apparent that the initial complaint in the referral is only a part of the issue and the party may wish to

---

2   MEDIATION UK, *Community Mediation Video*, 1996, Bristol: MEDIATION UK. For details see p 123, n 10.

talk about matters not directly associated with the conflict with the neighbours. The mediators will need to sort out these issues in order to look at the options for the next step.

First, there are those issues directly related to the dispute, such as noise, boundaries etc. Second, there is the history of the dispute and the relationship with the neighbour, and here the previous relationship may be important in looking for ways of resolving the dispute. The nature and extent of the breakdown in the relationship may be an indication of how entrenched the party's position is and why they have called in a third party. There are occasions when mediators find that the matter has never been raised with the neighbour who may be unaware that their behaviour has been causing a problem; on other occasions there is a long history to the dispute which may have involved other agencies such as the police, solicitors or the local authority.

Third, are there others who are either directly or indirectly involved in the dispute? Other neighbours, friends or relatives can play an important part in influencing the party's attitude and behaviour to their neighbour. Fourth, is there any other action being taken? If, for instance, the party is taking action through the courts, it is inappropriate to proceed with mediation unless the court action is held in abeyance.

There are then those matters which are not related to the neighbour: loneliness, depression and loss all play a part in making minor irritants into major problems and, while it is important not to be seen to minimise the complaint, it may be necessary to explore the possibility of work in this area by referral to another agency, as an alternative or in addition to continuing the mediation process, subject to the party's consent.

When David McBride contacted the Mediation Service, the worker who took the telephone call established that the McBrides lived on the fifth floor of a tower block and that his complaint was that the tenants in the flat above made a lot of noise doing DIY. This went on in the evening and disturbed his relaxation but even more importantly stopped their children from sleeping. The Service arranged for two mediators to call.

They established that the problem was mainly in the evening and came from the couple upstairs who were always doing noisy work sometimes until after midnight. David said that when he complained he was abused. Rose said that she used to be good friends with Leonie but now they did not talk. The mediators were able to describe the role of mediators and emphasised such issues as confidentiality and the unacceptability of racist or abusive remarks. Rose had passed on a racist comment about the other couple from her family, and this gave the mediators a chance to ensure that their position about racism was clearly stated. Although Rose and David were not convinced that Herman and Leonie would co-operate, they were willing for the mediators to visit them and try to establish a direct meeting.

STAGE TWO – FIRST CONTACT WITH THE SECOND PARTY

If the first party agrees, the next step is to contact the second party with an appointment. Unlike stage one, the contact is with someone who may not wish to be involved in mediation and may not perceive that there is any problem. The process may, therefore, stop at this point and the initiating party will be informed that the service is unable to proceed. This is usually the end of the service's involvement, although sometimes further visits may be made to talk through the first party's options.

In most cases the second party is willing to see the mediators and is sometimes very relieved that action is possible on a problem which is as upsetting to them as to their neighbour. The mediators will normally need to outline their role and seek the viewpoint of this party. It is particularly important that the mediators develop skills in establishing trust and impartiality, as otherwise they may be seen as coming on behalf of the complaining neighbour.

The confidentiality of the process must also be maintained. Mediators should only discuss issues from the first visit to which the first party has agreed – they are frequently under some pressure to reveal more of the issues complained about than is appropriate. The other tasks in this stage are similar to those in the first stage, with particular reference to discussing possible options and the party's willingness to proceed with a round table meeting or some other option.

> The mediators visited Leonie and Herman who were quite willing to see them because they had also found the bad relationship a problem. They were keen to show off the work they had done on their flat and were obviously very houseproud. The mediators had to withstand some attempts from Leonie to quiz them about what they had been told and this opened up the issue of confidentiality. Herman and Leonie had a number of issues which they wanted to raise. Leonie believed Rose was gossiping about her to other neighbours and ignored her now. They also complained that Rose and the children were themselves very noisy especially early in the mornings. Rose or David had also taken to banging on their ceiling (Leonie and Herman's floor) for no apparent reason. When the role of a face-to-face meeting was described they agreed to attend to put their points to Rose and David.

STAGE THREE – PREPARING TO WORK ON THE DISPUTE

At both visits some preparation work takes place to establish the views of the disputants. If both parties agree to meet in a face-to-face mediation, then such a meeting will normally be arranged as soon as possible at a neutral venue. If not, an assessment needs to be made of the appropriate next steps, which can include further visits to one or both parties, shuttle mediation, referral elsewhere or closing the case.

It is quite usual for the parties to have reservations about meeting and in most services it is only a minority of disputes that go to a face-to-face meeting immediately after the initial visit to each party. Services vary in their policy about further visits and undertaking alternatives to the face-to-face meeting. A party's resistance to attending a face-to-face meeting may come from a number of sources such as a lack of confidence in the process, a lack of confidence in their own ability to negotiate or a lack of confidence in the other party's willingness to change. Mediators need to be able to reassure parties about the level of control and safety of the process, and that the mediation will only go ahead with the consent of both parties, in order to help them feel empowered by the process. Mediators also need to encourage both parties to come prepared to play a positive part in trying to resolve the issues.

It is important that a face-to-face mediation takes place only when both parties consent and when there is some possibility of progress, however slight. An important first step is some acknowledgment by both parties that there is some behaviour which is the basis of the dispute, and that this behaviour has undesirable consequences for the people involved. This subject is explored in more depth in Chapter 7 and in Chapter 8, which includes a case which proceeded to a face-to-face meeting when the parties had such different views of the behaviour in dispute that there was little chance of reaching any agreement, so that the mediation was a series of accusations and denials which could not be moved on.

If the service is not continuing its involvement, they can refer one or both parties to other appropriate agencies, subject to their wish. For example, an elderly person may benefit and cope with her neighbours better if she is given support from a visitor from Age Concern, or a single parent may need help from various organisations which will help to diminish the cause of conflict. It is important for local mediation services to build up a good knowledge and network of these to support their mediation work. Mediators need to be prepared to discuss these options with the party whom they visit and may include this as an option for discussion even when it is intended to proceed with mediation.

If both parties are agreeable, the next stage is to arrange a face-to-face or round table meeting. This should be arranged at a neutral, comfortably furnished venue which should be accessible to both parties. The venue must allow sufficient room to be able to keep the parties separate if needed, both on arrival and during the mediation session, to allow for the possibility of breaking into caucuses[3] or separate meetings. Arrangements for the reception

---

3   See later in this chapter for definition of caucus, page 60.

of the parties (including reception staff) and the layout of the room need to be considered and issues of health and safety taken into account.

Figure 3.2: Possible layout of a mediation session showing positions of two parties (P1 and P2) and two mediators (M1 and M2).

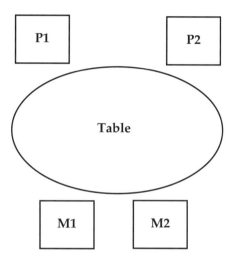

The selection of mediators to conduct this meeting is an important part of the process. In many cases this follows automatically from the visits, with the same mediators following the case throughout the process. There are occasions, however, when a mediator may feel that they would find neutrality difficult because of feelings aroused by the visits, or when one of the parties requests different mediators. Where there has been previous contact and a resolution has not occurred, it may be felt by the service that a fresh approach by different mediators is necessary. A change of mediators at this stage is not necessarily a disadvantage, as it is the issues raised at the meeting that will be the focus of discussion and not previous meetings. Some mediation services provide separate visitors (for the first meetings) and mediators (for the face-to-face meeting) as a matter of routine practice.

> The mediators had prepared the participants for direct mediation during the visits by explaining the way it would operate and ensuring that they were giving informed consent to the meeting. The mediators now met to discuss any particular issues which needed to be taken into consideration when conducting this mediation. The parties had seemed sensible and reasonable and the risk factors did not appear high. David had mentioned that on one or two occasions he had lost his temper after drinking and this worried him. Some precautions, such as ensuring that he was separated from Herman by a barrier such as a table and that the mediators had access to the room door and a telephone, seemed prudent and would be taken in almost all cases anyway.

The mediators also discussed the roles they were going to take and had some discussion about how they might deal with the issue of race if it came up.

STAGE FOUR – SETTING THE SCENE AND HEARING THE ISSUES

After the introductions and welcome to parties individually as they arrive, the process starts with the mediators' introduction which will outline the procedures for the meeting and make clear the ground rules for the session. These are usually sent out with the invitation to the meeting but need to be looked at to ensure that the parties understand and agree to abide by them. They will cover issues of behaviour, confidentiality and an assumption that all will be coming in good faith to try to resolve the problems, as well as any practical issues about the venue such as smoking policy. Even where there is a standard set of ground rules for all face-to-face meetings, there will probably be additional matters relevant to the individual dispute which require clarification at the start of the session.

The mediators then invite each party in turn to outline the issues from their perspective, emphasising the need for each person to be allowed uninterrupted time. Often the party which made the initial contact with the service will be asked to speak first. There are also occasions when the mediators might wish to invite the other party to speak first, particularly when there appears to be an issue of power disparity. It may be important to give the less powerful or less articulate the first opportunity. The control by the mediator is vital during this stage and can set the tone for the whole session; if either party is left feeling that they have not had a fair hearing, then progress to an agreement is unlikely, or that party may agree to something but feel coerced, and will lack confidence in the agreement and the service.

After each party has had their uninterrupted time the mediators feed back a summary of what they have heard and, where necessary, seek clarification or specific details. They then try to bring the issues from both statements into an agenda and seek agreement of the parties to the list of issues and the order in which they are taken. It is important that this is done in as open and fair a way as possible to balance both parties' needs. Within this constraint, it is useful if there is an issue which looks fairly easy to resolve which can be taken first, particularly if it is one which both parties see as important.

After the mediators set out the ground rules and procedures, Rose described the problem from her perspective with David adding and confirming her comments. Leonie broke in with one interruption but after a relatively gentle intervention she again interrupted and was told politely but firmly that she would have her say in a minute. The only issue which David and Rose brought at this stage was the question of Herman's DIY and the noise it created. One of the mediators then summarised what had been said.

Herman then outlined his position, saying that they had gone out of their way to be civil to Rose and David but they had not responded and their oldest child was 'growing into a right little bastard'. After the mediators intervened to remind him that they had agreed to the 'no name-calling' ground rule he apologised but said that the child was already learning to taunt him. He went on to say that he did not do DIY every evening. Leonie then raised the issue of the banging on the ceiling and said that Rose was turning people against them. She said the children were throwing balls at their walls and staring at their windows. She pointed out that they used to be friends. The other mediator then summed up and outlined the issues to be discussed.

STAGE FIVE – EXPLORING THE ISSUES

After the structured opening there is then the opportunity to widen the discussion to allow an exploration of the issues by the parties. This can be difficult for the mediators as they have to allow the parties to explore feelings aroused by the dispute and express some of the anger and hurt. This period is likely to concentrate on the past and a key role of the mediators is to try to move the parties on to thinking about the future once this seems appropriate. The manner and timing of mediators' interventions is crucial in maintaining control of the process and in ensuring that power differentials do not cause distress and damage the hope of a workable agreement.

The mediators will intervene if they do not feel that progress is being made and the discussion becomes circular, repetitive or one-sided. If new statements are still being made and neither party is becoming more distressed by the discussion, then it is possible to allow a good deal of time to see if the parties themselves manage to move things on. Mediators can intervene in a number of ways, either trying to move the discussion on or, if necessary, suggesting a change in the process.

Attempts to move the discussion forward may involve asking the parties if they feel that the discussion is getting anywhere, seeking suggestions about how things might move forward, reminding people of the ground rules if they are broken, or attempting to return to the agenda set at the start. While the mediators need to use assertiveness skills in this process, it is important that the parties do not feel that they are being steamrollered, and interventions will often be in the form of questions to them. Checking whether the parties are hearing what each has said, for example, by asking them what they think the other party is saying, is sometimes a constructive way forward. It may be necessary to help parties to reframe what they are saying to allow them to be heard better. Angry statements that demand that the other person takes some action can be reflected as statements about how the actions made them feel. 'You must turn your music down' can be reframed by the mediator into 'You find the music very disturbing' and it is more likely that the other party will hear this statement.

More significant interventions may be necessary, from altering the agenda, calling a break, to moving to side meetings (see the section on caucuses later)[4] or even suggesting that the session ends and exploring the next possible steps for the two parties. Part of the introductory statement will have emphasised that anyone can call a break at any time and the reasons for this can range from the need for a natural break and/or a smoke, to allowing someone to compose themselves when very emotional. Sometimes it is appropriate for the mediators to undertake some work with the parties individually and this is what is meant by suggesting a caucus. This may be because of strong feelings which are hampering any progress or when other matters arise, such as where one or both parties appear to be holding back.

The management of caucuses can vary and may involve the mediators splitting and going with each party simultaneously or continuing to work as a pair with each party in turn. Two key principles need to be adhered to during this process, however it is managed. The mediators must maintain their role of neutrality and be seen to deal with each party equitably. They must also continue to be seen as a team working together and not be drawn into positions of advocates. Caucuses may be very brief interludes or result in 'shuttle mediation'. This will be considered in more detail later.

A key concept at this time is the attempt to move people from their stated positions to look at where their interests lie. Frequently the initial statements will be well-rehearsed positions which allocate blame and make demands for change from the other party. It is unlikely that these will be a good basis for negotiation and the mediators need to help the parties move on to look at what their real interests are and what outcomes would satisfy them. It is possible to use this to explore whether there is an outcome which would satisfy the interests of both parties and produce a 'win/win' solution which is the aim of mediation.

A frequently-used exercise which demonstrates the 'win/win' concept in a very simple form is 'the orange'. Two people both want an orange and there is only one. Various solutions may be proffered such as cutting the orange in half or getting another one, but neither would satisfy the positions taken by the parties who both want a whole orange now and cannot buy another one. Detailed questioning reveals that one person is making a cake which requires the zest of a whole orange for decoration and the other is making a cocktail which requires all the juice. Thus both can have their needs met without depriving the other. While this example is clearly an oversimplification, it illustrates the principle of moving from entrenched positions which seem incompatible, to interests which may be able to be fulfilled.

---

4   See p 60.

One process for helping this move from positions to interests is described by Katz and Lawyer[5] as 'chunking'. This is the altering of the levels of communication from generalities to specifics, chunking down, or specifics to generalities, chunking up.

An example of this process is that party A has complained about dog noise and takes the position that the solution is for party B to get rid of her dog. Moving from generalities to specifics, it emerges that the problem occurs when he is on the night shift once every three weeks and he cannot get his daytime sleep because the dog barks when it is left alone. His interests are that he wants to have sleep during the day and not be disturbed by the barking dog, and to return to the good relationship that existed previously with his neighbour before she got the dog. Party B's reaction to the original position is a clear denial of the problem but the chunking down process produces her interests. She wants to keep the dog as company and security, she is hoping her young dog will learn better behaviour and she wants to re-establish good relations with party A.

When both parties are able to see and accept the legitimacy of the interests of the other, it is often possible to bring out the fact that, not only have they some interest in common (in this case the desire to re-establish good relationships) but their other interests are not as directly opposed as their original positions might indicate. A solution might well emerge in which party B makes better arrangements for the dog, particularly when party A is on night shift, and uses dog training facilities to improve its behaviour. Party A in turn might make an effort to be less hypercritical of the dog and recognise that as it gets older and better trained, it will also add to the security of his home.

The essence of this process is in clear contrast to the more formalised means of dealing with such problems which rely on an adversarial approach, either through court action or complaints to the local authority. Court action or the keeping of complaint diaries start from a fault-based approach and often have the effect of entrenching the positions taken by the parties. As a party is building a case, or defending one, it becomes more difficult to look beyond the position of the 'opponent' and recognise any legitimate interests they may have. Mediation services try to avoid the terminology of confrontation and blame, such as 'complainant' and 'defendant', and such phrases as 'answering the complaint', and try to view the situation as two parties who each have a problem which requires attention and resolution.

Until this stage in the process is reached it is usual that the main concentration of the discussion has been on past events, and it is important that parties feel that their grievances have been aired and heard by the

---

5   Katz, Neil H and Lawyer, John W, *Resolving Conflict Successfully*, 1994, California USA: Corwin Press.

mediators, and to some extent, at least, by the other party. The past, however, is seen as the problem, and to find a resolution requires a switch of attention to the future; what does each party want from the meeting, what are their ideas about how they might live as neighbours without all the aggravation that has occurred? This requires some building of trust between them and it is often important to emphasise that they have both made an effort to come to a difficult meeting. Recognition that mediation is not an easy thing for either of them, and can only work if they are willing to participate constructively, can help build trust in the process and, by implication, with each other.

It is quite common that during the early stages of a mediation session, the parties address most of their remarks to the mediators. Mediators' interventions and attempts to move them from positions based on the past to interests for the future can encourage this tendency and mediators need to focus on encouraging direct communication of a more positive nature between the parties. Mediators need to resist the requests for 'solutions' or for their opinions of the others' behaviour. This needs to be done in a positive way by seeking reactions from the parties and emphasising their role rather than as a negative non-committal process. A mediator's 'solution' to the problem may not meet the needs of either party; they may accept it in the session but reluctant agreements are unlikely to hold. Later breakdown can then be blamed on the mediators because 'their ideas have not worked'.

> After the opening statements the discussion was widened and all parties contributed over a wide range of subjects. Leonie said that she had heard Rose's family making racist remarks and this led to the mediators intervening to establish that race was not an issue between the parties and suggesting at this stage they should concentrate on what was at issue between them. This period had seemed unproductive to all the parties but it is often necessary to get through some of the negative feelings before the parties are ready or able to move forward.

> The mediators then brought the focus back on to the DIY noise as the first issue to be tackled. All of the participants seemed more willing to focus on looking for constructive ways of going forward. Herman asked the mediators what they thought a reasonable time to stop DIY was in the evenings but they resisted this and sought the parties' solutions, by first asking David and Rose what time they thought reasonable.

STAGE SIX – BUILDING AGREEMENTS

Usually in any dispute there are several issues which need to be addressed and at Stage Four above we discussed the drawing up of an agenda. That may well have got lost during the exchanges and new information and ideas may have emerged that require some changes to it, so a start to building agreements can often be a redefinition of the problems that require attention.

Hopefully by this stage the parties are more able to view the problems from the perspective of their interests than from their previous positions. Priorities may have changed and the issues most amenable to progress may have become clearer.

The mediators need to deal with this period using problem-solving methods, trying to move from an atmosphere of conflict and hostility to one where there is a recognition of a problem which may be resolved by co-operative activity. The first stage of any such process is agreeing what the problem to be solved is.

Having reached an agreement on which issue should be tackled first, the next stage is to start generating options for its resolution; it is important that a variety of options are generated rather than jumping immediately to the first one that seems a possibility. Various methods may be used for this process, for instance, inviting people to express ideas without discussing them can generate a wide variety of options, giving a greater degree of choice and sense of participation to the parties. It is important that people are encouraged to think laterally and produce what at first sight may seem quite wild ideas and then to select from all of these the ones that could be viable.

The next stage is to assess each of these options, particularly focusing on the extent to which each meets the interests of each party and the feasibility. Some options will be easily discarded as unacceptable to one or both of the parties. Others will require more discussion and evaluation to test out each party's most favoured one. Mediators need to be prepared to test out the genuineness of each party's consent to any option, the extent to which it is within their powers to deliver it and the likelihood of it holding. Asking questions of a 'what if?' nature and trying to build in fall-back positions can prevent an option being taken up which will prove unfeasible in the long run.

An important principle is that any agreement can only be a commitment for action by those present and in many disputes there are others who play a part in the dispute but who are not present. Children, for example, can play a significant part in many neighbour disputes and it is important that any agreement focuses on what the parent present is going to say to them and how they will deal with their behaviour, rather than implying any guarantee of their future behaviour. A party may say that they will ask their visitors to park more carefully and to move their cars if they seem to blocking the neighbour's drive, but they cannot make a commitment about the visitors' behaviour. To say they will ensure that they won't do that again is easily done in a spirit of trying to resolve the issue, but it would not be realistic to make such an assurance.

Throughout the mediation session there may be some comments which could be seen as conciliatory and it is important that these are brought out and used to help progress. These may be in the form of offers, concessions, apologies or any number of comments that show some willingness to move and understand the other party's point of view. These can often pass unnoticed by the other party and it may not be appropriate for the mediators to intervene immediately but they need to come back and highlight them. Checking out whether the mediators' interpretation or memory is correct with the person who has made the gesture, needs to be followed with checking whether it has been recognised by the other party. The reaction of both parties to this can be used to explore whether it forms the basis of an agreement on an issue or whether it improves the communication, allowing progress on other issues.

In reaching an agreement it is important that it is seen as balanced between the needs of both parties and is drawn up to reflect this. Clear timetabling of any agreed action is important and, where possible, a fall-back position is agreed if some action is not taken on time. A mechanism for dealing with any future issues that may arise is covered. If a full or partial agreement is reached it is usually written down and then signed by both parties and the mediators. Both parties will be given a copy as well as a copy being kept by the service.

It needs emphasis that any agreement is voluntary and does not cover any statutory enforcement or legal status other than any other voluntary agreement made between two parties. There are good reasons to encourage the writing of an agreement. Committing oneself to paper is a demonstration of good faith and may demonstrate any balance in the agreement more effectively than if done verbally. A document that is signed and kept is more likely to be remembered and adhered to than a verbal agreement. There are, however, occasions when a written document might be thought to be provocative or misused by one of the parties and if it is likely to become the focus of future disputes it may be better omitted.

> The mediators reminded Herman that he had said that he had nearly finished the flooring which was the main source of the current problem, and then moved on to the practicalities of how much more time he needed to spend on it and when that could be done. This led to an agreement about this issue and they then turned to the issue of Rose banging on the ceiling. By systematically working through each issue they all achieved an agreement which was balanced between the parties.

> The following agreement was reached:

> - Herman will not make a noise after 9.00 pm next Friday and will aim to complete the current project before 7.00 pm next Sunday.
> - Herman will inform David and Rose if he does not complete in order to arrange a mutually satisfactory time for completion.
> - Herman will discuss any future noisy work with David and Rose to agree a timetable.
> - David and Rose will approach Herman and Leonie if there is a problem in the future and not bang on the ceiling.

- David and Rose will try to keep the children quieter before 9 am on Sundays.
- David and Rose will not play their stereo before 9.00 am on Sundays.
- Rose will not talk about Leonie and Herman to other neighbours.
- Rose and David will talk to their children about provocative behaviour and language directed against Leonie and Herman.
- Anybody may contact the service again if there are future problems.

STAGE SEVEN – CLOSURE AND FOLLOW-UP

It is important that the efforts made by the parties are acknowledged, whether or not an agreement has been reached. The mediation service will emphasise that it is available for further assistance should either party wish it, and will describe any follow-up procedure that may be undertaken; services vary in the manner of any automatic further monitoring contact. While some may do this routinely others, either because of a policy decision or because of lack of resources, may do little follow-up.

Follow-up systems can be designed to meet two needs. First, they ensure that the parties are given an opportunity to express any views about the process and the outcome of their contact with the service. This provides feedback to the organisation on how the process has worked and is a source of learning for mediators. Second, they provide statistical and anecdotal information about the working of the service. This provides feedback to funders and can be used to review practice for more effective operation of the service. Most funders now expect to receive such information routinely as part of any funding agreement.

Many services now have a formalised follow-up routine in which they send out a questionnaire to all parties either at the closure of the case or at a fixed period after the service's involvement with the case. Such questionnaires ask for feedback about the process, the behaviour of the mediators and about whether the parties' situation has improved. Sometimes direct contact is made either as part of the agreement or as a routine follow-up to allow discussion of the person's experience of mediation.

At the end of the mediation session the mediators explained that a feedback form would be sent to Rose and David and to Herman and Leonie after three months. This was done and showed that the agreement was holding and that the parties were satisfied with their experience of the community mediation service. There had been one or two minor incidents but they had managed to sort these out by direct contact.

CO-MEDIATING

Most community mediation services routinely undertake all the mediation work using two mediators working together, and this chapter has so far assumed this without looking at it in any depth. This may seem a resource-intensive manner of working which has to be justified and it also carries some logistical problems. There are risks that mediators may not find it easy to work together and a good deal of preparation and team building is necessary. Communication between co-mediators is vitally important before, during and after any work.

Co-working does have considerable benefits for the mediators, the service and the disputants. First, it offers some security, particularly when home visiting, and although the risks to mediators should not be overstated, they are working in a field where emotions can be very strong. There is also the safeguard of two mediators in the event of any complaint.

The main reasons for co-mediation centre on issues of the quality of the service offered. Mediation can prove very demanding and it is not always possible, even for experienced mediators, to conduct a session and also to be able to make appropriate notes, follow the non-verbal elements of communication and observe the process objectively. The flexible division of roles between the two mediators enables this to be undertaken more effectively and reduce the level of strain. Mediators' own experiences, views and attitudes are liable to colour their interpretation of disputes and the process; co-mediating gives a broader experience and can safeguard against mediators being trapped by their own experience into appearing to be closer to one party than the other.

Neighbour dispute mediation is a relatively new area of work and most services are young in experience of the work. Co-mediating gives the mediators a better chance of learning from each other and sharing their skills and experience, and allows newly-trained mediators to benefit from working with their more experienced colleagues. Debriefing discussions after each piece of work is a vital continuation of training as well as bringing a wider perspective to reports and communications about the session.

The co-mediators are able to offer the parties a model of co-operative working which exemplifies a positive partnership and demonstrates good practice in action. The broader experience of two people can be of benefit to the parties and help to offer a counterbalance to any power imbalance that exists between them. Ideally the mediators can reflect the sex, age, ethnic background, and economic and educational status of the neighbourhood which they serve, and this can help all the parties feel more at ease and identified with those who are trying to help them.

There may be times when the two mediators find a difference in their perceptions of the dispute and issues raised, and they will then have to discuss these to try to reach some consensus. There is, therefore, the need to have a means of resolving difficulties that may arise, and the role of co-ordinator or other person to assist in this process varies from service to service. Regular meetings and ongoing training sessions will be of value in helping to develop an atmosphere of team working between all the mediators within a service to enable co-working to be effective.

SHUTTLE MEDIATION

While most services aim to bring the parties together and may undertake more than one visit to the parties with this in mind, it is not always appropriate or possible. One of the parties may refuse a meeting, there may be threats, power differences, high levels of distrust or harassment that make a joint meeting undesirable and services may decide not to proceed (this is dealt with in more detail in Chapter 8). If shuttle mediation is then used it is an alternative to closing the case rather than to face-to-face mediation. On occasions both parties may wish to seek a resolution without meeting and the process of shuttle mediation is appropriate. In this the mediators have separate meetings with each party with a view to establishing some agreement.

Because an important aim of mediation is to help parties communicate better, this method of work is often seen as a second best. However, it enables some disputants to reach a resolution, so it is an important tool in a service's repertoire and, because it occurs usually where parties have refused to meet, it is liable to be used in the most intractable disputes and is, therefore, particularly valuable as a method. Indirect work can make some progress in improving communication and this can lead to direct mediation over unresolved matters later.

There are specific difficulties which need to be addressed. Issues of confidentiality need to be sorted out at an early stage to determine what can and cannot be discussed with the other party. It is important that the mediators are not seen simply as message takers going between the parties but are using their skills to the full. Most of these will be the same skills as have been discussed in the description of the process generally. Parties need to be helped to move on to consider their interests rather than be stuck in positions, and they also need to move on to think about the future rather than dwell on the events that 'caused' the dispute.

In particular, the process of defining and assessing options is crucial to successful shuttle mediation. Each party needs to look at what their options are and what the possible consequences of each option are. The possible areas of agreement will be identified and assessed separately before they are communicated to the other party and it is important that this process is done in an even-handed way rather than mediators just bringing proposals from one party for consideration of the other, thus limiting the exploration of other possibilities with that party.

THE USE OF CAUCUSES

The calling of caucus meetings during the mediation session has been briefly discussed earlier but requires a more detailed discussion. They can be called for a variety of reasons which may centre on relationship or communication problems between the parties; it may result from a feeling by the mediators that the process is not working and needs some individual work with the parties for progress to be made; or it may be that the problems are with the content and some options need exploring with the parties separately.

The calling of caucuses may lead to a period of shuttle mediation aimed at bringing the parties back together when there is the basis for an agreement but more often they are fairly short meetings. The issue of confidentiality within caucuses has to be made clear from the outset. It may be that it is managed as an open process with the discussion from each caucus being fed back to the joint meeting or it may be that there is an issue which requires confidential discussion, and therefore each caucus meeting is regarded as confidential and the parties have the responsibility for bringing anything back to the face-to-face meeting. Either is possible provided all parties are aware of the way issues are to be managed.

MULTI-PARTY DISPUTES

Many conflicts within a neighbourhood involve a number of people rather than a simple dispute between two households. Even in disputes between two couples it is important to recognise that neither couple may represent a single view. Partners may be more ready or less ready to reach agreement and their joint position is often a compromise. It is not appropriate for mediators to appear to be trying to exploit differences between partners or others within the same household, but it is equally inappropriate to treat them as if they were identical. It is important to check with each of them individually from time to time.

Where there is more than one party on any side it becomes even more relevant to ensure that they are each given their own identity as it is unlikely that they will represent a monolithic viewpoint. However, the basic principles of the process remain the same. In a mediation involving a larger group of people it is important to have a process which allows all participants to feel that they have a say and can contribute to the discussion. For example, in a mediation which involved two groups of about 20 people, a meeting with each group was arranged. At these meetings, after the introductions, the mediators went round the group asking them to give one issue each which they wanted to see dealt with, each person being given the right to pass. After the first round people could add any other issue which had not been identified.

After the issues had been identified and displayed on a flipchart, a discussion took place about how each might be tackled if there were a joint meeting with the two groups. From the two preliminary meetings there emerged an agenda which was brought to a joint meeting and, although conducting mediation in a room with about 50 people has its particular demands, not least a loud and firm voice at times, the skills and techniques remain the same.

The issue of power is an important consideration in any dispute which involves more than one party and it is important that mediation is not used where a number of people are likely to 'gang up' on one or two others. In such cases shuttle mediation may be the most appropriate way of avoiding the imbalance of numbers from aggravating situations rather than ameliorating them.

ATTENDANCE OF NON-DISPUTANTS

Disputants often wish to have a friend or supporter present for the face-to-face session and this requires some thought. If such a person is invited to even up a power imbalance or bring an extra dimension to the discussions, their presence can be constructive. It is important that they are not coming to act as advocate and spokesperson as this can undermine the central aim of helping the parties to communicate directly.

Bringing people as 'witnesses' is sometimes suggested but it needs to be emphasised that mediation is not a quasi-judicial hearing and does not operate in this way. The terms evidence and witness are rarely appropriate as the mediators are not trying to determine the truth or rightness of what is in dispute. It starts from the premise that each party's view is partial but equally valid. The parties are the ones that have to determine the outcome and hear each others' viewpoint. If an objective ruling on what is true is necessary then mediation is not the appropriate mechanism. In some disputes, such as those concerning boundaries, factual information may be important but its importance lies in helping the parties to assess the options and alternatives for their actions rather than as a determinant of the basis of an agreement.

Persons attending to support one of the parties can prove very useful if they are able to bring a perspective which is less emotionally involved with the dispute. They may be hearing the view of the other party for the first time and, therefore, see the situation in a new light. Experience suggests that it is often their intervention which moves the process on and influences the party they are accompanying to seek a way forward. The reverse can be true but this seems less common and has to be handled by assertiveness and possibly caucusing when it does occur. If a party is going to be negatively influenced in the mediation it is likely that, had that person not been present, they would have been able to influence the party subsequently and thus undermine any agreement reached.

OTHER INFLUENCES ON THE PARTIES

It needs to be recognised that everyone has influences, some recognised and some covert, that affect their behaviour and freedom to negotiate. Within any conflict each party has such a constituency of relationships which may help or hinder a mediation process. Gregory Tillett[6] describes these influences in various terms and ascribes them roles. There is a network of friends and other neighbours who may act as advisers or scriptwriters, giving the participant a brief and suggesting courses of action or offering help to make their case more effectively prior to mediation. Then there are those who will act like cheerleaders, whipping up support and seeking ultimate victory for their side. The less active supporter also influences a party, making them less able to compromise, and the wider audience of neighbours who are aware of the conflict without taking sides may equally make it more difficult for a party to be seen to have climbed down from an entrenched position.

The mediators will normally have no contact with or even knowledge of these pressures but they need to recognise that, to a greater or lesser degree, they will affect the behaviour of each party. A party may well feel that they are fighting the cause for others as well as for themselves or that they cannot be seen to have given way. In the majority of cases that come to face-to-face mediation, these influences are not significant, and provided the process is properly run and any agreement genuinely owned by the parties with fall-back arrangements, they will not prevent an agreement being met and sustained.

SUMMARY

The structure of any mediation process is important to give a consistent and balanced approach and a good quality of practice. Within that structure it is necessary to be flexible and deal with each case on its own merits and any process description needs to be seen as a generalised guideline rather than a

---

6   Tillett, G, *Resolving Conflict*, 1991, Melbourne, Australia: Sydney University Press.

prescription. Whatever variations may occur, the stages described are likely to be present to some degree, and the issues raised subsequently need to be seen as fitting into, rather than conflicting with, the overall structure.

CHAPTER FOUR

MODELS FOR DELIVERING MEDIATION

Marian Liebmann

INTRODUCTION

The last chapter looked at the stages in the mediation process and its variations, as practised by community mediators when they are assigned to a particular case. This chapter will look at the different models for delivering mediation, that is, the organisational structure which lies behind the mediation process. There is considerable variation between mediation services, depending on factors such as history, philosophy, funding and the nature of the area where the service is located. These different models are also changing as mediation becomes more established as a mainstream option in the UK.

These variations will be examined by looking at several crucial dimensions, including:

- different organisational structures;
- how a community mediation service is funded – from minimal through grant-aid to contract-based;
- use of paid staff/volunteers and their roles – from services which use only volunteers to those using only paid staff;
- referrals, cases and record-keeping;
- geographical situation – from densely urban through small town to very rural;
- philosophy and ethos.

Several small case studies will show how or why a particular model of service delivery has been adopted.

The chapter will make use of research studies carried out on these aspects of mediation services, such as the Grubb study on Southwark Mediation Centre,[1] the OPUS study on Newham Conflict and Change Project[2] (both several years ago), current research by Sheffield University (especially the Community Mediation Service General Survey 1995)[3] and an interview with

---

1   Quine, C, Hutton, J and Reed, B, *Community Mediation of Disputes Between Neighbours*, 1990, London: The Grubb Institute.

2   OPUS, *Newham Conflict & Change Project*, 1989, London: OPUS (An Organisation for Promoting Understanding in Society).

3   MEDIATION UK, *Community Mediation Service General Survey 1995*, 1996, Bristol: MEDIATION UK.

Bridged Canavan, who has worked with five London community mediation services at various stages in their development.

DIFFERENT ORGANISATIONAL STRUCTURES

The following options are all ones which have been tried in the UK – there are advantages and disadvantages in each.[4]

Training existing staff to be specialists in mediation

Several housing associations and local authorities have adopted this as an interim measure after identifying the need for mediation. The advantages of this approach are that the service is kept under the control of the host organisation (which usually funds it), and is relatively quick to implement. However, the disadvantages are that there can be a possible clash of roles, between being independent mediators and being enforcement officers of regulations. This means that housing officers, for instance, are not seen as impartial. There is also a problem concerning community involvement: as local people are not involved in any way, they may not feel any sense of ownership of the mediation service, or see the service as one they would wish to use.

Using freelance mediators

In this model, external freelance mediators are brought in to resolve neighbour disputes. This can work in situations where there are few disputes, and the main groundwork has been done previously. The advantages are that the mediators are preserved as independent and impartial, and the model does not require a large organisational infrastructure. The cost is also directly related to the number of cases handled. However, such mediators may be seen as very remote from the community, and problems of access and availability may increase the cost and lead to frustration.

This model has been used successfully with the Housing Associations Tenants Ombudsman Mediation Service, set up to resolve disputes between tenants and their local housing associations (usually derived from unresolved neighbour disputes), once all local remedies and efforts have been exhausted. The contract for this mediation service was awarded in 1993 to a national commercial mediation service, with a number of trained mediators in several areas; they also call on mediators from local community mediation services as and where necessary. The mediators travel to the housing association where

---

4   Crawley, J, *Neighbours, Nuisance and Mediation*, 1994, Baldock: Conflict Management Plus.

the conflict exists, talk to both parties and carry out the mediation. It works because the housing association does all the background preparation, bringing parties to the point of mediation.[5]

This model was considered in the setting up of a rural mediation service in the south of England, as superficially it looked attractive to invite mediators from Surrey (the nearest community mediation service at the time) to deal with cases as they arose. However, one only has to consider the nature of the community work involved (people out, cancelling at short notice, wrong addresses and so on) to realise that mediators travelling 100 miles to do a first party visit, only to find that they are out, could soon become an expensive and ineffective option. In fact, no community mediation service has opted for this model, as, apart from the practical difficulties, it does not allow for the community development work and raising of awareness which is needed to run a community mediation service effectively.

In-house mediation service

In this model, the mediation service has a co-ordinator who is subject to the management structures of the host organisation, but usually recruits volunteer mediators from the community to undertake the actual mediation of disputes. The advantages of this model are managerial control, often by the funding organisation, while using community involvement through community-based volunteers. The mediators are also seen as independent, as they do not have other roles within the organisation.

One of the disadvantages is that the service may have difficulty in being seen as impartial, although this can be achieved to a considerable extent by an independent multi-agency steering committee to oversee independence of operation as far as the mediation of disputes is concerned. There is also the danger of co-option of the mediation service towards the aims of the host organisation, and coming to be seen as the soft arm of enforcement.

Arguments about funding advantages and disadvantages can cut both ways. On the one hand, funding for an in-house service can be more stable, with an adequate budget, as part of a larger organisation, which is keen to set it up and see it succeed (having presumably decided that mediation is a more effective way of solving certain disputes than other well-tried remedies). This also releases the staff involved from the necessity of fundraising, so that they can devote their time to the actual work of running the service. On the other hand, some argue that in-house services with only one source of income are very vulnerable to budget cuts, and to changes of managerial policy.

---

5   Lickiss, R (with Giddings, P, Gregory, R and Karn, V), *Setting up the Housing Association Tenants Ombudsman Service: The debate and the outcome*, Research Report 2, 1996, London: HATOS.

There are a few community mediation services in the UK which have been set up in this way, usually by housing departments. They have been going for several years and shown considerable stability, and achieved a good reputation for their work; and there have been no complaints of partiality or failing to meet community needs. They all take care to keep their day-to-day operations independent of their host organisation, by being housed in separate premises, by recruiting volunteer mediators and by involving other agencies in an advisory committee to ensure good practice.

Independent community mediation service

In this model, the local mediation service is set up as an independent organisation, often a registered charity, with a management committee which oversees the general running and the co-ordinator, who in turns manages a group of mediators, usually volunteers from the local community. There are several advantages of this way of organising community mediation. In the first place, it guarantees community involvement both in the management committee (which is drawn from a wide cross-section of individuals, agencies and community organisations) and through the volunteer mediators. It also helps to build skills in the community by training volunteers and thus spreading mediation skills. The service is seen as independent and impartial. Its independence means that many different agencies can refer cases to it, and all these agencies will be able to save their officials' time.

The disadvantage of this model lies mainly in its vulnerability to funding pressures. With no statutory organisation to undertake long-term funding of the community mediation service, considerable time, effort and resources have to be put into raising funds, often from charitable trusts and businesses, as well as from statutory sources. (On the other hand, the fact that they draw funds from many sources may sometimes be a source of strength, in not relying solely on one source of funding.)

New services often have to rely on short-term project funding, which is made available locally or nationally for new initiatives, but which then needs to be replaced by longer-term funding after one or two years. In the early 1990s, many community mediation services started in this way, often supported by the government Safer Cities[6] initiative, but then became very

---

6   The UK government Safer Cities initiative provided central government funds for a variety of local projects centred on crime prevention in its broadest sense, including social methods (such as mediation, youth activities, community action, and so on) as well as the more usual tangible methods such as bolts and better lighting. It started in 1990 and local groups, including local authorities, could make bids for this funding. In 1995/96, this funding ceased, and its functions were taken over by the Single Regeneration Budget (SRB), which replaced all other funding for deprived or inner city areas. Some mediation services are beginning to access this funding, although it is much harder to do so, requiring a three-way partnership between voluntary agencies, local authorities and local business.

short of funds (particularly core funds – the funds needed to keep the basic service going) after two or three years, just when the benefits of mediation were becoming better known, and the services more experienced. More recent developments in the UK may alleviate this problem, in that more local authorities are now prepared to make contracts with local community mediation services, to handle a certain number of disputes *per annum*.

Broadly speaking, there is now a consensus that the independently organised community mediation service is the option that fulfils best the needs for independence of operation and community involvement. Many local authorities are now promoting independent community mediation services as the best way forward for them as well as for the community. They are often prepared to fund a development worker to do the preparatory work needed to involve the local community and launch an independent service, substantially funded by local authority agencies.

Setting up an independent community mediation service

There are several stages to this process, which can last up to one or two years. The most common stages in this process are as follows:

- Establish why the service is needed – this is usually done by undertaking a survey of agencies (such as housing, environmental health, police, Citizens Advice Bureaux, social services, probation and local churches) and disputes which are difficult to resolve with current resources.

- Form a steering committee – this will ensure that the service is independent in its operation and is seen as impartial. The steering committee will usually include members of statutory agencies such as the housing department, police, probation service; also voluntary agencies such as Citizens Advice Bureaux, tenants' associations, councils for voluntary service; other members may be representatives from religious denominations and the local community.

- Decide the status of the mediation service – whether it should be independent or part of another agency.

- Decide the structure of the mediation service – whether it will have paid staff, volunteers or both. Most community mediation services need at least one or two paid staff, even if most of the mediators are trained volunteers.

- Raise sufficient funds to start the service – from all the sources outlined above. Contact with the local authority will be especially useful at this point.

- Look for resources and equipment – an office and basic furniture such as telephone, photocopier and filing system, will be necessary before the mediation service can start.

- Decide on how records are to be kept.

- Recruit co-ordinator by advertising locally and also in national mediation journals.
- Recruit (volunteer) mediators – this needs to be done by all means possible eg word of mouth, publicity in the local media, posters and leaflets, using other networks. There will also need to be selection and training of volunteers, and a probationary period. (This is dealt with in more detail in Chapter 6.)
- Publicise the new service – using press, leaflets, talks, community-based networks and other opportunities.
- Seek referrals – by all the means described above.

If the mediation service is to be independent of other organisations, then the following will also be needed:

- Apply to become a registered charity – this will enable the service to attract funds from sources which will only give to registered charities.
- Set up a management committee to oversee the running of the service. The management committee is often a continuation of the steering committee, but can be composed of different people. The management committee must be voted in at the first Annual General Meeting (AGM).
- Hold AGMs and provide annual reports.
- Decide whether to register as a company limited by guarantee – this is extra work, but can protect management committee members, who are otherwise personally financially liable for any debts incurred by the service.[7]

Community mediation services are keen to serve their whole community, and this means paying attention to equality of opportunity. There is some legislation to consider and mediation services also need an equal opportunities policy. An important part of this will be to ensure equality of access to the service – and might lead to consideration of publicity or access facilities for disabled people. It will often also include a commitment to recruit volunteer mediators to reflect the local community; and this needs to be monitored, to check that it is happening – and if not, find ways of addressing this. Such a policy will also include how to handle direct discrimination, whether racism, sexism, ageism or any other way of discriminating on the basis of a person's background, beliefs or appearance.

Mediator training can be provided by a number of different people and organisations. With the growth of mediation and especially of community mediation services, there are now many mediation trainers within mediation services and also several freelance trainers who are well equipped to undertake this task. Usually a new mediation service will use an outside

7   MEDIATION UK, *Guide to Starting a Community Mediation Service*, 1993, revised 1996, Bristol: MEDIATION UK.

resource such as this for its first one or two mediation courses. After that, local trainers who have done the training course and acquired skills in mediation are able to take on the task. In this way, as more trainers become competent, more mediators are trained and mediation skills are spread wider and wider.

Community mediation service as a base to develop further services

Although community mediation services spend the bulk of their time on community and neighbour mediation, many services later develop other kinds of mediation services. Sometimes services start out with two strands from the beginning. The most common other kinds of mediation are schools mediation and conflict resolution work, and victim/offender mediation. The Community Mediation Service General Survey 1995[8] showed that some community mediation services also undertook work in the following areas: commercial, employment, domestic violence, education special needs, inter-agency and debt mediation. Several also undertook resolution of family conflicts, as family mediation services usually only accept referrals from separating or divorcing couples. One mediation service is investigating adding on family mediation (see Geographical Situation, pp 78–80), while another (the only one to offer such a broad range so far) is offering community, victim/offender, schools, domestic violence and family mediation! This parallels the situation in the USA, where mediation services often offer all kinds of mediation.

HOW A COMMUNITY MEDIATION SERVICE IS FUNDED

This is an all-important topic for community mediation services because the service is almost always provided free at the point of delivery. There are several reasons for this. Most of the work undertaken by a community mediation service is an alternative to a statutory process, which is provided free of charge by law. Environmental health officers have a duty to investigate complaints, housing departments have a duty to respond to tenants' complaints, and so on. If mediation is only available on payment, this is a disincentive to use it. Most community mediation clients cannot afford to pay anything, many living on impoverished housing estates.

There are very few cases where community mediation deals with disputes which would otherwise result in a court case, as happens in commercial mediation and family mediation, where mediation often saves clients considerable legal fees. The only neighbour disputes which are comparable are boundary disputes, which often end up in a court of law.

8   See footnote 3 for details.

Nevertheless, there are one or two community mediation services which are trying out the idea of asking for 'sliding scale' payments from clients. These services include some wealthy districts, where clients are willing to contribute – and it assumes enough awareness of the benefits of mediation that clients are willing to pay. Mediation clients who are unable to pay can still receive the service free of charge. However, this income will not be anywhere near sufficient to fund the service, so the problem of funding still remains – as it does for the large majority of services where it is not felt appropriate to charge at all.

The first three organisational structures outlined above will usually be funded by the host organisation, because the mediation service is usually started at its initiative, to fulfil needs which cannot be met in other ways. Even so, host organisations may apply to other sources of funding to help with costs, in particular special project funding from national or local government.

Independent mediation services are usually funded from a variety of sources. Often they attract start-up funding for six months to three years from national or local special project funding, eg Safer Cities, Urban Programme, Home Office Programme Development Unit, City Challenge, Community Safety Fund, Environmental Action Fund etc, many of which have recently been replaced by the Single Regeneration Budget. The latter fund is one which is accessed via local authorities, with a three-way partnership between voluntary organisations, local government and local business.

Community mediation services may also attract ongoing local government revenue funds, as mentioned above, especially from housing and environmental health departments, which are the ones which usually have the greatest need for mediation resources. Occasionally social services, probation, police and health authorities may also help – and the local education authority for any schools-related work. Community development funds are also sometimes available.

Until recently, most such funding was given in the form of a local government agency grant, for a period of one to three years. Now many local authorities are being required to purchase services by way of local contracts, and more recently still, by compulsory competitive tendering (CCT), where the local authority is legally obliged to ask for tenders for services which it previously provided. The advantage of contract-based funding is that community mediation services can expect much more secure funding, in return for providing services. The disadvantages are the serious implications of failing to complete the contract, and the increased requirements from the local authority, often accompanied by considerable bureaucracy and paperwork.

In the CCT situation, it is also not possible for a 'fledgling' community mediation service to tender for the work, as it is unable to prove its track record. In one recent instance, a grass-roots community group starting to work towards a community mediation service learned that the local authority had become interested in supporting mediation. However, because of CCT, the local authority had to hire a consultant to draw up a brief for a community mediation service, then advertise this and invite tenders from existing mediation services who could prove their viability and were interested in taking on another area as an expansion of business. The local group was not in a position to compete. Fortunately, in this instance, a neighbouring community mediation service put in a bid, was successful, and appointed a local co-ordinator to develop the service along community-based lines. This still left the local group rather out of the picture, although a possible source of volunteer mediators, and the group decided to turn its energies toward a different kind of mediation.

Another possible disadvantage of contracts is that different departments may wish to make different contracts for the work, eg the local housing department may wish to make a contract for disputes concerning local authority housing tenants only, and the environmental health department may wish to make a contract in respect of noise disputes only, leaving other kinds of neighbour disputes unfunded. However, several local authorities have co-ordinated their efforts towards funding a community mediation service for all the citizens in a particular area. This is easier in those areas where housing and environmental health are administered under the same directorate. A recent development, especially since housing associations have taken over the provision of social housing from local authorities in some areas, is that housing associations may also have contracts with local community mediation services.

Most community mediation services receive some funding from the charitable sector. This may either be to start up the mediation service, or to supplement funds from the sources already mentioned. As mediation has gained a higher profile in the UK, so the charitable trusts and foundations have been more willing to fund such services. However, this funding tends to concentrate on innovative work, eg the first rural mediation service, the first mediation service to undertake a particular kind of work, and so on. Most charitable trusts are not willing to pay for a community mediation service *ad infinitum*, or to allow more than a small percentage of their funding to go towards core costs.

Many community mediation services, once they are running well, develop training and publications as a supplementary service which brings in some money towards funding the service. However, there are no community mediation services which can fund themselves entirely in this way, without diverting all their effort into training, and ceasing to run the mediation service.

Local mediation services also look to local companies to help in a variety of ways, with grants, secondment of staff or with gifts in kind, such as office furniture and computers.

The mediation service may also have a membership scheme, and try to raise funds from members of the community, local churches and fundraising events.[9]

The Community Mediation Service General Survey 1995[10] showed that the five largest sources of funds for community mediation services in 1994/95 were (in order): local authorities, the Scottish Office, Safer Cities, local charities, industry/commerce.

USE OF PAID STAFF/VOLUNTEERS AND THEIR ROLES

The most usual model which has developed is that of a paid co-ordinator (or manager, where there are several staff) who recruits volunteer mediators and arranges for them to be trained in mediation skills. Larger services also employ further administrative help if they can afford to – and there are many ways of developing different roles, such as intake worker, volunteer co-ordinator, volunteer supervisor, fundraiser, and so on.

A few community mediation services operate with volunteers only. For the most part, these are smaller services, sometimes rural or based in a small town, which have not attracted sufficient funding to appoint a paid co-ordinator, or where the workload does not justify such an appointment. Sometimes, sadly, this is the case for mediation services in sizable towns, where start-up funding has not been followed by regular income, but volunteers keep the service going from their own sense of dedication. Where this situation is only a short-term problem, this can tide a mediation service over the gap until further funding becomes available; but if it continues long-term, this can be very debilitating and lead to the gradual demise of the service. Although this has happened to a few services, it is remarkable how few, given the national trends in cutting back services in general over this period.

In a different category are one or two quite large community mediation services which deliberately use volunteers only. The main reason they give for this is one of principle: all those involved give their time freely to the community. A secondary reason, also quite important, is that the service is more likely to survive in a harsh financial climate if it only requires small amounts of money (for volunteers' expenses, telephone bills, etc). It also obviates the need for large-scale fundraising, so that all efforts can go into running the service.

To achieve this, the co-ordinator roles rotate around a number of different people. In practice, this depends on a few very dedicated and highly skilled

---

9   See footnote 7 for details.
10   See footnote 3 for details.

volunteers who are prepared to spend large portions of their week undertaking professional work without remuneration. This makes these services vulnerable to changes in circumstances of the volunteer co-ordinators. Despite their lack of financial resources, they can provide a service which is just as good as those with paid co-ordinators – in fact one such service was one of the first four to gain MEDIATION UK Accreditation in 1994.

An opposite trend to this is the payment of mediators in a few community mediation services. Although this goes against the 'volunteers serving the community' ethic of most community mediation services, there are plenty of precedents in other kinds of mediation. Commercial mediators are all paid; family mediators are paid sessional rates; victim/offender mediators are sometimes volunteers and sometimes paid sessionally. (Payment of course need not stand in opposition to community service: nurses, social workers and teachers are all paid to serve the community.) Training in community mediation skills is almost always paid for, at conventional training rates. Supervision of volunteers is sometimes a volunteer task (eg a member of the management committee), sometimes paid – either someone internal or someone external to the service.

One of the newer community mediation services was started by a steering committee which included several people from the local family mediation service. They felt very strongly that it was exploitative to use volunteers for such a skilled task as mediation, and that it should be paid. They applied to a national charity for the funding to start the first community mediation service with paid mediators. These posts were advertised in the normal way, and the service operates with a full-time co-ordinator, part-time intake worker and six part-time paid mediators. It is being evaluated as a condition of the funding.

One or two other services have decided to opt for paid mediators for circumstantial reasons. One of the oldest services, based in the Midlands, started by recruiting volunteers but found them hard to retain. A new co-ordinator came and did much of the mediation herself to learn the ropes. She operated the service in this way for several years, until the workload became too big. The service then tried again to recruit and train volunteers, but had a poor response. At this point they opted for another paid worker, as they felt continuity was important, and it cost no more to have two part-time paid mediators than continually to recruit and train groups of volunteers.

One of the larger London services with several paid staff uses paid workers to do all the intake work and preparation for mediation. They do much of the work with the individual parties on the telephone, and do not undertake home visits. They feel that using staff for the initial stages is less complicated, provides greater consistency and is less vulnerable to volunteer turnover. Cases going to mediation are then handed over to trained volunteer mediators, who are recruited from time to time as the need arises. Such a service, with a large staff input, can manage with quite a small volunteer group, as many cases do not get as far as a face-to-face mediation session.

Here we see again the tension between the aims of, on the one hand, volunteering and developing mediation skills in the community, and on the other hand, running an efficient and reliable community mediation service. The first emphasises the importance of volunteers, the second the most effective way of providing a mediation service. Often of course both can be accomplished using volunteers, but the examples above show circumstances where service delivery has been given priority over community development.

In many smaller community mediation services, co-ordinators also act as mediators. Sometimes this is a matter of necessity, sometimes it is concerned with induction of new volunteer mediators, sometimes it is a matter of choice, especially if the person concerned has trained as a mediator and wishes to 'keep his/her hand in'. In one London service, the co-ordinator undertook practically all mediations himself, taking different volunteers with him as the second mediator. If the co-ordinators are paid, then this is another way of using 'paid mediators' in community mediation.

In larger mediation services, co-ordinators rarely mediate – they have too much else to do. They are responsible for the overall running of the service, for talks and publicity, for relating to local agencies, often for fundraising, sometimes for other staff, and many of the matters relating to being an independent voluntary organisation.

The Community Mediation Service General Survey 1995[11] showed that in 1995 there were nine community mediation services with no paid staff (ie all volunteers), seven with one part-time paid person, and 15 with one or more paid members of staff. Only four mediation services had three or more full-time-equivalent staff, and all were large urban services.

REFERRALS, CASES AND RECORD-KEEPING

Referrals to a community mediation service come from many agencies and quarters. Some services insist that disputants refer themselves, but most are happy for agencies to make referrals, provided that the disputants have agreed. This can be helpful where disputants do not have access to telephones and are not happy writing letters. Agencies making referrals may include housing departments, environmental health departments, housing associations, police, social services, probation services, race equality councils, victim support, tenants'/residents' associations, Citizens Advice Bureaux, advice centres, law centres, solicitors, doctors and health centres, religious organisations – and self-referrals, or referrals from friends or relatives.

Referrals may be concerned with disputes in any of the following areas: noise (from home improvements, televisions, stereo systems, washing

---

11   See footnote 3 for details.

machines, dogs, cars etc), boundary disputes, children's behaviour, pets, rubbish, drainage, vandalism and damage to homes, abusive behaviour, racial harassment, parking problems and cars being mended; these are only some of the possible issues.

The community mediation service usually records basic statistics, including the source of the referral and the nature of the dispute. It may also record (for both parties) housing, employment, sex, age, any disability, and ethnic origin. Some services also record mediators' ethnic origin, sex, age and any disability. Obviously services record the number of 'cases', although this may not be a simple matter, and there has been great variety between services as to how they do this. For instance, one mediation service may record only cases asking for mediation, while another may record all enquiries. Some mediation services record all enquiries as cases, others only if mediators make an actual visit.

The Community Mediation Service General Survey 1995 showed that 10 services (mainly rural ones and those based on small towns) received less than 50 referrals over a 12-month period. At the other end of the scale, the two oldest London services received over 300 referrals, and two large experienced urban services outside London over 200 referrals. Large towns and small cities received 100 to 200 referrals. These numbers seem to reflect both the size of the population being served and the time the service has been running. There can be considerable fluctuations in referrals, depending on how well the service is known, the attitude of local agencies and seasonal variations.

As well as recording the total number of enquiries, mediation services also record the number which turn into 'mediation cases', and what happens to all of these along the way, ie where visits are made to first party, second party, and those cases which proceed to face-to-face mediation. Some mediation services only consider cases as mediations where both parties agree to meet, while others are happy to offer 'shuttle mediation' and consider this just as valid a form of mediation as meeting face-to-face. Obviously these differing philosophies will be translated into very different records and statistics.

Services also record their evaluation of success, although the indicators chosen can vary quite significantly, from productive work with one party, to achievement of a face-to-face mediation with both parties – or improvement of the relationship between the parties by whatever method. Records also show the number of agreements and any follow-up that is undertaken, such as a measure of whether agreements are still holding after a period of say, six months.[12]

This variety of recording systems of local mediation services has made it difficult to obtain an accurate national picture of community mediation across the UK. The recent research project on the cost-effectiveness of mediation,

---

12   See footnote 7 for details.

undertaken by MEDIATION UK, therefore also included an attempt to co-ordinate such recording systems, and achieve consensus on how to record referrals and what happens to them, so that a national database can be compiled.

The research team from Sheffield University (see Chapter 12) accomplished this by compiling a list of the most common referral categories, and then piloting a number of 'success criteria' with the MEDIATION UK Executive Committee. The resulting criteria were sent out in advance and then discussed at a meeting of the MEDIATION UK Community Mediation Network (a twice-yearly gathering of community mediation services to discuss matters of common interest). Most local services were very positive about the possibility of a national database, as they felt this would strengthen their local credibility. In January 1996 all local services received a questionnaire based on the agreed categories and criteria, to cover the year 1996, returnable in May 1997 (to allow for completion of cases started in 1996). At the time of writing these returns were not yet due, but it is hoped that they will provide an annual and comparable picture of the development of community mediation in the UK.

The schedule for the annual returns, together with guidance notes, is shown in the Appendix to this chapter. It shows the current 'state of play' in the debate on what is important to be counted. The debate continues, however, and one of the next issues to be raised is the question of who has the right to judge the success of a mediation. The form in the Appendix is set out in such a way as to assume that the community mediation services will make this judgment, usually via the mediators. Some services have already suggested that the disputants should be doing this, in line with the empowerment ethos of mediation – and then of course there might be two (or more in the case of multi-party disputes) opinions. Many community mediation services do try to do a follow-up client satisfaction survey, but there are also many which do not have the resources to undertake this at the moment.

GEOGRAPHICAL SITUATION

When community mediation services started in the early 1980s, it was implicitly assumed that neighbour disputes were a largely urban problem, exacerbated by a number of factors such as overcrowding, increasing lifestyle differences, poor house conversions leading to thin walls, shortage of housing (leading to problematic housing allocations), heterogeneous ethnic mix and so on. Early services were started with the explicit aim of helping people from a variety of backgrounds to live together more peacefully.

In these densely populated areas, transport is not usually a problem. However, there may be problems associated with particular neighbourhoods, so that – quite apart from the mediation considerations for having two co-mediators – safety may also require this. Most such services try to recruit volunteers who either live or work in the area concerned, so that mediation clients can identify with them as local people. Training usually takes place at the local mediation service premises or somewhere central to the area.

As large urban mediation services grow, they may need 50 or even 75 volunteer mediators. It then becomes impossible for volunteers to continue meeting as one group to hold case discussions. One way of handling this situation is to assign volunteer mediators to small groups which can meet these needs more appropriately (see Chapter 6). Regular social occasions can provide larger meeting points and help to retain a sense of belonging to the larger service.

Many of the community mediation services which started in the early 1990s were funded by the government Safer Cities initiative, aimed at intensive crime prevention on identified high-crime housing estates. It proved difficult to recruit mediators from these estates, so such services used volunteers from other parts of the same town or city. Most of these services soon received referrals from other districts and sooner or later obtained funding to become city-wide.

More recently several rural mediation services have started. Although the pressures of the inner city are absent, there are disputes which cause great distress to those concerned, and mediation services have been welcomed as fulfilling an identified need. However, they experience some problems which urban services do not.

The most obvious of these is the wide area covered by most rural services. This makes car ownership a near necessity for volunteer mediators, and the large distances to be covered in visits and mediations means that rural services need to raise considerable funds for travel expenses. Distance also makes attendance at the initial training course problematic for some – so some rural services alternate venues for training courses, to attract volunteers from different parts of their 'patch'. They may also arrange training in weekend blocks, rather than weekly evenings, to cut down on travel needed.

With smaller caseloads, the variations in the flow of cases also affect rural services more, especially when the end of a training course coincides with a lull in cases! One rural service has received fewer referrals of neighbour and community disputes than expected from the needs survey prior to starting – but a growing number of couples seeking family mediation, as there is currently no family mediation service in the area. It is therefore considering widening its brief to include family mediation. Rural services may become the first 'all-purpose' mediation centres because it makes sense in geographical terms.

Some rural mediation services deal with their large area by opening small sub-offices which may be staffed by one or two volunteers once a week for half a day. This enables the service to have a more local profile. The nearest volunteers may also undertake all the mediations in those areas, and have a stronger identity with their patch than volunteers in an urban service. However, this raises the problem of being too well-known to be seen as neutral, so that there may be occasions when volunteers from far afield have to be mobilised.

The organisational consequences of being an urban or a rural community mediation service are not unique to mediation – they are common to most voluntary organisations. Urban voluntary organisations have the benefit of larger numbers of cases and volunteers, and the problems of overload of cases and turnover of volunteers (both standard features of urban life). Rural voluntary organisations receive fewer referrals and have fewer volunteers, who may stay longer; their problems concern travel time and costs, and keeping the organisation going throughout fluctuations in referrals.

PHILOSOPHY AND ETHOS

This has already been commented on briefly above, and will be developed further in this section. It also takes up the threads of the trends noted in Chapter 2.

In Chapter 2 we noted the two strands of thinking which informed the community mediation movement from the start. The first was community-based with an emphasis on independence, volunteer help and community learning. The second was more agency-led, with an emphasis on problem-solving and effectiveness, and the procedures to achieve this most efficiently.

These emphases are still apparent in 1997. Those services which emphasise community-based learning tend to have much greater involvement of volunteers as a point of principle. Volunteers undertake the initial casework as well as the mediation, and also have a place on the management committee. Such services have a large volunteer group (never enough!) and regular, well-organised training courses, often twice-yearly. They often have more applicants wishing to join than training places. They try very hard not to reject volunteers but to use those unable to learn mediation skills in another capacity, such as helping in the office. They see their task not just as training a volunteer workforce, but as training the wider community. In these services, the volunteers are the life force of the organisation.

Those services which emphasise service delivery tend to have more paid staff, who do a larger proportion of the work. Volunteer mediators are still often used, but in a smaller role, and they are recruited as and when necessary rather than as part of a regular philosophy. As they may not be recruited in very large numbers, it can be difficult to organise specific training courses for them, so they may be trained 'on the job'. Some of these services, as we have seen, have dispensed with volunteers altogether.

As community mediation becomes a more mainstream activity, and more local authorities are prepared to provide funding, some people see a danger that mediation will necessarily become agency-led, with service delivery as the main aim – and that this is the price to be paid for becoming 'part of the establishment'. These fears parallel developments in the USA, where mediation is often the only alternative on offer for poor people, and mediation sessions concentrate purely on achieving a solution to the problem.

This dichotomy in the USA has been expressed by Bush and Folger in their book *The Promise of Mediation*,[13] which contrasts the 'satisfaction' story, in which mediation concentrates on settlements, and the 'transformation' story which helps people to understand each other and through this to change how they view the problem situation. This is developed further in Chapter 13.

However, there are factors which suggest (as in mediation and conflict resolution generally) that we need not contemplate an either/or situation. The readiness of local authorities to acknowledge the benefits of independent community mediation services suggests they are interested in community involvement and 'ownership'. Several of the larger, more established services, with substantial local authority funding, still maintain a vibrant and growing volunteer group. Moreover, most British community mediation has as its aim the increase of understanding between people rather than settlement pure and simple – so would see the 'transformation' story as 'what mediation is about'.

CONCLUSION

This chapter has looked at several important factors in the organisational structure which is needed to deliver the mediation process – the organisational structure itself, how the service is funded, whether paid staff or volunteers are used (and for which tasks), ways of keeping records, the geographical situation and the philosophy of the service. There may be other factors too which affect a community mediation service – such as the personality and background of the co-ordinator, and the way a management committee operates – but I have tried to confine the discussion in this chapter to those factors which are more systemic and generalised.

The interaction of all these factors is what gives each local community mediation service its own special flavour. There is a continual learning process as different factors are emphasised, and mediation services come

---

13   Bush, RB and Folger, JP, *The Promise of Mediation, Responding to Conflict through Empowerment and Recognition*, 1994, San Francisco: Jossey-Bass.

together (at the Community Mediation Network meetings and the MEDIATION UK Annual Conference) to discuss and develop better ways of delivering their service.

As a national organisation, MEDIATION UK is committed to 'good practice' but not to uniformity. Its accreditation procedure (see Chapter 11) deliberately emphasises diversity and developing practice to suit local circumstances and conditions. There are many good ways of delivering mediation services, and it is important to maintain a lively dialogue concerning the advantages and disadvantages of all the facets of differing structures and locations.

APPENDIX

MEDIATION UK Community Mediation Neighbour Dispute Survey

FIELD 1	REFERRAL PERIOD TO WHICH FORM RELATES: January 1996 – December 1996

FIELD 2	REQUESTED DATE FOR RETURN OF FORM TO MEDIATION UK: 31 May 1997

FIELD 3	IDENTITY OF MEDIATION SERVICE PROVIDERS

Name of Community Mediation Service *(please write in space provided)*	
Contact name and address *(please write in space provided alongside)* Tel Fax	

FIELD 4	KEY STATISTICS ON VOLUME OF CASES HANDLED DURING ABOVE PERIOD

Total number of **requests for assistance** involving 'neighbourhood' disputes during the current referral period *(please see field 1, above)*	
Number of 'neighbourhood' disputes **accepted by** the service during the above period	
Number of accepted cases during the above referral period which were **concluded** (ie no further involvement planned) by 31 March 1997	
Number of accepted cases during the above referral period that were **still ongoing at 31 March 1997**	
Number of **previous cases** that were referred before the start of the current referral period and not concluded until then	
Other enquiries involving neighbour disputes that do not fall into any of the above categories	

FIELD 5	BREAKDOWN OF CASES REFERRED TO SERVICE BY ISSUES RAISED
	Please indicate the **number** of cases that featured each of the following elements

Noise problems	
Family or relationship problems	
Children's behaviour	
Anti-social behaviour (not involving children)	
Abusive behaviour (including non-racial harassment), threats etc	
Racial harassment	
Boundary/property disputes including damage, drainage etc	
Untidiness/gardens/rubbish/smells	
Animals including dogs	
Cars, parking etc and vehicle repairs	
Mental health element, care in the community, personality disorder	
Other dispute not falling into any of the above categories	
Total number	

FIELD 6	**MAIN SOURCES OF REFERRALS**
	Please indicate the **number** of cases coming from each source mentioned below

Self-referrals (please see guidance notes for definition)	
Housing Departments	
Environmental Health Service Departments Other council departments, eg social services, education	
Housing Associations	
Citizens Advice Bureaux, Advice Centres, Law Centres, etc	
Police	
Solicitors	
Councillors or MPs	
Other referral agencies not included in the above	
Referrals where the referring agency is unspecified or not known	
Total number	

FIELD 7	**FORMS OF MEDIATION USED IN ALL NEIGHBOURHOOD DISPUTE CASES CONCLUDED DURING 1996** Please indicate the **number** of cases in which each of the following methods was used

Direct mediation (face-to-face meeting between the parties)	
Indirect mediation (shuttle diplomacy, go between)	
Combination of direct and indirect mediation	
Work with one or more parties not involving any of the above	

FIELD 8	KEY STATISTICS ON OUTCOMES REACHED FOR CASES REFERRED DURING 1996 (OR PREVIOUSLY) WHICH WERE COMPLETED BY 31 MARCH 1997 (Please indicate the **number** of cases involved for each of the following outcomes)

Problem resolved and agreement reached on all presenting issues	
Partial agreement on the presenting issues	
No agreement but **evidence of improved communication or better understanding** between parties	
Assistance given to one party removes need for further involvement	
Problem resolved without intervention by the mediation service	
Mediation felt to be **inappropriate and parties referred elsewhere**	
Mediation felt to be **inappropriate** and no other solution available	
Closure following a **withdrawal** (or refusal to get involved) by one of the parties	
Closure because of irreconcilable differences between the parties	
Closure for some **other reason**	
Total number	

FIELD 9	LONGER-TERM OUTCOMES DISCLOSED BY FOLLOW-UP MONITORING

Does your service undertake follow-up monitoring of cases?   **No** ☐ **Yes** ☐

(If the answer is yes, please answer the questions below; otherwise please go on to the next section)

Do you monitor how clients feel about the mediation process?   **No** ☐ **Yes** ☐

Do you monitor how clients feel about the outcome?   **No** ☐ **Yes** ☐

Do you monitor the state of relations between the parties?   **No** ☐ **Yes** ☐

(Please answer the following questions, if appropriate, by filling in the number of cases monitored that were dealt with during the referral period and also the relevant interval)

	Number	Interval
Agreements known to be holding in full after monitoring		
Agreements known to be holding in part after monitoring		
No resumption of conflict in cases where there is no agreement		
Agreements known to have broken down (or conflict is known to have resumed)		
Number of cases in which we are unable to ascertain current position		

FIELD 10	REPEAT REFERRALS

How many cases from the current referral period (see field 1) have had to be reopened again following a resumption of the problem or renewed conflict between the parties? ....

FIELD 11	EQUAL OPPORTUNITIES MONITORING

Does your mediation service regularly conduct equal opportunities monitoring?

No ❏   Yes in respect of clients ❏   Yes in respect of mediators ❏

Thank you for your assistance in completing this statistical return

Requested completion date: 31 March 1997
(please see accompanying notes)

Requested return date: 31 May 1997
(please see accompanying notes)

Please return it to: MEDIATION UK
Alexander House
Telephone Avenue
Bristol BS1 4BS

Guidance Notes to accompany the Neighbour Dispute Survey Form for Community Mediation Services

The accompanying survey form is intended to provide MEDIATION UK with selected key statistics about the operation of mediation services in relation to neighbour disputes only. Its main purpose is to enable MEDIA-TION UK to respond more accurately to requests for such information and, hopefully, to strengthen the case for more secure funding in the future. It has been designed in consultation with mediation service co-ordinators to try to ensure that it is compatible, as far as possible, with existing data collection systems, and, hopefully, to minimise the work involved in completing it.

The primary aim of these guidance notes is to assist you to complete the form in a way that will maximise the consistency and reliability of the information that is provided, since not all services record their statistics in the same way. The form itself is divided into a number of sections or fields which are numbered in the margin. Please refer to the following notes when completing each section.

Field 1 identifies the **referral period** to which the form relates; no action required.

Field 2 indicates the date by which you are requested to return the completed form to MEDIATION UK at the address shown below; no action required.

Field 3 **identity of mediation service provider:** please write in the appropriate boxes giving the name of your service and also a contact name and address, plus phone and fax numbers (where applicable) in the spaces provided.

Field 4 **key statistics** on **volume of cases** handled during the current referral period:

’**requests for assistance’** – please enter here the total number of cases in which you were asked to provide advice or assistance for someone involved in a neighbour dispute irrespective of whether it technically counts as a referral for your own recording purposes;

’**number of cases accepted by the service’** – please enter here the number of cases that appear to satisfy your referral criteria (eg geographical, tenure status of parties, type of dispute) irrespective of whether a visit has been made and irrespective of the wishes of other parties to the dispute to become involved or not;

'number of concluded cases' – please enter here the number of cases taken on during the current referral period (see field 1, above) in which no further involvement is planned by the service after the date indicated, irrespective of whether you have formally 'closed the books' on the case; [NB some services only do this after a period of follow-up monitoring];

'number of ongoing cases' – please enter here the number of cases taken on during the current referral period and which had not been concluded by the date shown (31 March 1997).

'number of previous cases' – please enter here the number of cases that were taken on by the service before the start of the current referral period (ie those that were ongoing from the previous year) and concluded during the current referral period;

'number of other enquiries' – please enter here any other enquiries relating to specific neighbour disputes that do not fall into any of the above categories (eg requests for factual information about the service itself; but not including press enquiries, requests from MEDIATION UK, researchers etc).

Field 5 **break-down of cases** referred to the service by type of case or issue raised:

please indicate for those cases taken on during the current referral period how many of them involved each of the issues mentioned. NB it is probable that the total number requested for this section may exceed the total caseload for the year since some cases may involve a number of issues, or may be characterised differently by each of the parties.

Field 6 **main sources of referrals:** please indicate here the number of cases that were known to be referred by each of the main agencies listed. Please include, if known, both direct referrals, using a formal procedure, and also indirect referrals, possibly as a result of informal advice. As far as possible, therefore, the category of self-referrals should be confined to those who approached the service on their own initiative, or at the suggestion of some other individual (eg a previous user of the service) as opposed to an agency of the type listed.

Field 7 form(s) of mediation (process): please enter here the number of cases dealt with under each of the headings specified. The term 'direct mediation' is intended to include any case resulting in a face-to-face meeting between some or all of the parties together with any preparatory meetings that might have been required to set up such a meeting. The term indirect mediation is intended to include any 'arm's-length' or 'shuttle' negotiations aimed at resolving a dispute.

Field 8 key statistics on outcomes reached for cases taken on during the current referral period (including ongoing cases from previous years) and concluded by 31 March 1997: please indicate the number of concluded cases dealt with in each of the ways mentioned in this field. NB the total number of cases should correspond to the number of 'concluded cases' referred to in Field 4.

Field 9 longer-term outcomes and follow-up monitoring: not all services conduct follow-up monitoring; if yours does, please answer all the questions in field 9 including the monitoring interval in the box provided. If it does not, please indicate this in the appropriate box and proceed to field 10.

Field 10 repeat referrals: please show the number of cases (relating to the current referral period – see field 1 above) that have had to be reopened following a resumption of or renewed conflict between the parties. NB if only one of the parties is the same, please count this as a 'new case'.

Field 11 equal opportunities monitoring: please indicate whether or not your service regularly conducts equal opportunities monitoring of the kinds referred to.

Requested dates for completing and returning the survey forms

The form provides for a follow-up period of three months from the end of the relevant referral period which should allow time for most of the more recent referrals to be concluded. This is referred to as the completion date and will be 31 March of the current year. However we are not asking for the forms to be filled in and returned to us until the return date, which is 31 May of the current year. We hope that this will allow sufficient time for the forms to be filled in after the end of the financial year.

CHAPTER FIVE

GROWTH AND DEVELOPMENT OF A SERVICE

Marion Wells

INTRODUCTION

This chapter focuses on one particular mediation service and describes its origins, development and current working methods.

Bristol Mediation is chosen because it is a mainstream mediation service which has been running for five years, and is typical of good practice as this is generally understood. It is a fairly well-resourced service in an urban area with paid office-based staff and a large number of volunteer mediators. It offers community mediation for neighbours and schools, and has a number of special projects to its credit.[1] It has an experienced and well-respected team of trainers.

THE BEGINNINGS

In 1986 a Quaker peace group met in the city centre. As people walked home they found themselves in the middle of a violent disturbance – around them rushed police cars with sirens going and they could see that barricades were being erected. This experience, together with anxieties about rising urban tensions, riots and talk of arming the police, led to a small group being formed at a Quaker Meeting House to consider ways of dealing with urban conflict. One possibility was mediation. After much discussion the group set about planning a community dispute resolution project. They brought their ideas and proposals to a large meeting in December 1986. There followed a lengthy period of enquiry and research before the Quaker Meeting would consider raising funds to set up the project. £6,500 was donated by Quakers in the autumn of 1988 and in the following spring a charitable foundation gave £10,000. There was now enough money to appoint a co-ordinator, Hermione Legg, and undertake some training work, but not enough to run a community mediation service. The steering group was formalised into a management committee and by September 1990 the mediation scheme was both a registered charity and a company limited by guarantee.

During the first 18 months, 20 people were recruited and trained in basic mediation skills by the most qualified pair of trainers in the vicinity, who

---

1   There are published reports available from the service: see Appendix 1 for address of Bristol Mediation.

developed a basic training course based on the *Mediator's Handbook* by Jennifer Beer.[2] This was seen as the most suitable, inexpensive handbook for community mediators at this time. The first group of mediators included several trainers, some from the group described above and some who were trainers elsewhere in counselling and communication skills. These trainers quickly became involved in helping to run the training courses.

Time was usefully spent, during this extended formative period, spreading the concept of mediation and developing the team of mediators. Part of the initial brief was to provide day training courses in mediation and conflict resolution skills for interested people who could see that mediation skills would be useful to them in their work with people. Visitors from abroad were a very significant catalyst: experienced mediators came from the United States and Australia and talked about their work.

DEVELOPMENT OF THE MEDIATION SCHEME

At this point Bristol Mediation was invited to join an inter-agency crime prevention group set up by Bristol Safer Cities[3] at the invitation of the Residents' Liaison Group in Southmead, a housing estate to the north of the city. Hermione Legg describes what happened in her report *Creating a Climate of Trust*:[4] 'From Bristol Mediation's point of view, its presence within the Safer Cities orbit gave it access to the statutory agencies at the highest level and enabled it to secure funding for its neighbour mediation service. It also gave the opportunity to extend the use of mediation into the area of community safety and crime prevention. Residents expressed a sceptical view of the value of mediation for neighbours in dispute but were extremely interested in getting their children to learn non-violent ways of handling differences.'

For three years until mid-1995 Hermione was the mediator-in-residence two and sometimes three days a week in Southmead. The work was funded until 1993 by Safer Cities. When these funds were unexpectedly curtailed, the Joseph Rowntree Charitable Trust agreed to fund the continuation of the work – in particular to explore further the use of mediation in an area of high urban stress. This concentration on working in one area of a city is quite a common starting point for mediation services.

As a charismatic first co-ordinator, Hermione attracted many supporters, in the capacity of committee members, mediators and funders. She was a

---

2   Beer, J, *Mediator's Handbook*, revised May 1990, Philadelphia: Friends Suburban Project of the Philadelphia Yearly Meeting, Society of Friends (Quakers). A more recently updated version, 1997, is available from New Society Publishers in the USA and Jon Carpenter Publishing in the UK.

3   A central government source of funds for inner city initiatives in the early and mid-1990s.

4   Legg, H, *Creating a Climate of Trust: Time to Listen*, Bristol Mediation Southmead Project 1991–95 Report, 1997, Bristol: Bristol Mediation.

mediator and innovator, and knew how to get publicity and develop trust from different groups of people. Soon premises were found and office systems set up.

An intake worker was appointed to receive enquiries, keep records and allocate cases to mediators. By the time a city-wide neighbour mediation scheme was launched in October 1991, 21 trained mediators had mediated 66 cases. Clients' most frequent presenting problem was categorised as harassment.

A NOISE COUNSELLING SERVICE

Noise was the second most common presenting problem, and funding became available from the Department of the Environment's Environmental Action Fund. Bristol Mediation decided to put together a proposal (in February 1991), to provide a pioneering service to help Bristol residents who were having problems with neighbours over domestic noise. The idea was encouraged by the city council's housing department and also by the health and environmental services department. The application was successful, and the project started in September 1991, with Paul Holder, a trained mediator, being appointed as the country's first noise counsellor. The first four months were spent setting up the service. Referrals were taken over the following 26 months and, as further funding was not available, the last month was given over to winding down the project and writing a report.[5]

The project's main aim was to provide an independent noise counselling service to enhance the work of the city's health and environmental services department, exploring more effective ways of resolving certain types of domestic noise complaints. These resolutions often included addressing circumstances which had social, personal and interpersonal aspects. Paul summarised his results: '102 domestic noise cases were dealt with over 26 months. 69% of clients who responded to an evaluation questionnaire said they experienced a change for the better after the service became involved. The project also gained useful knowledge into the nature of domestic noise problems. In particular, it was found that successful resolutions were facilitated by also giving support to the following issues, which were implicated in the noise complaint: housing/tenancy, mental health, personal life, physical health, family, and pet welfare.'[6]

---

5   Holder, P, *Noise Counselling Service September 1991 – March 1994 Final Report*, 1994, Bristol: Bristol Mediation.

6   *Ibid*.

BECOMING SKILLED NEIGHBOUR MEDIATORS

The mediators who took on the casework of the mediation scheme arranged to meet once a month for support and feedback. A small group of them worked on Good Practice Guidelines[7] which were then widely discussed, revised and agreed. Overall this early period was one of experimentation, not with the essential concept of mediation, but with a variety of ways of proceeding at different stages in the mediation process. The debate, which is still ongoing, surrounded matters such as the importance of persuading parties to come to a face-to-face meeting, the value of shuttle diplomacy and the number of visits it is reasonable or useful to offer to clients. Practising mediators had, and continue to have, differing views.

THE SCHEME BECOMES A SERVICE

Good publicity has always been actively sought and mediation promoted at every opportunity. Potential funders and users of the service were often confused as to what mediation was or could be expected to achieve: was it meditation misspelt or, 'Surely it's the same as arbitration really?' Care was taken to write and circulate suitable leaflets and prepare competent funding applications.

To adopt its more formal existence, Bristol Mediation had to have a written constitution, a properly elected management committee, annual general meetings and annual reports. Committee members were invited to stand for election based on their individual commitment and skills rather than as representatives of external organisations. They were and remain a highly motivated and available policy-making committee. For each of its areas of work, the organisation developed a task culture in which each project got the management structure best suited to it. Groups or sub-committees were changed or disbanded as the task changed. Bristol Mediation changed its description from scheme to service to reflect a sense of establishment and continuity.

BUSINESS PLAN PRODUCED 1993/94

A business plan was prepared over several months with help from someone seconded to advise on the process. It included a mission statement:

---

7   Bristol Mediation, *Good Practice Guidelines for Mediators*, first published 1994, updated regularly, Bristol: Bristol Mediation.

This service exists to promote and provide mediation and other forms of conflict resolution as processes which can empower all people to manage conflict and changes creatively. We strive to encourage and enable others to explore ways of coping with and resolving conflicts in their own lives and in the life of their community.

There were statements on values, policies and the background and role of the service. Strategies were outlined for the following six areas of work:

- Mediation service.
- Community development.[8]
- Special projects: noise counselling.
- Schools: peer mediation.
- Training and consultancy work.
- Education, research and development.

The business plan included statements on funding strategies and forward planning. It was an invaluable exercise both as a process and for its product. Later a schools project business plan and a training and consultancy development plan were also produced.

AN OUTLINE OF THE SERVICE FIVE YEARS ON – WINTER 1996/97

There are now 50 trained volunteer mediators, a schools group of four (paid sessionally) and six paid office staff – manager, intake worker, administration worker, volunteer co-ordinator, schools co-ordinator and promoter/fundraiser. Only the intake worker is full time. The management committee has nine members. The office has been three cramped rooms on three levels, but is thankfully moving (again as a subtenant of MEDIATION UK) to a clear space on one floor in an office building in the centre of Bristol.

The Community Mediation Service had 246 enquiries in the last year which related to neighbour disputes. All these were handled by the intake worker. One hundred and twenty-eight were allocated to mediators, 118 were dealt with by the intake worker alone. Cases are taken on if they come from within Bristol or its immediate surroundings and the first party is willing to consider mediation. Recently the caseload has been very heavy and staff have drafted a policy for case management. This includes time limits for allocation of cases and each stage of the process through visits to face-to-face meetings. Cases will no longer be classified as 'on hold', they will be ongoing or closed.

---

8   At that point this was inter-agency work on a housing estate, later it was taking mediation
      into areas of disadvantage in the city and recruiting local people to be trained as mediators
      for their community.

Of the presenting problems, noise is recorded as the most prevalent (in nearly 60% of cases) with children's behaviour and boundary disputes coming next (30% and 18%). Calls come from all over the city: 62% are self-referred, 26% come through housing or health and environmental services departments. Recently there has been a large increase in self-referrals as the existence of the mediation service becomes more widely known and satisfied users recommend it to their friends or not-so-near neighbours!

To gauge how the service was experienced by clients, Bristol Mediation made enquiries of other services about their monitoring practices. From the many views received, it was decided to send out stamped, addressed cards for parties to circle their preferred response and add any comments. The responses were analysed over a year, and showed that 35% of postcards were returned. Of these, 90% reported that the situation had improved; nobody found the mediators biased and over 60% found them to be helpful and friendly; 85% said the office was efficient. Responses will continue to be monitored in this way as part of an ongoing evaluation of the service provided.

The percentage of face-to-face mediations has increased from 10% to 14% – probably attributable to more effective encouragement by mediators. All but one face-to-face meeting resulted in an agreement. Also significant is the increase in shuttle mediations – at 22%, this is more than twice as many as in the previous year. Another 14% involve visits to both parties but sadly 50% do not get beyond first party visits.

Throughout each mediation process the emphasis has always been on the wishes of the parties involved. Much useful work has been achieved working with one party only, but efforts to bring both parties to mediation are being strengthened. This change may reflect the greater skills being shown by the mediators in promoting and managing the process. There is also a noticeable increase in knowledge and confidence on the part of the public.

To establish a common and clear understanding of Bristol Mediation's expectations of its mediators and its commitment to them, a number of documents have been produced. A job description and a volunteer agreement were written and trainers' contracts for external training were prepared. (Basic and ongoing training is mostly provided by in-house trainer/mediators. Several of them also offer training and consultancy to other organisations, including new mediation services.) Health and safety issues were discussed and addressed.

The special Southmead Project came to a halt as funding could not be obtained after 1995. In her report Hermione Legg writes, 'While the value of the work is recognised at a local level, local budgets have no heading for local facilitation and mediation, or available resources. This means that payment for this work has to go to a higher level where there is still no experience of long-term mediation, and where mediation is still not part of the grant-making process.'[9]

Schools work is flourishing. A peer mediation scheme manual has been published.[10] It sets out a programme for use in junior schools where peer mediation is being introduced. The children learn how to mediate in pairs, in the school playground, using a process similar to that used with adults, only much quicker. As a young mediator explained, 'Children haven't got time to waste; there's life to be getting on with'. The resulting reduction in playground conflicts is dramatic. It is hoped that these skills will be carried forward into secondary schools and become part of each student's life skills. Schools mediation has a high profile – it appears to be very effective and seems likely to expand into a large number of schools in and around the city if funding is available.

Media interest in mediation is increasing. There have been television programmes and newspaper articles as well as radio interviews. These usually take up much time and energy and sometimes end up conveying a rather insubstantial message of what mediation is about. The media prefers the personal angle on either users of the service or mediators, and is less interested in the mediation process itself – witness such headlines as 'When home is a living hell ...'; 'Big tribute to the neighbour peace makers'; 'Warring neighbours in peace and love bid'.[11]

Fundraising is never easy and ongoing core funding (to keep the basic service going) is particularly difficult to find. The service employs a part-time fundraiser and regards this as cost-effective. Applying in the right way to carefully selected charitable trusts is crucial to achieving a reasonable success rate. A bid for funding in 1995 for a volunteer development project from the National Lottery Charities Board was successful.

RECRUITMENT, SELECTION AND TRAINING OF MEDIATORS

Considerable effort is made to recruit potential mediators from a variety of backgrounds. Advertising, invitation and 'word of mouth' are used to bring around 15–20 people to an introductory day, at which they learn about mediation and the mediation service, and test some of their skills and potential for becoming a mediator. Recently the number of applicants has doubled, and two introductory days were needed for the last intake of volunteer mediators.

---

9   Legg, H, *op cit*.

10 Major, V, Smith, V and Mnatzaganian, N, *Peer Mediation Scheme Manual*, 1995 (revised 1997), Bristol: Bristol Mediation.

11 Newspaper headlines taken from the *Bristol Evening Post* during 1995/96.

A job description and person specification is sent out with the application form to be a volunteer mediator. Trainers on the introductory day have been implementing a selection process based on the person specification. Assurances are required that there is a commitment to attend all the training sessions and to work as a mediator for Bristol Mediation if the training is successfully completed. The basic training course is about 30 hours long, and is now based on MEDIATION UK's *Training Manual in Community Mediation Skills*.[12] (A basic training review is being undertaken and changes in the introductory days, training course and selection procedures are likely.) At the end of the course those who have demonstrated an appropriate level of competence are invited to become practising mediators. Initially they work with an experienced co-mediator (mediators always work in pairs). Mediators have volunteer mediator agreements which stipulate a commitment equivalent to offering one evening a week (12 hours a month), although this is not always achieved.[13]

A DAY IN THE LIFE OF THE INTAKE WORKER

To give an impression of what it is like being the person who receives the incoming calls to the mediation service, there follows a short account from Steve Woodward, Bristol Mediation's intake worker:

> Come in, switch off the burglar alarm and pick up the morning's post. The answerphone is flashing at me. Listen to the messages and start ringing people back. One woman in particular is very angry – she recorded the sound of drilling from next door on the answerphone.
>
> Two fresh cases come in during the morning. One is about the upkeep of a fence. The other involves a fight between children that spread to the respective parents. Listen to them and send out details of what to do. Fingers crossed, I should be able to allocate them both this week. Several mediators ring to update me on where their cases are at. A face-to-face meeting might be happening – I make several calls to find what venues are available near the clients. All of this whilst compiling a monitoring report for one of our major funders. Oh, the joy of multi-tasking!
>
> In the afternoon one of the clients rings. She is convinced next door has killed her cat. Listen to her and ask what she would like us to do. It turns out that perhaps English classes for speakers of other languages might help her deal with her neighbours – she has the basics but finds negotiation difficult. I do some research into classes available. Someone calls from another mediation service – what do we do about supervision of mediators?

---

12 MEDIATION UK, *Training Manual in Community Mediation Skills*, 1995, Bristol: MEDIATION UK.

13 See Chapter 6 for a general account of how mediators are selected and trained.

I ring several clients to check they are still on for mediation and allocate the cases to several mediators. Not for the first time, it strikes me that combining mediator and client availability, not to mention fixing up those with cars with those who haven't, makes blindfold chess in space seem a cinch. Send off the reports, back up the day's work on the computer and run to catch the last post. When I get back the answerphone is flashing.

A MEDIATION STORY

This account of a mediation (from this writer as mediator) gives an impression of the whole mediation process and how it works in practice:

A phone call from the intake worker. I had said I would like a case, so yes please, send me the details.

The referral sheet gives date of first contact, who referred (a housing officer of the local council housing department), date allocated, a reminder to dial 141 before ringing clients (so they can't ring me), names and addresses of both parties, and phone number of party A. It gives brief notes on what the problems are about and the name of my co-mediator. I ring him. We have not worked together before so we have an initial chat and look at our diaries for possible dates for visits. Agree I will phone party A and make an appointment.

Party A is expecting our call – she has had a letter from the office. She is quite keen to see us but doesn't think we can do anything. Visit date arranged. I inform co-mediator and arrange to pick him up with time to spare for planning how we will work together.

We meet and discuss our approach. I will introduce the mediation process and set an approximate time limit for this visit. We ring the doorbell. An elderly woman shows us into her living room. The television is on very loud and there is a man who hovers and corrects her story frequently. We politely ask for the sound to be turned down a little. I get to explain our role, and the man sits down and opens a large folder of letters and notes to do with the complaints they have against the young woman in the upstairs flat. By degrees we establish that there are problems over dogs barking, particularly when left most of the day in the flat, very rude remarks from the young woman, door banging and washing machine noise late at night. Yes, we may approach party B but no possibility of a meeting. 'She's scum', they say.

Co-mediator and I conclude the visit with a summary of what we have agreed we are going to do and say. We debrief in the car and on getting home we have a feedback session on how we did. There is a checklist for this process. We phone the intake worker and ask him to send party B a letter which gives a date when we will visit unless she wishes to change it or does not want to see us at all. Ringing the bell of party B is often an uncomfortable moment. This time it is terrifying. The shape of two enormous leaping hounds appears behind the frosted glass door. They sound ferocious. Nothing else happens. We write a note saying we called and could she phone the office please. I fear the dogs will eat it.

Two days later party B phones. She had meant to be there but somehow wasn't. She wants to talk to us but only by phone and leaves a number. Co-mediator concurs with this suggestion with considerable relief. We meet to make the call. Party B has a lot to say about party A. Very loud telly, very rude people. What can she do anyway? – she is waiting for a transfer to another council property so not prepared to put down carpet, but she is open to negotiation over mutual noise nuisance. She will trade washing machine noise for television noise. She's fine about meeting party A as long as we stop them insulting her. She says we can pass on everything she has said to us to party A.

We feel we are getting somewhere and arrange to call on party A. She is astonished by the offer to meet and negotiate. She is not at all optimistic about the possibility of a transfer for her neighbour. 'I'll be dead and gone before then'. Let's make a start on what we can do, we say. Back to the office to arrange a venue for a meeting.

The meeting is turbulent. Each party is strongly accusatory and demanding. We work hard keeping boundaries – halting abusive language and unhelpful references to people not present. We wait for a shift of emphasis from past experience towards the future. We prompt by inviting the parties to imagine a time when things are better and to tell us what has changed to make it so. The forward movement comes suddenly when party B makes a tentative offer that she might not run the washing machine at the weekends.

Eventually a written agreement is signed. It has a weekend and night-time limit for the washing machine. The television will be moved to the back room and the sound will be lowered if the window is open. The situation will be checked in a week's time by party B calling on party A. If this doesn't happen, 'Cos I may forget', either party may contact the mediators. They agree to be civil which means saying good morning to each other in the street.

A week after the meeting party B has got her transfer notice! We know because party B went to see party A and told her. Party A then rang the office to tell us. 'Such a pleasant young woman', she said.

RECRUITMENT, SELECTION, TRAINING AND DEVELOPMENT OF PAID STAFF

Paid staff posts are thought about carefully before funding is sought. Once it is obtained the process is as follows:

- A job description (JD) and person specification (PS) are drawn up by the manager and a member of the committee.

- A timetable for advertising, application deadline, shortlisting and interview is prepared.

- The job is advertised in publications which are chosen for appropriate circulation, while also bearing in mind the cost of advertising.

- A job pack is prepared. It includes the job description, person specification and application form, with a note to remind applicants to use it to give evidence of their ability to meet the person specification. Also in the pack are an equal opportunities monitoring form, information about the service and a covering letter with details of the interview date.

- The selection panel usually consists of three people, a man and a woman and another man or woman.
- The panel prepares suitable questions based on the JD and PS.
- Equal opportunities procedures are adhered to throughout the process.
- Shortlisting is done anonymously.
- Interviews are managed with the intention to help applicants to express themselves as well as possible and to give a full interview. Selection is made after all the applicants have been interviewed and the successful applicant will be offered the job immediately (by telephone the same day if possible), subject to a satisfactory reference. When the reference has been received, a formal offer is made.
- Unsuccessful applicants are phoned as soon as possible and offered feedback on their interview if they want it.
- Once the offer is accepted, a starting date is agreed and an induction programme arranged.

All staff are on permanent contracts, although inevitably with insecure funding, job security is not a viable feature. An induction period is considered preferable to a probationary period. Any information or training needs can be identified during this initial period, and an interview with the chair of the management committee at the end of three months checks its satisfactory completion.

The manager of the service has external supervision monthly and in turn supervises the other staff. Staff meet weekly and have access to members of the committee for support and advice. Joint progress reviews are held, and staff are encouraged to identify their further training and development needs and look for appropriate ways of meeting these. There is a staff development budget to help with this.

We found it was helpful to offer an existing employee, who applies for a new post, some support from a member of the management committee not involved in the selection process. If the internal applicant is not offered the job, this support may be very much needed. It is also important to consider with all staff the interconnections between roles and any necessary changes to existing job descriptions which the new post suggests.

MANAGEMENT COMMITTEE ROLES

The relationship between the manager and the chair is a very close one in this organisation, and is based on friendship and trust. The chair has to have plenty of time to offer – a good part of two days a week when there is a lot going on. A clear understanding of each other's role is essential as well as knowledge of and respect for each other's strengths and weaknesses. The vice-chair shares many of the chair's duties. Meanwhile, the treasurer has to keep a careful watch over budgets whose margins are often slender.

Members of the committee are not expected to represent other organisations but to be there in their own right as people seriously interested in conflict resolution and able to bring considerable knowledge and experience from related fields. Each member of the committee is involved specifically with one or more aspects of the service (schools, funding, premises, training and consultancy, new projects, staff support etc). Staff and committee are therefore closely connected. An annual 'away day' for them all has helped develop and maintain this rewarding relationship. The agenda is set on the day and the participants facilitate it themselves.

Management committee meetings are held monthly except in August and December. They are kept to two hours maximum and papers are circulated (and read) beforehand. If there is a report from a member of staff, he or she may be invited to attend and discuss it with the committee.

The constitution requires members to retire after two years but they are able to stand for re-election. There is no maximum length of service. Written nominations are sent in 35 days before the AGM. It has been found that people serve for as long as they are able to make a considerable contribution to the organisation. New members are sought when there is a vacancy or particular expertise is missing. The volunteer mediators are informed of committee activities through personal contact and the service's regular newsletter, and are encouraged to consider standing for election to the committee if they are interested. There is also a membership scheme for outside supporters, who pay a small fee to receive an occasional newsletter and the annual report – and volunteer mediators receive these as well.

AGMs are widely publicised as there is always a presentation around a new approach to conflict resolution immediately after the business meeting. Questions are answered and participation is invited and encouraged. Topics have included the Alternatives to Violence Project (which runs workshops in prisons), mediating in South Africa and peer mediation in schools.

COMMUNICATION

Communications within the organisation, with people in the city, with other services and MEDIATION UK, and with the outside world, are constantly in need of active focus. They are so crucial to the well-being and development of good understanding that it may be useful to dwell on some of the ways good communication has been and is being achieved. Many of these will be familiar to anyone involved in running a small voluntary sector service with a largely volunteer workforce. However, mediation has particular needs for strong lines of communication: it deals with a highly emotional subject – conflict; it is a relatively new and often misunderstood kind of community work; its boundaries and opportunities are constantly being reviewed.

Within the organisation, communication amongst paid staff is promoted by regular staff meetings, supervision sessions and daily contact. People, of necessity, spend considerable time covering for each other during leave, sickness and times of acute pressure of work. Too much pressure of work, particularly someone else's, sometimes leads to misunderstandings, duplication or working at cross purposes.

Support and supervision for volunteers is generally accepted as essential in order to retain their services, and to maintain and enhance their level of skill and commitment. To help achieve this, a system of progress reviews is being implemented.

Communication with and between mediators requires effort from all concerned. There is a monthly newsletter which encourages two-way communication but does not always achieve it. The appointment of a volunteer co-ordinator as the number of mediators climbed towards 50 was highly effective. As the number and variety of mediators expands, so new ways of communicating are explored.

When the number of mediators increased beyond a dozen or so, the pattern of a monthly support group meeting became ineffective. Several mediators stopped attending, some newer ones felt meetings were an unnecessary burden and never got into the habit, and some were unable to make the date, time or place. A long period of consultation and research by a small working group resulted in the implementation of support and feedback groups for six to eight mediators who could plan their own meetings. These groups were set up at half-day group-building events facilitated by members of the trainers' group. The details of this model are described in Chapter 6. A year later five groups were working satisfactorily, two had disbanded and one wanted to regroup. Larger meetings of mediators are arranged as day, half-day or evening forums. Agendas are entirely or partially set on the day, and these occasions are reasonably well attended.

Social events are regarded as valuable and usually include staff and management committee members. Visitors with relevant experience are most welcome, and open sessions to meet and talk with them are enthusiastically attended. Training events also provide opportunities to consolidate practice, revive feelings of belonging to the organisation and share experience. No one method of communication is sufficient, and we also have to remind each other that it is a two-way process.

As the number of mediators grows, the early strong feelings of camaraderie fade and some degree of lethargy inevitably sets in. People stop attending events regularly and lose contact with most of their colleagues. There comes a time when commitment to being a mediator has to be tightened. When mediators are reminded that they are required to attend meetings and to take cases on a regular basis, some mediators will leave and others will show disaffection. However, the quality of the service will be maintained and improved, and the commitment of the remaining mediators will be strengthened. Nevertheless, it is an uncomfortable stage to manage, and tests the bonds of support between mediators and managing staff, and between staff and management committee.

Communication within the organisation between different areas of work requires effort. It seems to work best if the onus is on people working in each area to put out information about what they are doing which may be of interest to others, together with contact names for further information or receiving comments.

The diagram below shows the structure of Bristol Mediation and its constituent parts, and shows some of the lines of communication.

Figure 5.1: The structure of Bristol Mediation.

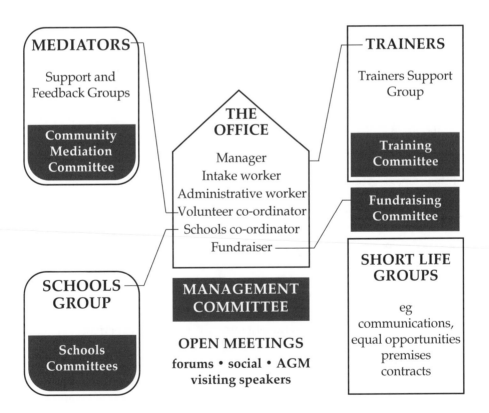

ROLES AND FUNCTIONAL FLEXIBILITY

In a small organisation there is often the challenge of keeping to a specific role when so required: many people can wear different hats. The same person may be talking to the intake worker about a mediation case as a volunteer mediator at one moment, and then need to change to a conversation in which she or he is the chair of the management committee talking as an employer to an employee.

At this stage in the organisation's development there is a clear hierarchical structure of management committee, several subcommittees, a manager and a staff team with line management. There is also a network of working groups, some permanent, some set up for limited tasks. As the membership of these groups is varied and includes people from all parts of the organisation offering themselves in different roles, there is a democratic freedom that seems to bring out the best in people and ensures the vitality of the organisation.

POLICYMAKING

Policymaking is seen as a committee responsibility. Advice from staff and practitioners is sought, and consultation on draft proposals is normal practice. Policy implementation decisions are delegated to subcommittees. There are subcommittees for funding, publicity, training, community mediation and schools . These work well in that they are concerned with a particular area of work, and each member has a special interest and contribution to make in that area. These subcommittees bring together into a close working relationship paid staff, management committee members and volunteer mediators.

CONNECTING WITH OTHERS IN THE FIELD AND BEYOND

There are now good networking systems with other services and with regional and functional groups. The service maintains close connections with MEDIATION UK and thereby both receives benefit from and contributes to the national forum which is regarded as essential for establishing good practice and credentials for community mediation.

In addition to community mediation, Bristol also has both family mediation and commercial mediation services. A close understanding of what each can offer makes cross-referral easy and unconfusing for potential clients.

The mediation service has always sought and cultivated connections with other organisations in the city such as the probation service, the police, social services and city council departments – housing and health and environmental services. There are links with community centres and churches, schools, the Citizens Advice Bureau and voluntary organisations, such as Victim Support.

SOURCES OF FUNDING

Initially funding came from Quakers, a charitable foundation and Safer Cities. Other charitable sources were added. Employing a paid, skilled fundraiser greatly expanded the range of funders to be approached. However, there remained the problem that most charitable trusts prefer to fund innovative projects rather than contribute to core funding. The service was committed to community mediation being its central work. It seemed that the core might wither while the periphery buzzed with potential growth. As other community mediation services have found, the way ahead lay in approaching the city council for case funding.

It required considerable negotiating skill on both sides before a service level agreement was achieved with the city council housing department. The contract that was signed states that Bristol Mediation will provide mediation for an agreed number of cases referred by the housing department for a certain sum per case.This agreement was followed by another with health and environmental services which had been supportive of the noise counselling service. Training sessions were run for housing officers to help them appreciate the purpose and processes of mediation, and to help them identify suitable cases for referral. A similar contract is now also in place for taking on some paid casework for housing associations.

MONITORING AND EVALUATION

For its own needs, and for funders and potential funders, the service is obviously required to provide competent monitoring and evaluation reports. There has been considerable debate about how and what to monitor in individual cases, particularly the advisability of following up a case some months later. It is timely that there is a national interest in establishing an agreed format for monitoring and evaluating community mediation cases. However, defining the measures of success is not a simple matter.[14]

14 See Chapters 4 and 12 .

CONCLUSION

How does one measure the achievements of the service, both internally and externally? Looking inward, it has well-organised office systems and clearly defined employment practices. It has consistently worked to its business plan. There is a clear organisational structure for policy and decision-making and good processes for consultation and implementation. Significantly people have shown they are capable of recognising, acknowledging and managing their own conflicts within the organisation – aiming to practise what they preach.

Anita Gibbs, a member of the management committee, described recently her impression of the service's collaborative model of working together. 'The atmosphere created is one of acceptance and equality, which is not based on the attributes of particular people but on the assumption that everyone has a valid contribution to make. Individual members 'own' what the organisation stands for and have a sense of belonging to it.' This is only partially true and there remains the difficulty of bringing this sense of ownership to all the mediators.

Outwardly the service has been successful in the renewal of service level agreements. Promotion and funding are competently pursued. The user survey reports the majority of users expressing some satisfaction – this is limited, sadly, by the fact that so often it is not only neighbour disputes but also housing conditions and poverty which provoke conflict.

Providing a cost-effective and efficient mediation service requires a continuously evolving process of development and experimentation. There are always opportunities for development, both within the organisation and in what it can offer the communities it serves. This leaves no room for complacency but plenty for challenge!

CHAPTER SIX

MEDIATORS: RECRUITMENT, SELECTION, TRAINING AND SUPPORT

Gavin R Beckett and Marion Wells

INTRODUCTION

In considering the question of who or what a community mediator is, there are a number of possible answers. Some people may consider mediation to be an art, others that it is an activity requiring an instinctive ability to do it. Yet others, and we fall into this camp, believe that almost anyone has the potential to become a mediator. What makes a mediator is the set of processes through which a volunteer recognises and learns the skills and attitudes involved in mediation. In this chapter we aim to describe the path that a new volunteer follows to become a community mediator in the UK. The processes we discuss are partly 'best practice' as conceived of by MEDIATION UK, and partly the practices as used by the four mediation services that we, the authors of this chapter, have experience of working in and for. We will look in turn at recruitment, selection, training and support.

RECRUITMENT OF MEDIATORS

Community mediation services wish to involve their local community in the service they are offering. They want people to become aware of mediation as a useful conflict resolution process and to have access to this service. Most services recruit and train volunteer mediators from the community in which they are based. A few services operate without volunteer mediators; they have instead a small number of paid mediators. To be suitable for selection as a community mediator does not require a specific type of experience, or academic qualifications, or a background of formal educational achievements. People with life experience and a willingness to develop the necessary skills, attitudes and knowledge are the broad target.

Initially a service may find it has enough potential mediators volunteering without making any effort to recruit. There are usually people who have some knowledge or experience of mediation who are ready and waiting for an opportunity to engage in it locally.

As an initial mediator training course is participatory and skills-based, it works best when there are between eight and 18 participants. With too few people, roleplaying becomes problematical and with too many it is difficult for trainers to attend to individual needs. A very large number of new mediators can be difficult to incorporate into the service as practising mediators.

A community mediation service needs mediators of all backgrounds, so that the local community can identify with it, and so that there is a wide range of mediators for different circumstances. To attract a range of interested people whose background adequately reflects the community served by the mediation service, it is necessary to consider very carefully how to go about recruiting, selecting and training. If a profile of the existing mediator team is kept, it will be easy to see whether targeting is necessary or desirable. Advertising to achieve an appropriate response may include local papers, journals, notice boards in public places such as libraries and doctors' surgeries, the mediation service's press releases, radio interviews and pamphlets or newsletters. The service can also maintain a list of interested people who have enquired about becoming a mediator. These will be invited to apply when a course is about to be run. Users of the service can be encouraged to consider becoming mediators.

Enquirers will want to know what the service does, what a mediator does and what skills they should have. It is helpful to give people written information and also to have someone available to answer questions. They need to be told about expenses and what will be covered. Will carers' expenses be paid as well as travel? What distances may they be expected to travel and how will they travel? It is important to check that people are not excluded by rigid requirements. They may particularly want to be assured about safety while working and that they would have support from colleagues. They will need to know about the training – where it is held, what hours, how long, and whether there is an induction period when starting work as a mediator. Some people will want to know what the training involves in detail. Will it include roleplay? Are there pass/fail tests?

Many services have developed an introductory day to which all interested potential mediators are invited. This provides a good opportunity for people to get answers to all these questions, to learn more about mediation and the mediation service, and meet the people they would be joining. Some will decide it is not for them. Trainers who are facilitating the day may be able to encourage the less confident and discourage any who are very clearly unsuitable (perhaps because they have no wish to be impartial in a dispute or are very disturbed by anger in others). Other services prefer to welcome all comers to the training course and leave selection of any kind till later. We will discuss this in the section on selection.

A decision has to be made early on whether to try to attract people who have, as yet, very few relevant skills and be prepared to help them acquire these skills, or to recruit people who have a background in some related field of working with people. Trainers will find a mixed ability group more challenging: there is a higher risk of individual disappointment when someone finds mediation is not appropriate work. The group may also get frustrated from time to time as people will be learning at different rates. The course will need to be longer and include more one-to-one support. It may be helpful to advise some prospective mediators to take a prior course, for instance, in basic counselling or communication skills. Those who have had no experience of a participatory style of learning have said that they felt at a disadvantage on a mediation course. The course itself will need to be adapted to suit the training group. It is wise to widen the horizons to include people and to identify and rectify restraining factors, if by doing so, a wide variety of people can be trained as community mediators. This upholds the belief that mediation skills are not esoteric but accessible to many.

SELECTION OF MEDIATORS

Mediation services operate selection procedures at one or several stages of the training. The service has a responsibility to its clients to provide mediators who will work towards 'best practice' and follow all the ethical guidelines that are necessary. Mediators will be involved in sensitive areas of people's lives, and the service must try to ensure that it selects volunteers who will respect the rights of the clients that they deal with. Services may carry out police checks on new volunteers before they begin to visit people at home. These checks will show up any criminal convictions that the individual has, and whilst many offences will have no bearing on their suitability to be a mediator, offences of a violent nature, especially against children, would usually be reasons to prevent the volunteer being accepted.[1]

The first point at which selection can occur is before training. Some services will encourage anyone who asks to join the next training course; in other services enquirers first come to either an introductory evening or a full day in order to learn about mediation in more depth. Volunteers can then assess for themselves, with the trainers, whether mediation is for them – some people select themselves out at this point. Other services might choose to ask for application forms, with references, followed by interviews, before accepting people on to the training course. All services use a number of methods of assessment during training, in order to build up a picture of the capabilities of the volunteers. We look at these methods later in the chapter. This assessment is rarely on a pass/fail basis; it is used more to provide the information needed for the trainers and the volunteer to discuss which skills they possess, which need improvement, and whether the volunteer is able to fit into and promote the values of mediation. This often happens in an

---

1   Although almost all of the community mediation services in the UK have volunteer mediators, there are also a few services that employ a small number of paid staff instead. For simplicity we refer to volunteers here because this is still the most common practice.

informal interview with the volunteer after the training. This interview is sometimes called an accreditation interview, but this does not necessarily mean that the volunteers have been following a formally accredited training course. More can be read about this in Chapter 11.

Application form

Questions that might be asked on an application form would be about the volunteers' previous skills and experiences, whether they have done voluntary work in the past, why they want to become a mediator and when they can offer time to the service. The service or volunteer co-ordinator can then build up a picture of the strengths and weaknesses of volunteers before they begin the training. With the application form, the volunteer should receive a job description, person specification and information about the service. Amongst the qualities asked for are the ability to observe confidentiality, to be flexible, to be open to learning, to be open to difference, to have and demonstrate a non-judgmental attitude, to be optimistic and to be committed to doing the work.

Training course

Through a mixture of group discussion, observation of the exercises, one-to-one feedback, and guided self and peer assessment, both verbal and written, the trainer seeks to evaluate how well trainees have grasped the skills, processes and values of mediation. In the early stages of the course, this evaluation will enable the trainer to help trainees focus on areas needing more work. In the later stages, if a trainee cannot grasp some aspects of the work, the trainer has to identify whether further training is needed, or whether the trainee simply will not be able to take on board the new ways of working he or she is being presented with. No one is expected to be fully competent at the end of the course, but a certain level of understanding is necessary for the volunteer to be able to go on to the probationary period, working with more experienced mediators. Some people find it very difficult to avoid being directive about the content of the dispute, cannot learn the skills of active listening, find it difficult to ask questions without interrogating people, slip into making judgments, and cannot keep their negative emotions about the situation or people from affecting their attitude, body language and expressions. The ability to learn to control the process without controlling the content or options for settlement; the ability to treat people impartially and show this through body language and spoken language; an understanding of how to use open, probing and clarifying questions in the process of active listening; and the ability to help people to problem-solve for themselves are all central skills for which the trainer will be looking. There is a much fuller discussion of present thinking about standards of competence and best practice in Chapter 11.

Interview

Many services follow up their assessment during training with an interview. Here, issues that arose on the training course are discussed, and volunteers can work with the trainer and co-ordinator to identify where they need more training. If some volunteers appear to be unsuitable to take on a mediator's responsibilities, they can be offered other ways in which they can help the service, or asked to repeat the training course at a later date, having discussed the particular areas where they need to pay attention.

TRAINING OF MEDIATORS

The rationale behind mediation is that often our usual ways of dealing with conflicts fail to deliver the positive outcomes that we want. Mediation offers itself as a new way of dealing with conflict, using new skills that most of us do not possess. But these skills have been identified by looking at what does work in those conflicts that have been dealt with positively. This means that there will always be some people around us who have some of these skills, and may already use them in some situations of conflict. Trainers are coming to recognise that one of the most important tasks of a training course is to elicit the skills and qualities that trainees already have. Trainees may already possess listening skills, problem-solving skills, a non-judgmental attitude or many other useful qualities and skills. However, trainees may not recognise these in themselves, and the training seeks to demonstrate that the mediation process uses a particular skill or quality in a certain way and at a certain point.

This is particularly important when training multicultural groups, or groups where the majority of people are from cultures other than the white, western, largely middle-class culture of the trainers. (This is itself a crude generalisation about who trainers are.) Different cultures have different ways of thinking about and dealing with conflict. What is helpful and constructive in one culture may be entirely inappropriate in others, so an elicitive model of training is essential here – in which these different effective ways of dealing with conflict are drawn out from the trainees, and tacit, unarticulated knowledge made explicit.[2]

Of course there are always some new skills and qualities for people to learn on a mediation course. The process itself has evolved in the USA,

---

2   For more on this model see Lederach, JP, *Preparing for Peace: Conflict Transformation Across Cultures*, 1995, Syracuse: Syracuse University Press.

Australia and the UK into a particular form which is new to most people. Few people have thought systematically about conflict, and the training attempts to ensure that mediators have an understanding of the dynamics of conflict as it arises and escalates. Other people find active listening to be an entirely new and difficult skill, and many are tested by the requirement of being non-directive about the content of the dispute. Mediation also requires people to be able to deal with sensitive cases, and distance themselves from potentially upsetting experiences. Mediation began in the UK with a lot of volunteers who were experienced in 'people work', who had already learnt how to let go of their cases after they had closed. Newer volunteers in recent years are increasingly drawn from more diverse areas of life, and many need the opportunity to learn the ability to let go. The training course allows people to confront these new ways of being, in a safer environment than on the job. Trainees can make mistakes on the course and learn from them without worrying that they are damaging someone's life.

This brings us on to a third major reason for training – introducing volunteers to the ethical issues involved in mediation. Mediators enter people's homes and hear about their private lives, often in some detail. They take actions that may have considerable effects on those lives. They therefore need to be very aware of the ethics of intervention. More is said about this in Chapter 13. During the training the mediators learn about confidentiality and equal opportunities policy and practice, and have the opportunity to make mistakes without serious consequences. Training aims to ensure a high standard of skills in people who will intervene in sensitive situations, so that trainees are competent in the skills and understand the attitudes and values of mediation.

Core content of a mediation skills training course

We are going to describe briefly the content of a sample training course from the MEDIATION UK *Training Manual in Community Mediation Skills*.[3] This content can be delivered in a variety of packages, depending on the circumstances of the local mediation service. Training courses are frequently run as evening sessions with one or two weekends for longer roleplay work; courses organised this way are more accessible for volunteers who work during the day. If the service is training people who will be paid mediators, or if it has established that a lot of volunteers are unemployed, the training course can be run during weekdays. New services, which may be using trainers from some distance away, might organise the training over two long weekends. Some services will use different formats for each course, aiming to

---

3   MEDIATION UK, *Training Manual in Community Mediation Skills*, 1995, Bristol: MEDIATION UK, p 328.

enable people who cannot attend evening sessions to come to the daytime course run a few months later.

Both ways of running courses have pros and cons. Evening sessions can be short and snappy, providing an easy way in for volunteers new to mediation. They also allow space for reflection in between each session. However, they can be somewhat too short, at two to three hours, to ensure that in-depth learning is possible. Spending whole days, up to eight hours long, continuously building up the repertoire of mediation skills, can be a better way to train. However it does prevent trainees from stepping back and reflecting, and after one or two days of intensive skills training, both trainees and trainer can become tired and less effective. We have chosen to describe the five-day course presented as a sample in the MEDIATION UK *Training Manual*, where each day's session is eight hours long. For each session we have provided an example of a training exercise from the *Training Manual*.

Day one

The first day introduces people to each other, and sets the ground rules to be used on the course. These generally consist of confidentiality, respect for one another's views, listening to one another, only volunteering yourself, and the right to pass, plus others depending upon the trainer and the suggestions made by the group. Having begun to establish a safe environment, the day then focuses on the personal reactions of the trainees to conflict, and how to develop a constructive approach to it. Following this there are exercises to aid understanding of disputes and disputants, and to show how mediation works. The trainees are introduced to the key skills and qualities of a mediator, and then begin to learn how to build rapport and use active listening skills with clients.

Sample Exercise: Conflict – Positive and Negative.

A 20-minute brainstorm and discussion exploring how people feel about conflict. The aims of the exercise are for participants to express and listen to views on what is involved in conflict; understand the idea that conflict has negative and positive aspects; and identify how they feel about this idea. The group brainstorms the words that come into their minds when they think of conflict, and the trainer collects them on a flipchart. The group then discusses differences and similarities and how people feel about what has come up. They are led to consider whether it has been difficult for them to acknowledge the positive or negative side. The positive and negative sides of conflict are flipcharted. The trainer then explains that mediation aims to draw out the positive side of conflict and minimise the negative, and gives out a handout from the manual.[4]

---

4   *Ibid*, p 25.

Day two

Day two begins by introducing the trainees to the distinction between positions and interests, and to the idea of win/win solutions. The trainers demonstrate the mediation process in a brief roleplay, and then the trainees begin to learn the stages of the process one at a time. During this day they would roleplay stage one, first contact with the first party, and stage two, first contact with the second party, as well as looking at perceptions and prejudices, and what effective doorstep technique is.

Sample Exercise: Win/Win and Win/Lose

This is a 30-minute exercise that aims to introduce participants to the difference between win/win and win/lose conflict resolution; to recognise the difference between positions and interests; to be able to identify people's interests in examples of neighbour disputes; and to come up with examples of win/win resolutions. The trainees work in pairs or threes, and go through a handout from the manual with two scenarios, working out what interests might underlie the positions expressed by each neighbour. After 10 minutes the group reconvenes and compares the variety of ideas from each small group. The ideas about possible interests are flipcharted. The trainer then provides some input on the importance of distinguishing positions from interests, the way in which uncovering interests can open up new options for a settlement and that it is the mediator's task to enable the disputants to do this. The trainees are then given a handout with suggested outcomes for the examples discussed earlier.[5]

Day three

On the third day trainees look at the different outcomes possible from the two first visits to parties in dispute. They then plan for the face-to-face roleplay, and spend most of the day doing the roleplay itself. Face-to-face/direct mediation is broken up into a number of stages that the mediators must grasp, and be able to recognise whilst they are mediating. These are: setting the scene, hearing the issues, exploring the issues, building agreements, and closing the meeting. There is more information about the content of these stages in Chapter 3.

Sample Exercise: Face-to-face Roleplay

A full face-to-face roleplay may take between one and two hours, including the preparation, briefing, roleplay, de-roling and discussion. There are a variety of ways of running the roleplay, but one of the most common is in small groups, with two disputants, two mediators and some observers. There may be enough trainers for each group to have a facilitator, or one trainer may move between groups as needed. Roleplayers are prepared by the trainer, who either outlines a dispute scenario, or generates one with the group. The individual roles have

---

5   *Ibid*, p 36.

briefing handouts, and people playing neighbours help each other to take on their roles whilst the people roleplaying mediators plan their strategy. A set of rules and guidelines are set up by the trainer to ensure that the roleplay is as safe as possible for the mediators to attempt to put the skills they have been learning into practice. When the roleplay begins the mediators have to set the scene and hear the issues that each party has brought to the session, they then have to help the parties to move into exploring the issues, and then building agreements. For each of these stages the manual provides key tasks for the mediator, guidelines for observers and suggestions for feedback. After the roleplay has reached some form of conclusion the trainer ensures that all roleplayers go through a de-roling process so that they leave any unresolved issues and feelings behind, and can step back into their own shoes.[6]

Day four

On day four another full face-to-face mediation roleplay is run, giving trainees who played disputants previously the chance to play mediators, and *vice versa*. It is followed up by specialist exercises which have been identified as useful through discussion between the trainer and the trainees. These might be on subjects like giving the opening welcome and establishing ground rules, managing conflict in the face-to-face mediation, reframing language, sorting issues, generating options, and constructing agreements, amongst others.

Sample Exercise: Reframing in Mediation

This is a pairs exercise, lasting 30 minutes, which aims to enable participants to understand the different frames of reference which affect the way people feel and think in disputes; to notice the effect of these frames of reference on communication; and to recognise that messages can be reframed to assist understanding. In pairs trainees read a handout containing statements made by two neighbours about each other, framed in emotive, blaming and abusive language. The trainer explains that the language used by the neighbours is likely to provoke hostile reactions, and trigger old cycles of anger and fear, so that the other party is unlikely to be able to hear and understand the underlying message. The group is asked to suggest which words and phrases would be most provocative and difficult to hear, and these are flipcharted. Then the trainees are given a handout with suggestions for reframing techniques involving changing the syntax of the message, the vocabulary, and the meaning. They use these to explore ways of reframing the difficult words and phrases. In group discussion the trainer checks out how people feel about the techniques, especially whether people feel that they may be manipulative. Trainees then work in pairs on a handout of statements, practising reframing them.[7]

---

6   *Ibid*, pp 239–57.
7   *Ibid*, pp 197–98 and 212–14.

Day five

The final day allows for further work on areas that the trainer or trainees have identified as difficult. Often trainees want more roleplay, so that they can practise particular parts of the process. It is also necessary for the co-ordinator of the service, who may not be the trainer, to discuss the procedures that the service uses for referrals, paperwork and further training.

Sample Exercise: Partnership between the Office and the Mediators

This is a mini-lecture with group discussion, lasting for 30-45 minutes, which aims to explain the administrative procedures involved in receiving and handling cases; to explain mediators' responsibilities; to identify case management skills and where to find support; and to explain the standards expected of mediators. Often, if the training has not been conducted by the mediation service's own staff or trainers, this session may be presented by the manager/co-ordinator of the service. A generic handout is included in the manual, but most services will tailor this session to their own materials. After an input on the way the service operates, trainees discuss in small groups issues of support, how to liaise effectively with the office and their own ideas about practice standards. Ideas are shared in the whole group and then a handout on good practice guidelines is given out and discussed.[8]

Following the publication of the *Training Manual* from which this course outline and examples are drawn, a MEDIATION UK working group created a Training Programme in Community Mediation Skills, accredited by the Open College Network and based on the materials available in the manual. This programme prescribes a set of learning outcomes that together describe a competent mediator. Trainee mediators must be able to demonstrate that they have these competences to obtain the Open College Network certification. Practising mediators might take all four units of the programme, each of which is suggested to take 30 hours, of which half is personal study and half is group training. Clearly this sets a high standard for the training of community mediators and begins to introduce more measures of professionalisation into the field. This trend continues with the imminent publication of standards for a National Vocational Qualification (NVQ) in Mediation.[9]

Training methods, style and expectations

Methods

Mediation training is based largely on experiential learning, in exercises and roleplays. Whilst the trainer often gives short presentations, using flipcharts

---

8   Based on *ibid*, pp 283–89.

9   For more information on these developments see Chapter 11.

and handouts, it is unusual for these to be more than a few minutes long. Trainers use visual aids to introduce new concepts and processes. Overhead projector transparencies are increasingly used alongside flipcharts, and MEDIATION UK recently produced a training video.[10] Mediation involves the use of a set of skills, and so the main thrust of the training is to give people the opportunity to practise these in pairs, small groups and large groups. Reflection on and consolidation of these skills happens in discussions after the exercises, and in the trainees' own time between sessions.

Because people have different learning styles, trainers should ensure that they provide a number of different ways of learning. One way of characterising learning styles is by distinguishing between activists, theorists, reflectors and pragmatists. Whilst most of us will have elements of several or all of these styles, one may be more dominant. Activists will benefit most from the participative, experiential and challenging exercises and roleplays; theorists will learn better from exercises that uncover the basis of the skills and processes involved, that require them to think, and give them time to do so in a structured way; reflectors need to be able to take a more passive role in exercises and observe the interaction of other participants, and learn from discussions where they have time to consider issues before contributing; lastly, pragmatists look for the practical link between the exercises and the 'real world' application of the skills that they are learning, and want to see that the trainer is a credible expert and that they are learning techniques that will meet a clear goal.[11] Trainers must therefore make sure that they encourage people to learn according to their own strengths, whilst helping them to stretch themselves.

Style

Mediation trainers aim to work in a participative and non-manipulative way, recognising the tensions between eliciting and validating prior skills, and introducing new ways of thinking and acting. Mediation involves a new set of skills, and a new way of looking at conflict, but these are also a very common set of skills. Often people simply need to be shown that the skills can be combined in the structured process. Mediation trainers are ideally open to two-way learning, realising that they do not have the only answers, and that trainees may come up with new insights. Good trainers aim to create a supportive environment for trainees, recognising that many people have fears about experiential learning, especially roleplays. At the same time it is the

---

10 MEDIATION UK, *Community Mediation Video*, 1996, Bristol: MEDIATION UK. This video is in three parts: (1) a 15-minute section on 'What is mediation in the community?'; (2) an 18-minute role play of a dispute, demonstrating the stages of mediation and the skills needed at each stage; (3) a series of 'trigger points' of difficult doorstep situations, for discussion during training.

11 Taken from material by J Patrick Associates, 159 High Street North, Stewkley, Leighton Buzzard, LU7 0EX.

trainers' task to encourage trainees to extend themselves and take the risk of trying new behaviours.

Expectations

In general mediation trainers expect that all (or almost all) people have the ability to mediate, that many of the necessary skills will already be there, and that people will commit time and energy to the training. Some people portray mediation as an art, an almost innate capability to deal creatively with conflict. But this puts many people off, making them think that they cannot be a mediator as they clearly do not have the inner resources. In fact, almost all of our interpersonal skills are a matter of learning and education, and with the proper attention, ensuring that learning starts from the level at which people enter the course, most people can learn new skills.

SUPPORT AND SUPERVISION OF MEDIATORS

Support is an essential feature of mediation practice, as mediation is a complex and often stressful process. All practising mediators need continual support and supervision in order to fulfil their role adequately, to remain committed to the work, to maintain the standards expected and to develop their competence as individual mediators and that of the service to which they are attached.

Most mediators are volunteers whose work as a mediator takes up a few hours a week. Mediation will be only one of several interests or occupations. There may be no requirement or possibility for volunteer mediators to meet many of the other mediators or staff in the mediation service's office. Therefore the overseeing of mediators has to be carefully considered and structured.

Support during and immediately after training

Clear messages should be given during the training period about how a trainee mediator can expect to be supported. Who is available, when may they be contacted? How open can a trainee be about difficulties, questions and doubts? Is it acceptable to talk about personal problems? Where are the boundaries of confidentiality? Many important issues arise and confront mediators as they come into contact with people in conflict situations. There are social justice issues, including unacceptable housing conditions, equal opportunity matters and so on. There are also strong emotions generated by conflict – new mediators may find that their own anger and feelings about unresolved conflicts get in the way and have to be addressed. Helping people often turns out to be not at all easy, and a regular opportunity and a safe environment for mutual support is essential. This enables mediators to bring out anxieties, fears, weaknesses and hopes – it helps to share these concerns and find others have them too. Much informal learning comes from meeting together in this way.

Post-basic training is a critical time for the new mediator. The co-mediator is a most powerful influence as is the person allocating cases from the office, so a good service chooses these people very carefully and trains them well. At this stage the new mediator will also need written guidelines on good practice, a clear understanding of office procedures relating to casework, and a regular support meeting to attend.

Support and supervision for all mediators

There are several models for providing support and supervision. These should be studied by a new service as it is setting up and the most appropriate model chosen. It is more difficult to introduce a new model of supervision into an existing service. However, a particular model may suit a small team of mediators very well but be unrealistic if the team expands later on, or initial enthusiasm wanes, and considerable consultation may be needed to choose the most appropriate model for the new circumstances. The word 'supervision' has a range of emotive connotations for people, from antagonism through fear to enthusiasm. There is general agreement in most people-orientated organisations, that all workers at every level in an organisation should have regular opportunities to discuss their feelings about the work they are doing. However, there are some mediators who do not see this as necessary, and a service may or may not feel it can risk this degree of independence or unconnectedness.

The main purposes of supervision are to:
- monitor work and work performance;
- evaluate work and work performance;
- clarify priorities;
- share information about work;
- provide an opportunity to discuss how the worker and supervisor (or supervision group) feel about the work;
- recognise and deal with existing and potential problems;
- discuss how external factors are affecting work;
- provide a framework for discussing and agreeing change.

There are three aspects of supervision for a mediator:
- normative: personal and professional accountability, standards, ethics;

- formative: a resource for support and challenge for self-development plus further learning of skills;
- restorative: allows the mediator to be heard, understood, respected as an individual, to let off steam, to show pleasure and enthusiasm and to put things into perspective.

The restorative aspect of supervision overlaps with support. A support session aims to provide a safe setting in which to express feelings, share experiences and develop skills and practice. Lack of support is often identified in exit interviews as a reason for giving up the work. Mediators may readily accept the need for support for themselves but be unmindful of their role in giving support to others, particularly from the less to the more experienced mediator. Support can be arranged on an informal basis, but it still requires arranging, and the less enthusiastic will always need encouragement to partake.

Problems and issues that might come up in supervision include difficulties working with a co-mediator, persuading parties to let them across the threshold, not getting a face-to-face meeting, or assessing whether a situation is mediable or not. A mediator may have anxieties about her or his skill level, have been frightened by unpleasant people or animals when visiting, or be uncertain how to bring a case to an end.

Supervision models

One-to-one sessions with a supervisor

This is a traditional model of a regular (probably monthly) one-to-one discussion focusing on professional concerns/problems and the development of the individual worker. This model is a particularly appropriate one for supervision for the manager/co-ordinator of a service. Usually the supervisor is an outside person and is paid for this service. Appraisals or joint progress reviews are based on a similar format but are held less frequently, and may have a structure defined by a set of prepared questions, resulting in a jointly agreed written summary.

Pairs: one supervisor supervises two workers

The advantage may be lower costs and a greater range of discussion.

One-to-one peer supervision: co-supervision

Each of the pair in turn takes the role of supervisor. Participants may change over at half time or take alternate sessions. The advantage is that it may be cost-free and it gives experience of both roles, but it requires monitoring and probably works best in addition to experienced supervisor supervision.

Attachment: a more experienced worker supervises a less experienced one

Again, this could be in addition to one-to-one supervision. It is a mentoring process which is often used when a new mediator works with an experienced co-mediator. A pre-prepared feedback process with a checklist is important and should be used after each mediation visit or meeting.

Group supervision with one or two supervisors

This model has the advantage of a group providing more material for discussion and group members being able to support each other. Members receive reflections, feedback and input from their peers as well as the supervisors. This setting is also less dominated by the supervisor. Another advantage is that there is the opportunity to use roleplay. The disadvantage is that there is obviously less time for each individual, and group dynamics may become a preoccupation. Shy people find groups hard going. Attendance at groups can be variable or fall away.

Peer group supervision

This model appeals to many services. It has most of the advantages described in the model above, if members take on the facilitator role in turn. The skills required are closely akin to a mediator's. It does not require paid hours of anybody's time and has a structure of equality that mediators tend to like. It has the same disadvantages as the model above. To have the best chance of succeeding, care should be given to the setting up of each group, and skills training offered to those hoping to be facilitators. Some group facilitation materials could be made available for each group to hold.

Three-person supervision

This is an extension of the training method of working in threes. Here the 'mediator' chooses a particular problem or issue and describes it to the 'supervisor'. The 'supervisor', by active listening and careful questioning, helps the 'mediator' work out an understanding and a way forward. The 'supervisor' avoids giving advice or rushing to solutions. The 'observer' notes the communication between the two and gives feedback on what went on, performing an enabling function. This model is often incorporated into group supervision as described above.

Whole team meetings

Opportunities for all mediators and others working for a service to get together are important for making and renewing contacts, and for communication of information and ideas.

Network supervision

This is a system for wider groups with common interests to meet and include supervision as part of their agenda. It can be very valuable and achievable when there are at least a few highly motivated members.

CONCLUSION

In this chapter we have discussed the processes of recruitment, selection, training and support that shape new volunteers into practising mediators in the UK. Equal opportunities for all are at the heart of these processes. People who have the desire and the basic capacity to learn and understand the ways of working that non-violent conflict resolution requires, can become mediators. From its early beginnings until very recently, community mediators have not had to face many strict assessments, and they have not been expected to come into mediation with a theoretical understanding of conflict and human behaviour or psychology. In this sense the recruitment and selection processes involved in becoming a community mediator have been fairly open, and services have had to consider carefully whether this raises questions of quality for clients, and whether volunteers are fully confident in themselves. To meet these questions most services have placed a strong emphasis on regular support and supervision as discussed here. Standards of quality and professionalism have been steadily rising over the past decade of mediation in the UK, from the point where 12 hours of training was considered enough, to today's situation where professional trainers offer foundation courses of 40 hours over five days, mediators can gain National Open College Network accreditation, and National Vocational Qualifications are around the corner.[12] Community mediators of the future will be more likely to hold one of a number of forms of accreditation, gained as a result of their initial training or through assessment of their mediation practice. How this will affect the nature of the body of community mediators in this country remains to be seen. However, it is certain that, whatever backgrounds new mediators will come from, they will be shaped as mediators through processes of recruitment, selection, training and support very much like the ones described in this chapter.

---

12   More can be read about these developments in Chapter 11.

CHAPTER SEVEN

DISPUTE ANALYSIS

Gavin R Beckett

INTRODUCTION

All mediators engage in dispute analysis in the first stages of the mediation process as they establish the issues of the case, the emotional context, and the relationship of the parties. Looked at from a more academic position, dispute analysis involves more than these points, also including attention to the structural background in which the conflict is occurring. In this chapter I shall look at both this wide sense of dispute analysis, and also the narrower sense with which mediators are concerned. My aim is to describe the typical characteristics of neighbour disputes, using an analytical framework developed by Paul Wehr.[1] I look at the history, context, parties, issues and dynamics of conflict, analysing each of these in the context of neighbour disputes. This then serves to underpin the discussion in the next chapter, about the process undertaken by the local mediation service, of selecting disputes for mediation.

This chapter also includes discussion of the limitations of mediation in the face of large-scale structural forces. Although mediation is an extremely effective and potentially transformative process for dealing with neighbour disputes, all forms of intervention are limited in their reach and efficacy; and to address all the elements of conflict, more than one method is needed. This idea is discussed in more depth in Chapter 13.

CAUSES OF CONFLICT

When the mediator first visits a client, one of the first questions asked will be a variation on 'Would you tell us about the situation?'. The people involved in the dispute will then present the issues they want the mediator to help them deal with. There is a fairly common set of issues found in neighbour disputes all over the country, including noise from a variety of sources; the behaviour of children, both very young and teenagers; noise and smells from pets; where and when people park their vehicles; smells; untidy homes and gardens; and many other issues often lumped together under the category of 'lifestyle clashes'.

---

1   Wehr, P, *Conflict Regulation*, 1979, Boulder: Westview Press. There are other frameworks for conflict analysis available in the literature, and used by practitioners, all of which have their strengths and weaknesses. I choose Paul Wehr's because it contains three main areas that mediation training considers in depth (parties, issues and dynamics) alongside other categories which are less commonly discussed (history and context).

These are the parties' reasons for the conflict, the things they tell the mediator when asked why they are in conflict. But they are not the only causes of conflict – there can also be structural causes of conflict, factors that arise as a result of the social and political structure, ie the groups and institutions of society, like the family, the economic system, the class system, cultural traditions, government policy and procedure. These are things that pre-exist the individuals who are born into them. They therefore condition the way that people act and think to a certain extent.[2] They enable some actions and ways of thinking, and constrain others. Thus some causes of conflict cannot be changed by individual action, and this will influence how far mediation can be appropriate or effective.

MAPPING CONFLICTS

When they first visit the parties involved in a conflict, many mediators use a simple technique of 'conflict mapping' to help themselves and the parties to analyse the dispute. One such model, presented by Shoshana Faire and Helena Cornelius, maps the issues of the conflict, the parties involved, and the needs and fears of each party.[3] So a conflict could be mapped as follows: the issue might be a noisy, fierce dog; the parties could be Mr and Mrs Allen and Mr Bates; Mr and Mrs Allen's needs could be for peace and quiet to enable them to relax, and their fear is of the large dog; Mr Bates's need could be to feel secure in his home, and his fear is of being the victim of a violent burglary.

In order to consider elements of structural context and conditioning as well as people's reasons for conflict, I am going to make use of a more complex conflict mapping model proposed by Paul Wehr.[4] To get a full picture of a conflict, mediators need to consider as many of these elements as possible; most mediators do this informally, even if they do not use this exact model.

Conflict history

The history of the conflict is usually extremely significant for parties in conflict. Mediators need to recognise its origins and major events, and their relationship to the present. The story of the conflict often becomes a central

---

2   Although they do not determine what we do and think. Structures present us with opportunities for and constraints on action, and when we act we are at the same time producing, reproducing and transforming structures. We are neither wholly free nor totally constrained. See for instance Bhaskar, R, *Reclaiming Reality. A Critical Introduction to Contemporary Philosophy*, 1989, London: Verso; and Giddens, A, *Central Problems in Social Theory. Action, Structure and Contradiction in Social Analysis*, 1979, London: Macmillan.

3   Cornelius, H and Faire, S, *Everyone Can Win*, 1989, New York and Sydney: Simon and Schuster, pp 117–29.

4   *Op cit*, Wehr, pp 18–22.

element of people's lives, and frames their view of events in the present. Of course, there will usually be two different histories of the conflict, one from each side (assuming that there are only two sides). These two histories may also have variations, especially when there are several members of a family involved, each of whom may have a slightly different understanding based on their involvement and personal perspective. Nevertheless, each side's story will have a number of agreed elements that reoccur each time it is told. Mediators will hear this history, sometimes in a coherent story, sometimes in separate or jumbled up parts, and they will probably be asked to listen to it several times. Some mediators are willing to hear the story as often as it takes for the person to feel heard and validated. Others try to introduce the 'future focus' of the mediation process very early on, and move people on as soon as possible. Whatever their style, all mediators have to try to help the parties redefine the importance of their history of the conflict. Mediators will not attempt to dispute or to verify the truth of these histories, but they will try to challenge the way in which people use them to justify continuing the conflict.

Conflict context

All conflicts have a specific context, which affects both their history and their current state. This context involves the local geography, for instance how housing estates are laid out, and where neighbours live in relation to one another; political structures and relationships, including the effects of housing policy, regeneration programmes, local taxation and criminal justice; and social structures and relationships, including relations between and within social classes, the nature of the family, cultural traditions and differences, and problems of poverty. Technology also plays a part in conflict: for instance, the decline in building standards due to financial constraints, combined with the increased power of modern home entertainment technology, does a lot to exacerbate noise problems.

I said at the beginning of the chapter that conflicts had structural causes as well as psychological causes. These structural causes would frequently be identified by the mediator and the parties as the context of the conflict. If they are aspects of reality which cannot be changed, then the deepest causes of the conflict may be unaffected by the mediation process. However, even when such causes can be removed or diminished, these things are often outside the control of the individuals involved in the mediation process. For instance, if owner-occupiers realise that the root of a particular problem lies in certain physical features of their homes, and that these are alterable – such as better soundproofing for walls, floors and ceilings – then, given the financial resources, this root of the conflict may be removed. However, the same problem occurring in houses on large council estates with hundreds of properties, in the present economic situation, is very unlikely to be resolved in the same way. Social housing providers simply cannot afford to carry out large programmes of soundproofing houses and flats. The individual disputants and mediators will not usually have any power to influence the social landlord on such large-scale questions.

Indeed, the inability to deal with physical problems of housing is not solely within the power of the housing provider either, as it stems from larger structural problems, such as the relations between local and central government, and the particular ideology of central government which prioritises other areas of expenditure. Were local authorities to have access to capital receipts from the sale of council houses, which have been denied to them by central government policy, significant sums of money would be available, and could possibly be used in major refurbishment of estates. (The new Labour government is releasing some money from capital receipts.) Central government is constrained in turn by the global market and national political climate.

Furthermore, other structural causes of conflict, such as the structured relations between social groups, whether based on culture, status or class, come into the picture through their effect on individuals' personal identities, beliefs and prejudices. In the short and relatively superficial mediation process, such deeply embedded aspects of individuals cannot be transformed. Mediators may challenge prejudices, but they cannot change them. Deep social and political structures provide the context in which people form their identity, their sense of who they are, and the interests that flow from that are frequently a cause of conflict. Mediators have to be aware that the parties may be unable to loosen the grip of their personal biographies sufficiently to reassess their interests. However, mediation provides a process in which these elements of the conflict can be recognised, something that is not so easy to do within the more adversarial forms of dispute management. Moreover, if mediation can help people take positive actions to deal with conflict, positive changes in their attitudes may come as a result.

People's perceptions of difference are also formed within social and political structures, and within communities. In contexts where intolerance and bigotry are common responses to difference, people's behaviour towards neighbours who are members of different classes, ethnic or national groups, who have a different occupational status, whose sexuality is different, amongst other things, will often feed into neighbour conflicts. Moreover, intolerance and bigotry are not only responses formed by psychological processes but are also affected by social conditions. The processes that lead to stereotyping of 'outgroups' are more likely in situations of hardship and social and political stress. Members of communities under social, political and economic threat feel insecurity more sharply, and this seems to lead to a tendency for individuals to act in prejudiced ways. The structural context thus challenges mediators, who cannot affect the large-scale social, political and economic processes which provide the backdrop for conflicts over difference.

Our present society in the UK is rich in its diversity of culture, having been the settling place of migrants for thousands of years. British culture is a polyglot culture, with earliest influences from a variety of European sources, and in recent centuries influenced by many cultures from all over the globe. In our urban and (to a lesser extent) our rural communities we live with or near to European, South-east Asian, African, Caribbean and Middle Eastern influences, each of which could be split up into dozens of different cultures. This diversity of cultures leads to diverse ways of living, and these can bring people into conflict over how it is acceptable to live. Mediation can play a role in such conflicts, in enabling people to reflect on their actions and beliefs, the effects they have on their neighbour, and whether they want to change their behaviour and attitudes. However, the caveats about the effect of large-scale structural contexts on personal and social identity and interests still apply.

Having recognised that there are limits to what mediation (and indeed any form of third party intervention) can achieve, I want to look at some aspects of conflict that the mediation process can affect.

Conflict parties

It is important to identify all of the people involved in the conflict, and their degree of involvement. Mediators cannot afford to assume that they already know who is involved when they receive a referral. On hearing the story of the primary individuals involved (who may be single people, couples, whole families or even entire streets), it becomes clearer who else is involved. Frequently the children of the adults involved are part of the situation, and sometimes people can be completely mistaken about the source of the problems they have attributed to their neighbours.

Primary

Primary parties are those who are in direct confrontation over incompatible goals, and are in structural positions such that they come into conflict with each other. These include the next-door neighbours who suffer from the poor housing conditions that exacerbate noise problems, or have different lifestyles, different views on pets etc and who come into direct personal contact with one another. They are the people who are referred, or who refer themselves, to the mediation service.

Very little statistical research has been done on the characteristics of disputants.[5] At the moment we do not know whether one kind of person becomes involved in neighbour disputes more than others. It seems that

---

5   One of the few pieces of research in this area is Tebay, S, Cumberbatch, G and Graham, N, *Disputes between Neighbours*, 1986, Birmingham: Aston University.

anyone can become involved in conflict with their neighbour. Owner-occupiers, private tenants, local authority tenants and travellers can all come into conflict with their neighbours, as can rich, poor, and middle-income households. Mediation services have recently been finding themselves as useful in rural areas as they have been in urban areas, and people of many nationalities, religions and races come to them for help.

The relationships between primary parties can vary considerably. In some cases disputants begin as friends, often helping each other in several ways, such as watching out for each other's security, sharing tasks in the garden, and speaking to each other in a friendly way. In other cases neighbours may never speak to one another, but are quite happy to live alongside each other in this way. It is when a difference arises in neighbours' perceptions of what the relationship should be, that conflict is likely to result. If an incumbent neighbour believes it is good behaviour to be very welcoming and do a lot for new neighbours, when the latter want to be left alone to arrange themselves in their new home, tensions can arise. The first neighbour may begin to feel they have done a lot for their new neighbours in return for little gratitude or reciprocal help. The other neighbour may feel overwhelmed and stifled before they have found their feet. Even with long-established good relationships, when a problem arises over a new issue, it is easy for small events to alter the dynamics of the relationship. In these situations neighbours are also likely to feel hurt and upset.

Secondary

Secondary parties are those who have an indirect stake in the outcome of the dispute, but do not feel directly involved. Extended families are often secondary parties, because they have an emotional investment in the conflict, and are frequently involved in supporting their relations who are the primary parties. Sometimes secondary parties come to be seen as primary parties as mediation progresses, if it becomes clear that it is they who are most concerned, or who are causing the problem. The primary parties can be in conflict over events which were actually caused by secondary parties. Mediators have to look out for such situations, and try to include in the mediation process those people who are responsible for the problem and can act to change the situation.

One case (see Chapter 9, pp 157–61) referred to a mediation service involved a couple, Mr and Mrs Patel, who lived next door to a family of four, the Brauns. The Brauns were directing their initial complaints at Mrs Patel, but the mediators soon discovered that it was actually her grandchildren, and their parents (Mrs Patel's adult children), who were acting in ways to which the Brauns objected. One of Mrs Patel's issues was that her neighbours should not expect her to be responsible for her adult children's behaviour, or their children's behaviour. The mediators had to consider whether to widen the process to include these people, who were responsible for the actions that had caused the conflict. In another conflict, during the mediation process it became clear that one party was mistaken about the identity of a child causing problems for them. The child was not related to their neighbours at all, and a large part of the conflict had therefore been based on wrongly interpreted perceptions and a failure to communicate.[6]

Issues

One of the goals of mediation is to help people come to agreements, so clearly it is crucial for the mediators and the parties to be clear on what the issues are. When a mediator enters a conflict, issues have usually proliferated from the original cause of the dispute. This means that the presenting problems may actually be symptoms rather than causes. Paul Wehr breaks issues down into four types.

Facts-based

These issues arise out of 'disagreement over what is because of how parties perceive *what is*'.[7] Conflict arises out of different judgments or perceptions of events and actions. So, for instance, people may be in conflict over responsibility for rubbish being left in common hallways, each seeing the rubbish as evidence that the other makes the mess. Or they may be in conflict about alleged abusive language or behaviour. Something has definitely happened in these cases, some actions or events, but what is at issue is the meaning of these things. One side may tolerate more expletives than the other. Or perhaps neither party is responsible for littering, but one or both has a different perception. In noise cases, one party may complain about excessive loud noise, or noise played late at night. Both of these complaints are based on standards that are relative to the perspective of the complainant. The parties will often have different ideas about whether music is being played loudly because they do not perceive loudness in the same way. In other cases, conflicts may be maintained because people perceive the interactions with their neighbours as abusive or disrespectful, and they frequently generalise this to the whole personality of their neighbour. The mediation process has to address these perceptions of what their neighbours are like, to enable people to take part and negotiate in good faith.

---

6   The term 'misperceptions' is often used in conflict resolution, but this implies that there must be a correct perception that someone has failed to see. There can only be different perceptions, especially in mediation where right and wrong are essentially irrelevant to the process. It is people's interpretations of perceptions that matter.

7   Wehr, *op cit*, p 20.

Values-based

These issues arise out of 'disagreement over *what should be.*'[8] People often talk about 'lifestyle clashes' as causes of conflict. What is at issue here are competing values about how life should be lived. Neighbours may disapprove of unmarried couples, of single-parent families, of child-rearing practices different from their own, of different sexualities from their own, and many other less central elements of how people live their lives. Conflict can arise as people's sense of what is right and wrong is offended by the actions or inactions of their neighbour. Noise caused by children playing together may be interpreted as indicating a lack of common values about peace and quiet. Developing a jaundiced view of one's neighbour as a result of such a value clash, will of course add to the likelihood of a clash of perceptions about what is going on. Where one party sees noisy brats who are out of control, the other sees joyful and exuberant children. Values can cause problems for mediators, who are not there to pass judgment on the differing values of the parties.[9] If the parties do not recognise any shared values and oppose each other's views of the future, it is difficult for negotiation to begin. Sometimes, however, the actual process of mediation can play a part in challenging the rigidity of people's values.

Interests-based

These issues arise out of 'disagreement over *who will get what* in the distribution of scarce resources'.[10] These resources are not just the concrete ones like land and economic benefits, but also include less tangible things like power, privilege and respect. We could see noise disputes as being centrally about people's interests. On the part of the noise-maker, playing loud music may be a way of relaxing, or spending their spare time enjoyably. On the part of the suffering neighbour, peace and quiet may be necessary for exactly the same reasons, or because they need their sleep to function well during their working hours. The scarce resources here are time and airspace, which the parties have to find some way of sharing. Interests are connected to values, through identity. People's sense of who they are, and what they hold dear, also affect their interests. People who see themselves as good parents, who bring their children up with values of right and wrong, have an interest in being publicly recognised as good parents. Thus they will be triply antagonised by neighbours who criticise their child-rearing practices or their children's behaviour: their interest in a good reputation, their value system and their identity as good parents, are all under attack. Interests in scarce

---

8   *Loc cit.*

9   There are limits to mediators' non-judgmental stance; and mediation itself is based on certain values. See Chapter 13 for further discussion of this.

10   *Loc cit.*

resources can also cause neighbour disputes about fences or constructions blocking access previously regarded as shared. Problems can also arise if the amount of sunlight in a neighbour's garden is reduced, or if the neighbour thinks that a new structure diminishes the attractiveness of their property, perhaps reducing its monetary value.

Relationship-based

These issues concern the ways relationships between neighbours affect conflicts, and include such things as people's communication styles.[11] If neighbours do communicate to each other about the dispute, it is often in a manner that makes the dispute worse rather than better. They may confront their neighbours in an aggressive way, shouting and using abusive language. They may not use words at all, instead thumping on walls or the ceiling, or simply glaring at each other. These things can all add to the intensity of the dispute, and may be offered to the mediators as an issue to be dealt with, ie 'Our neighbours are rude and aggressive people and we want them to be polite to us.'[12]

Dynamics

These are the processes of change that take place in the course of a conflict. Wehr notes five stages of importance, although there are of course other ways of describing these dynamics.

Precipitating events

Parties in conflict often name significant events as the beginnings of the conflict. These are the events that are offered to the mediator in response to the question 'When did this all begin?' or 'What started the dispute?'. They may not be the root causes of the conflict, but they are the markers for the transition to overt conflict. In a noise dispute, the precipitating event may be remembered clearly as the first time that a noisy party disturbed their neighbours. In other cases, small incidents may be ignored, but resented, until a particular event causes one neighbour to complain.

---

11 *Loc cit.*

12 Paul Wehr uses the term 'non-realistic' for this category, which makes these issues seem unimportant, because they are not 'real'. Andrew Floyer Acland and some others also use these terms in their analysis of conflict. However, there is little to gain by labelling some elements of conflict 'non-real', as they do not seem any less real than other elements of the conflict. In any case, who makes the judgment of what standards reality can be measured by? See Acland, AF, *A Sudden Outbreak of Common Sense. Managing Conflict Through Mediation*, 1990, London, Hutchinson Business Books, pp 45–46.

Issue emergence, transformation, proliferation

Mediators seldom intervene in disputes at their beginning, much as they would like to. As they hear the story from the neighbours, it becomes clear that emergent issues are transformed over time: the impersonal becomes personal, specific complaints become more general, and as the conflict continues the issues multiply. Mediators often have to untangle carefully the strands of the conflict, to determine with the parties which are major and which are subsidiary issues. Initial complaints about noisy children may become transformed into accusations of deliberate intimidation or harassment; proliferate into issues around child-rearing practices, the attitudes and behaviour of the parents; and then spread to other sources of noise and the various ways in which the neighbours react or fail to react to the complaints.

Polarisation

There is a clear tendency for neighbours to become polarised as the conflict goes on. Parties look for allies amongst family and friends, consolidate their positions, increase the internal consistency of their story and outlook, and put psychological distance between themselves and the other side. Unfortunately mediators often arrive in a dispute after the parties have become polarised, and this can make their work extremely hard. Because the parties have developed the internal consistency of their stories, and these stories of course contradict each other, mediators can find it difficult to draw parties into a mutual agreement about the content of the dispute. In one case, the mediators found almost completely equal and opposite stories from both parties, and no matter how they tried to explore the situation, they could not discover any common perception about each other's behaviour. Neither party would agree that they were doing anything that the other accused them of, and simply told the mediators that it was the other side who was doing it. In such a situation no issues can be found as a focus for discussion; and mediators risk becoming conduits for accusations and denials. In such a polarised situation, the only way to break the stand-off may be to bring the parties face to face so that they have to confront each other's different perspectives. Paradoxically this is often too risky a step to take because of the frightening image of the other that they have developed.

Spiralling

Over time the conflict is very likely to escalate, as each party reacts to the other in a more hostile and destructive way, leading to a reciprocal increase in intensity from the other. Mediators aim to initiate de-escalatory spirals, where the parties reciprocate in reducing hostility. Sometimes the escalation of events can be extremely serious: the initial event may cause angry words to be exchanged, and this may lead to more abusive language, which may lead to threats of violence, which may then be carried out against property and/or the person. Mediators will have a very difficult job if they find themselves entering a conflict that has already reached a violent stage.[13]

Stereotyping and mirror-imaging

A central part of polarisation is the demonisation of the other. As the internal consistency of the party's story is increased, so the actions of the other become correspondingly unexplainable. The other party is set up as a mirror image, whose lies, duplicity, aggression and rigidity is contrasted to the honesty, straightforwardness, peacefulness and flexibility of the first party. Because both parties are involved in this process, each mistrusts the other, and communication becomes very difficult, as each interprets the other's actions and words with suspicion. Such attitudes often make it difficult to get parties to agree to a face-to-face meeting, because their image of the other is so bad that they dare not risk a confrontation, and also do not trust them to act in good faith. Nevertheless, it is in such a confrontation that disputants are most likely to be able to move forwards towards a new relationship. Shuttle mediation is often used when parties will not meet, but its drawback is that people cannot see their neighbours react to their side of the story, and hence the human connection is absent.

Alternative routes to a solution of the problem

Mediators will often find in their initial analysis of the dispute that the parties already have ideas about solving the problem. Alternatively, the parties may not immediately be able to suggest ways forward, so the mediators provide a problem-solving framework for them, helping them to analyse the situation and come up with new options. This helps to emphasise from very early on that it is the parties who must create and own the settlement or resolution of their dispute. In some cases, neighbours may come up with the same idea, but be unable to communicate because of the deterioration of the relationship. One such case involved two elderly people living in flats one above the other, unable to speak face to face without shouting abuse at one another; yet they both recognised that their problems would be solved by the man upstairs moving to a ground-floor flat. As a result of the mediators' visit, the man upstairs decided to take action and was able to move fairly quickly. Of course mediators often find that each party has his or her own ideas about what would solve the problems, and negotiating over the best way forward is a central part of any mediation.

---

13 Many community mediation services do not accept referrals where violence is involved, but it is not always easy to know the full facts before becoming involved. See Chapter 8 for more detailed discussion of this.

CONCLUSION

This chapter has described and analysed the characteristics of neighbour disputes under the headings of the history, context, parties, issues, and dynamics of conflict. My aim has been to show that conflicts between neighbours, which often seem to be solely rooted in individual personalities and circumstances, have an important structural context that plays an equal part in creating the conflict. When mediators enter into a conflict and begin to unravel its tangled strands, a framework like this will enable them to think clearly about those strands that can be dealt with head on, those that can be affected indirectly as the mediation process changes the relationship between the neighbours, and those that will remain unchanged during and after the process. The latter will include the deeper structural causes of conflict described at the beginning of the chapter, particularly those rooted in large-scale economic and political structures. Mediation cannot change these structures, but it can affect the way in which people react to them. Instead of viewing each other as the problem, neighbours can change their perceptions as a result of mediation, and recognise that they stand together, equally affected by these structures.

CHAPTER EIGHT

SELECTING DISPUTES

John C Patrick

INTRODUCTION

The process of case selection varies in detail from service to service, so this chapter will look at the general procedures and principles governing the process. As the parties can withdraw from mediation at any time, and the second party may not wish to participate from the outset, we will look mainly at the service's considerations in deciding how to proceed.

In practice, most services 'select out' cases with which they will not proceed, rather than selecting those with which they will work. This selection occurs for a number of reasons. Some cases are not considered suitable for mediation because of the attitude and behaviour of one or more of the parties. Other cases may require a ruling either through the courts or through some form of arbitration. Services work with limited resources and may need to target their work where it is likely to be most effective, or may have to work within restrictions imposed by their funding; this can mean taking on only cases which are funded.

Mediation requires some motivation on the part of the parties to reach a solution, and is most effective when both parties wish to keep or establish a positive relationship with each other. Mediation may be easier when the dispute is in its early stages, and relationships are still good; and also sometimes when the dispute is of long standing and the disputants have exhausted other ways of resolving the issues, and are more prepared to seek compromise.

As the selection process continues throughout the work with each case, this chapter will look at the decision making at each stage in the order of the mediation process.

REFERRALS

The first point at which selection may occur is on initial contact from a party or a referrer. Community mediation services receive their referrals from a variety of sources. Most services accept referrals from agencies on behalf of disputants, but some insist that the disputants themselves contact the office. A self-referral means that the party is coming to the service voluntarily, thus taking the first step towards a mediated settlement. If the referral comes through another agency, the service will check with the party on their first contact, whether they really want mediation.

In many services, even though they receive most or all their work from self-referrals, the parties may have heard of the service from other agencies. Some of these self-referrals will not be appropriate or may feel they are coming to mediation under duress, and mediation services need to work closely with potential referring agencies.

The first contact in the majority of cases is by telephone, as services vary in their accessibility for personal visits and in their ability to deal with these. Services based in the middle of their area, or near the offices of agencies who may refer cases to mediation, may receive some of their referrals by a personal visit from the complaining party. Many services, working on limited funds, are unable to staff their offices full-time and rely on the telephone answering machine to handle incoming work.

In most cases the initial contact will be handled by an employee of the service who is usually a trained mediator and may undertake some mediations her/himself. Where the reception staff are not mediators, they will have received some training in handling referrals and dealing with people in a distressed or angry state. At this stage, basic information will be taken about the nature of the conflict, along with the details of the person contacting the office.

At the referral stage, the motivation and attitude of the party, and the nature of the problem, may give an indication of the suitability of the case for continuing the work. Sometimes the person taking the referral may be able to make some suggestions for the party to try to deal with the matter personally, with a view to coming back if the matter is not resolved. On occasions the complaining party may not have said anything to the neighbour, and a suggestion to raise the issue may be sufficient, at least as a first step, before arranging anything further.

In the majority of cases, a visit by mediators will be arranged. The co-ordinator or intake worker will select the mediators for the visit on the basis of the information gained and the availability of the mediators, who are usually working voluntarily in their own time. There may be clear indications about the nature of the party or the conflict which help in this selection. Issues of age, sex, experience and race may affect this choice, and the staff undertaking this will know their mediators and their preferences, interests, strengths and weaknesses. It is also important, where possible, to maintain a balance between the two mediators, and a knowledge of how well they work together may be a factor to consider. While matching is attempted where possible, the major factor in allocation usually comes down to the availability of mediators.

REFERRERS

An important issue is the manner in which cases come to a mediation service and the work the service needs to do with potential referrers and parties. The voluntary nature of community mediation needs to be stressed in any publicity material and in discussions with the main referral agencies. It is equally important to make clear the difference between mediation, advocacy and arbitration. Some people come to a service seeking help but want the mediators to act on their behalf and tell the neighbours their problem, others come seeking an arbitrated solution and concentrate on trying to prove to the mediators that they have right on their side.

When a referral comes on the advice of an agency with authority for taking other action, such as a housing authority, environmental health or the police, the party may feel obliged to come to the mediation service, to get further action from that agency. If someone is seeking a housing transfer, for instance, they may feel that coming to the mediation service will enhance their application, and so may not wish to see the matter resolved and their case for a transfer diminished.

When they are seeking advice to take legal proceedings, they may be advised to try mediation as a means of enhancing their case and demonstrating their reasonableness. In such cases it is important that the two processes are separated. Their willingness to accept an informal and non-enforceable resolution needs to be explored, and if mediation is to proceed, any court action needs to be suspended during the process.

ASSESSMENT PROCESS

In the majority of cases coming to any service, a visit is arranged and this allows a more detailed opportunity to assess whether mediation is an appropriate way forward. Mediators will be looking at the nature of the problem and the motivation of the people involved to seek a solution. Different options are discussed and the mediation process explained in some detail, emphasising its voluntary nature.

If it is agreed to try mediation, the next stage is usually to arrange a visit to the other party involved in the dispute, to hear their view and assess the possibility of a face-to-face meeting. On occasions, the first party may not be willing to try this, and mediators have to consider whether to continue to work with that party in the hope of progress towards mediation at a later stage, or whether to help the party look at other ways to resolve the issue.

The willingness of the second party to participate is crucial and a number of cases are closed because they will not co-operate. If they are willing to discuss the issue, the mediators again need to assess the way forward that seems likely to be most effective; this is discussed with both parties.

Mediation services vary in their approach to the second party, and many services are becoming more proactive in their efforts to make contact with them. A letter, putting the onus on them to contact the office if they do not want a visit, has proved effective, and if they do telephone the office to cancel an appointment offered, this gives an opportunity to discuss the situation and clear up any misunderstandings about the role of the service and the purpose of the visit.

LIMITING FACTORS

Although most services try to undertake some work with almost all those who seek their help, there are a number of limiting factors. The mediation service's governing documents such as its constitution will be the basis for some of these. If the service is registered as a charity, it must work within its constitution which has been endorsed by the Charity Commission, and this may limit the geographical area and the types of dispute undertaken. Contracts with funders may also influence case selection: for example, funding from a housing authority may be earmarked for work with tenants of that authority; funding obtained for noise problems may exclude cases involving other issues.

Most services develop policies for decisions about work to be taken on, and lack of resources may mean that rationing of cases takes place. However, there are also several other factors which could preclude mediation service involvement.

The research project completed by Jim Dignan et al[1] (see Chapter 12) showed that the average rate of acceptance of referrals by community mediation services was just under 80%, with six services reporting 100% acceptance. Some of the differences between services may be explained by differing interpretations of what constitutes 'accepting' a referral. Services gave a variety of reasons for not accepting a referral, although all the reasons were mentioned by only a minority of services surveyed.

Geographical restrictions were mentioned most; other factors included the existence of court proceedings, a history of threats or violence, racial harassment, mental illness, power imbalance and the unwillingness of the parties to participate. Although some information on this may be available at the time of referral, most will only be clear after an initial visit and an assessment. While for some services these factors would lead to an absolute decision not to accept the referral, for others they would be considered in assessment and influence decisions about whether and how to proceed with mediation.

---

1   Dignan, J, Sorsby, A and Hibbert, J, *Neighbour Disputes: Comparing the Cost-effectiveness of Mediation and Alternative Approaches*, 1996, Sheffield: University of Sheffield.

ASSESSING SUITABILITY FOR MEDIATION

A conflict's suitability for mediation is assessed at each stage of the process by the mediators in consultation with the parties. A fundamental part of this is the assessment of the parties' willingness to continue to participate. Mediators will usually look with each party at all the options including mediation, as well as the possible consequences of not dealing with the conflict. The problem often arises of one party being willing to continue while the other is not, and this will be discussed later in this chapter.

In assessing suitability for mediation, it is useful to look at three interlinking areas:

- the attitude of each of the parties;
- the relationship between the parties;
- the nature of the conflict.

Parties' attitudes

Where each party recognises that there is a problem which needs resolution, and that such a resolution would have some benefit for them, the chances of a successful mediation are enhanced. It is important to assess the extent to which each party wants to retain some control over the situation, to ensure that mediation is the appropriate way forward. When one or both parties are looking for someone else to decide the issues, then mediation may not be appropriate and other means of conflict management need to be explored. Many people initially look to some form of arbitration from mediators because they lack confidence in their own ability to find a solution and do not understand the nature of the mediation process. Exploration of this can frequently lead to a change of view, and many people find that the empowering processes of mediation lead to a greater sense of freedom and self-confidence. Others may feel unable to accept the responsibility for making decisions about the conflict, and so will not respond well to a mediation approach.

Some people may be so entrenched in their positions that they find it impossible to move; they may have very mixed feelings about the conflict, but would find any compromise or adjustment of their attitudes or behaviour more difficult than the continuation of the aggravation with their neighbours. Others are used to achieving their goals by forcing the issue and being aggressive; they have little or no interest in their neighbour's feelings or the establishment of any better relationship. By contrast, there are those for whom the relationship is so important that they may be prepared to give too much in the mediation, only to regret it afterwards, and agreements reached in this manner are likely to break down. While both these groups of people may be involved successfully in mediation, the chances of achieving a resolution are reduced and particular effort is required.

Relationship between the parties

The history of the relationship between the parties is important assessment information. While it is not impossible to mediate where the relationship has been bad from an early stage, it is often considerably easier if one can point to a previous period of good relationships. Disputes often arise between parties who have enjoyed a satisfactory relationship, and restoring this is a strong motivation to try resolving the issues.

If the relationship has deteriorated to the situation of abuse, threats or even violence, it may not be possible to bring parties together. Even if the parties are willing, mediators may have reservations about their ability to control the situation; and the safety of all is a factor in deciding whether and how to proceed. Some services are not prepared to arrange mediation at all where violence has been a factor, and all services will take particular care in making arrangements for such a meeting.

A further factor is the difference in power between the two sides. A significant difference in power makes direct mediation difficult and, unless well handled, it can be counterproductive; here alternative processes such as shuttle mediation may be considered. The power issue and its influence on the mediation process are considered in detail in Chapter 10.

The nature of the conflict

Mediation is not an appropriate means of resolving some disputes because of their nature. Where there is a need for some higher authority to determine an outcome, or make a ruling over disputed facts or interpretation of facts, the matter requires a judicial hearing. For example, in a dispute over ownership or position of a boundary, the mediation service might be able to help sort out peripheral issues and improve communication so that the substantive issue can be resolved amicably – but it is not the role of mediators to give a ruling, or even an opinion, on a disputed fact. (Of course, in many boundary disputes, there are few 'facts', and mediation is then one of the few means of resolving the dispute.)

Where the alleged behaviour of one party amounts to a criminal offence, it is not normally appropriate for a community mediation service to deal with the matter, unless or until the criminal matter has been resolved either by prosecution or by a decision not to proceed through the criminal law. Even then, unless the behaviour described is admitted, mediation could result in an unproductive session of accusation and denial.[2]

2 In these situations, mediation becomes more like victim/offender mediation, where mediation takes place on the basis of an admission of responsibility by the offender.

A particular example of this occurs when a neighbour makes accusations about the abuse or neglect of a child. While mediators normally operate to conventional standards of confidentiality, there can be occasions where general concern about the welfare of children takes precedence. Where the concern arises from the comments of a neighbour, the mediator will help that neighbour take his or her concerns to the appropriate authority, usually the local social services department, police or NSPCC (National Society for the Prevention of Cruelty to Children). If the mediators' concerns arise as a result of their own observations or the comments of a member of the household where the abuse is alleged, the mediators themselves may need to report the matter. In general, it is inappropriate for services to undertake mediation in these circumstances unless the issue of the alleged abuse is dealt with first.

Most services will not accept a referral if there is a civil law suit taking place, although they may do so if legal proceedings are suspended to try to resolve the matter through mediation. On occasions county courts have adjourned disputes between neighbours to allow mediation to be tried. While this is not yet common practice, the growth and establishment of community mediation services may encourage this trend.

Mediation may not be appropriate, except as a mitigating activity, where the dispute centres on one or both parties' fundamental belief system. Complaints about the water and noise of car cleaning on a shared driveway may derive from one party's strong religious beliefs when the events happen on their Sabbath. It may be possible to work to reduce the conflict in practical terms, but the beliefs in religion or the worship of cars are values that mediation cannot change. Some beliefs, such as racism, need to be challenged and the service's position on equal opportunities made clear. This in itself can render mediation inappropriate, and it is a matter of judgment for individual services, on a case-by-case basis, whether they can intervene in cases where oppression results from fundamentally different sets of beliefs. However, mediation can be used to help deal with misunderstandings and miscommunications which are often part of the backdrop of oppression and value-based beliefs.

WORKING WITH ONE PARTY

Where it is not possible to continue work with both parties in a dispute, a service has to decide whether to continue working with one party only. Return visits and follow-up work with the complaining party may occur when the second party will not co-operate or a decision is made not to proceed to mediation for other reasons. Such work needs to focus on how the person is going to deal with the conflict and what other help they may need. When mediation does not seem possible or appropriate, some mediators find it difficult to limit their involvement, because they may be dealing with someone who is very distressed by the conflict with their neighbour. It is important to have a knowledge of other agencies to whom the person can go for advice or counselling.

The main task with a single party is to help them look at the options that remain. Are they going to pursue other means of resolving the conflict? If so, how? If not, how can they learn to live with the conflict? An analysis of the alternatives and an unbiased look at the advantages and disadvantages of each, is an important part of the work of a mediation service. Having undertaken that analysis, the mediators need to be able to discontinue their involvement and avoid getting into general support and counselling.

SELECTION AND EFFECTIVENESS

This chapter has been looking at the current practice of case selection, which is based mainly on experience, intuitive analysis and anecdotal evidence, with little work on systematising it on the basis of effectiveness. To consider such an approach it is useful to try to categorise differing sorts of dispute. The research at Sheffield University by Jim Dignan et al[3] (see Chapter 12) discussed a six-fold categorisation of disputes, and considered the implications for mediation of each of them.

These categories are:

- disputes resulting from inconsiderate or mildly anti-social behaviour on the part of one or both of the parties;
- disputes involving a more serious personality or lifestyle clash;
- disputes involving a degree of harassment and/or minor criminal acts relating to the dispute itself;
- disputes where the neighbour nuisance element is an incidental by-product of some other activity or problem (eg domestic violence, drug abuse etc);
- disputes involving serious harassment (including racial harassment), or where one of the parties is involved in serious criminal activity;
- disputes involving 'care in the community' cases or those in which one of the parties appears to have mental health problems.

1 Inconsiderate or mildly anti-social behaviour

This category forms the bulk of work undertaken by mediation services, as it is generally viewed as the one most amenable to mediation. The cost to other

---

3   *Ibid.*

agencies of such 'minor irritants' may not be great, however, and, from a cost-benefit point of view, mediation may be seen as relatively expensive. However, many cases that may appear to the outsider as trivial, are viewed very seriously by those involved and can cause a disproportionate amount of unhappiness. Furthermore, disputes that start as apparently minor episodes often escalate into more serious ones, with the behaviour of the parties deteriorating with every incident. The Sheffield University research project quotes a case of manslaughter which started with the barking of a puppy.[4]

Work with this category of dispute can mean earlier referrals to the service, which means that mediation can take place before the relationship has deteriorated too badly and attitudes have become hardened. As each minor event in a conflict occurs, the positions taken by the parties tend to become more extreme and fixed, making mediation more difficult and resolution less likely. Nic Fine and Fiona Macbeth describe the development of conflict using the metaphor of a fire going through the stages:[5]

- The fuel – contact between people always has the potential for conflict and people vary in their combustibility.
- The spark – the incident that ignites the conflict.
- Smouldering – conflict simmers under the surface and feeds on rumour, gossip and resentment.
- Fanning the flames – further real or imagined incidents build up anger and hurt.
- Stoking the fire – social and environmental pressures intensify the situation.
- The blaze – the conflict has escalated to the point where it is out of control and damaging to those involved.

While it is possible to intervene at any time, it is often most effective to work with the spark before the smouldering process has gone on for too long. The rate of escalation of conflict, like that of fires, can vary considerably, depending on the nature of those involved, the behaviour and the social pressures. Undertaking mediation at the earliest possible stage is likely to be the most effective intervention.

2 Serious personality or lifestyle clashes

Jim Dignan *et al* argue that it is this category that has the greatest potential for cost-benefit. These cases are time-consuming and expensive for housing and environmental health departments, and conventional legal remedies are

---

4   *Ibid*, p 35.
5   Fine, N and Macbeth, F, *Playing with Fire*, 1992, Leicester: Youth Work Press.

generally ineffective. Such cases do present particular difficulties for mediation services, but mediators can help people accept their differences and learn to live with them. It is often possible to bring parties together, help them listen to the other's viewpoint, and find some resolution to the behavioural problems, without trying to remould people's lifestyles or personalities.

Sometimes the experience of mediation also achieves some change in people's attitudes. Helping people to work with their differences and negotiate with each other, can achieve a better means of dealing with the issues now and in the future. This highlights one of the major differences between mediation and other forms of conflict management.

3 'Minor' harassment and/or criminal acts

This is a category which causes some problems for mediation and, as we have discussed, may result in cases being selected out by services as unsuitable for intervention. Mediation does not make judgments about behaviour, so if it is important to demonstrate society's disapproval, then action other than mediation is required. Where mediation is seen as appropriate, it is important that the focus is on looking for ways to change unacceptable behaviour.[6]

4 Dispute as a by-product of other activity

Sometimes behaviour that causes the nuisance is not directed towards the neighbour, but is a by-product of some other activity. Here it is important that mediation concentrates on how the neighbour is affected, and the dispute is only likely to be resolved if there is parallel action by others to deal with the main behaviour.

5 Serious harassment or criminal activity

The discussion under category 3 above applies even more to this group of neighbour complaints, and it is likely that such behaviour will require other action (such as prosecution or a court injunction) which would render mediation inappropriate. Many services do not accept such referrals unless they have a victim/offender mediation service as part of their organisation. In some areas this work is done alongside community mediation, and this offers an appropriate model for dealing with this type of problem by mediation. A prerequisite for such work is that the offender accepts responsibility for the behaviour.

---

6   See also footnote 2 on victim/offender mediation.

6 Mental health problems

Some services are reluctant to become involved in cases resulting from one of the parties' mental health problems. Where they do, it is necessary to assess that party's ability to cope with a face-to-face meeting before direct mediation can be tried. Mediators need to distinguish eccentricity and unusual thinking or behaviour, from behaviour resulting from a recognisable mental health problem. This is particularly important when the disputant is of a different cultural background or has a different belief system from the mediators. The key determining factor is the person's ability to accept responsibility for their behaviour and their ability to play a meaningful part in mediation.

CONCLUSION

In this chapter I have described the issues considered in the selection of cases for mediation. This process is based on the shared experience of mediators, which has led to the development of guidelines, with some input from the theoretical analysis of conflict. The major factor in selecting cases remains the willingness of the parties to be involved in a voluntary process, and most community mediation services try to work with the vast majority of such cases that come their way.

CHAPTER NINE

CASE STUDIES

Compiled by Marian Liebmann

INTRODUCTION

This chapter has been compiled from case studies contributed by Gavin Beckett, Jim Dignan, Marian Liebmann, John Patrick, Marion Wells and several community mediation service co-ordinators. They are drawn from Bradford Mediation Service, Bristol Mediation, Milton Keynes Neighbour Dispute Service, Mole Valley Mediation Service, Rochdale Mediation Service, Sandwell Mediation Service and two local authorities, to whom thanks are due. All names have been changed to preserve confidentiality.

Mediation is a broad and diverse activity which cannot be neatly encapsulated by one or two typical examples. Mediation cases reflect the communities where people live, and these differ markedly from region to region, and even within the same town or city. The case studies presented here are drawn from a wide range of situations and geographical locations, from small towns as well as large urban centres. They give an idea of the variety of situations where mediation can make a positive contribution.

The variety of case studies – and mediation services – means that we have received the contributions in many different styles. Although it can be tempting to impose some uniformity of format, we have decided to leave the different styles, to reflect the diversity of experience.

The tendency in quoting case studies is to present only the success stories. But sometimes there is as much to be learnt from situations that were not resolved, and we have deliberately included two such cases. It is also good to remember that people in dispute can often sort things out themselves – not everyone needs mediators; so we have included a case which resolved itself while on the waiting list.

The chapter is structured in the order of the mediation process:

- cases where mediation was not tried, but where it might have been useful;
- cases where mediation was tried but no way forward was found;
- cases where the parties resolved the matter without mediators;
- cases involving shuttle mediation;
- cases involving face-to-face meetings between parties;
- cases involving multi-party mediations.

Each case study is introduced with a brief summary of its essence, so that readers can select the most relevant case studies for their purpose.

MEDIATION NOT TRIED

Noise, abuse and harassment

Neighbour disputes can cost housing departments considerable time and money, and still remain unresolved. The suggestion of mediation was introduced, but only after the dispute had escalated into entrenched positions, with many agencies involved.

This dispute involved an elderly couple who complained of deliberate noise, abuse and harassment from their neighbours. The couple had lived in their house for around 50 years. The neighbours, a family consisting of two parents and three children, had lived at the address for about four years. The complaint was mainly brought to the housing department via the elderly couple's son who did not live with his parents, though the latter are referred to as the complainants.

The first entry on the relevant property file was dated 6 January 1994. Following an incident on 16 April to which the police were called, seven taxis arrived at the complainants' house during the course of the night, necessitating further police involvement. The son then complained to the area housing office by telephone and letter. The initial response by the housing officer was to inform the local community police officer who agreed to visit the elderly couple and report back. Visits were made by housing officials to both parties to the dispute, but the alleged perpetrators denied there was a problem, unless of the complainants' making. For their part, the elderly couple indicated that they no longer wished for any further action to be taken.

Further complaints were made, but most of these were instigated by the elderly couple's son. He repeatedly alleged that his parents were intimidated by and lived in fear of their neighbours, though it is not clear what part this played in their seeming reluctance to take the matter further, or even to complete a diary of events in relation to the noise complaints, as had been suggested.

At this stage it is clear that the area housing office took the view that not all the complaints were well-founded and, since the couple had previously complained about neighbours living on the other side (who were also relatively new tenants with children), it was concluded that the complainants just did not wish to have young families as neighbours.

From around September 1995 – 20 months into the dispute – the dispute appeared to be at least as much to do with the way the complaints had been handled by the council's housing officers as with the original grievances, and only one fresh incident was reported after this.

In response to a letter from the complainants' MP, the senior management officer wrote explaining that, while both parties clearly had problems with one another, neither was in breach of their tenancy agreement and, although the police had been called on several occasions by both neighbours, no charges had been brought. Consequently, no action would be taken for the time being. The letter also stated that, while the complainants' neighbours had indicated that they would be prepared to attend a mediation service, it was believed that the complainants would be unwilling to do so.

It was not clear from the file whether the possibility of mediation had by this stage been raised with either party, and this was one of a number of points on which the complainants' son took issue in subsequent correspondence with both the council and the MP. The first recorded mention of mediation being actively encouraged, was in a letter sent to the complainants' son by the senior management officer on 20 October 1995, which also enclosed a leaflet advertising the local community mediation service.

In January 1996 the complainants' son wrote to the director of housing complaining about the department's handling of his parents' problems with their neighbours. Up to this point the area office was still refusing to take the matter any further, in view of the complainants' unwillingness to proceed with the complaint. However, in March 1996 the area manager offered to meet the complainants' son, and during the interview which followed, the possibility of using professional witnesses was discussed.

Subsequent investigations by the area manager revealed that the complainants' neighbours could actually be involved in illegal activity, and that the noise late at night might be a result of this. At the time the case history was concluded, the matter was being investigated by the police.

Over its 26-month life-span, the dispute had by this stage occupied an estimated 17.75 hours of housing officer time, involving personnel at virtually every level in the department. The direct costs to the housing department were estimated at £333.23. Despite the active involvement of all these officials, the police and the MP concerned, the dispute had still not been resolved by the time the case history was written up.

The scope for mediation in this particular case is unclear. The possibility does not appear to have been mentioned until 19 months into the dispute, by which time it was clearly too late, since attitudes had already become entrenched. Had it been attempted earlier, the prospects might have been much better. At the very least, it might have provided a non-threatening environment in which the concerns of the elderly tenants themselves could have been raised and addressed.

Possession awarded in favour of council

This neighbour dispute involved several complainants and several different local authority departments, costing thousands of pounds. Again, mediation was suggested too late to be of use, and in a half-hearted way, and the case went to court, with the result that the defendants were evicted and made homeless.

In this dispute complaints were made about the large number of animals belonging to a tenant's adult daughter. There were said to be 17 dogs (including four Great Danes), four Persian cats in cages and a number of cats which ran free. The family had occupied the house since September 1991, though in practice the daughter lived on her own with the animals at the property, which was a three-bedroomed house. The official tenants, her parents, primarily lived elsewhere.

The complaints came principally from the next-door neighbours, a couple who had lived at their property since August 1994. There were also a few complaints from another tenant. Specifically the complaints were about intimidation and noise nuisance from the daughter's many dogs, the erection of an unsightly fence and cat run, and strong disinfectant smells and their effect on the next-door neighbour's garden.

The problems really started in February 1995 when the next-door neighbours and neighbours in the house adjoining the rear of the property complained that the dogs were frightening people. The dog's owner offered to raise the fencing around the property. This appeased the neighbours at the rear of the property, but not the next-door neighbours, who apparently broke down the fencing one evening. The police were called to this incident but no action was taken.

The next-door neighbours' main complaint was about the smell of the strong disinfectant used to wash out the dog runs twice daily. They also complained that this disinfectant ran off on to their garden. The owner of the dogs refused to compromise on the type of disinfectant used.

There was also much argument about the type of fence to be erected between the properties. The owner of the dogs initially wanted a totally concrete fence, while the next-door neighbours wanted a normal 'waneylap' fence. After inspection and consultation, the housing department proposed that two concrete slabs topped off with 'waneylap' might be a reasonable compromise, but specifically asked for work not to proceed until both parties had agreed to it. Despite being asked to wait, the owner of the dogs erected a fence which included more concrete than the proposed compromise and was topped off with unsightly timber boards.

During the course of the dispute there was some suggestion that the next-door neighbours might not be entirely innocent, in that they were accused of provoking the dogs. While the dog owner said she had witnesses to this, she never provided their names, although one neighbour did tell the housing office that she had seen the next-door neighbour provoking the dogs.

Six months into the dispute, the dog owner enquired about the possibility of mediation, but the complainant seemingly refused to go along with the suggestion, so this proposal was not pursued.

In the end, possession of the dog owner's property was granted by the county court in December 1994, on grounds of nuisance. After two adjournments to the eviction date, amid complaints from the tenants that they should still be allowed to continue with their 'Right To Buy' application, the tenants were finally evicted from the property in March 1996. The council refused to rehouse them as they had made themselves intentionally homeless through their anti-social behaviour and were deemed not to be in priority need.

The eviction did not mark the end of the matter as the family complained to the Local Government Ombudsman. The Ombudsman's enquiries were closed after a brief investigation, as the Ombudsman decided that the complaints had been satisfactorily dealt with by the court when it considered the proceedings for eviction.

Throughout the course of the dispute, 18 letters were written to the perpetrators, two to the complainants and three to MPs or councillors. There were five telephone conversations with the complainants and four with the dog owner, and there were 11 interviews with the complainants and 12 with the dog owner. Environmental health services were involved and there was some contact between them and the housing department. There was also obviously a considerable amount of communication between the housing department and the legal services department. In total the dispute consumed an estimated 62.3 hours of housing staff time at an estimated direct cost of £2,419.42.

The case also involved a considerable amount of legal and administration time, resulting in a massive bill of £2,713.70 for the 82.25 hours' work. The total cost of the dispute for both sets of departments amounted to £5133.12.

MEDIATION TRIED BUT NO WAY FORWARD

The Patels and the Brauns

In this case it was not clear whether both parties really wanted mediation, as one neighbour seemed only interested in a court ruling, and was directed to mediation by the judge. Shuttle mediation was tried, but the parties disagreed on the basic realities of the case, accusing each other of similar behaviour. As they had the same interests in a peaceful life, a face-to-face meeting was suggested, to help them realise this. The second party agreed but the first party refused, so the case was closed.

This case started with a referral to the local victim/offender mediation service by the solicitor representing the Brauns. The co-ordinator recognised it was a neighbour dispute, differing from most victim/offender cases (where victim and offender live in different areas), so assigned it to two mediators, one of whom had trained originally as a community mediator. Support and guidance were provided by the neighbouring community mediation service.

An assault had allegedly taken place, but there had been no formal charge nor a court case. The Brauns had pursued an injunction against the Patels, but when the case came to court, the judge told the parties there were no legal grounds for a ruling, and they should try mediation. As there was no identifiable offence, the case was handled as a neighbour dispute, with the agreement of the parties involved.

The Brauns were a family, comprising a mother, a father of German origin, and two girls, one studying for 'A' levels and one a toddler. There was a baby on the way, which was born during the time mediation was being tried. The Patels were a married couple, the husband being Asian. They had grown-up children, and about 10 grandchildren who lived in other houses on the same housing estate. The Patels and the Brauns lived in houses on the corner of a road, as shown in the plan below.

Figure 9.1: Plan showing positions of the properties of the Brauns and the Patels

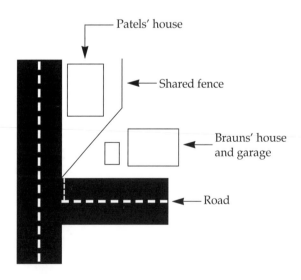

When the mediators visited the Brauns, they heard about racist abuse, rubbish being thrown over the fence, swearing and rowdy children, people staring at them over the fence, and damage done to their gate and their car. The Brauns described all these events as deliberate harassment, and only agreed to try mediation because the courts had not provided them with the results they wanted. Mrs Braun told most of the story in a rapidly spoken and lengthy way. Mr Braun stayed silent most of the time, occasionally making loud and vehement interjections over the top of his wife's words, before lapsing back into silence. The Brauns were distressed by the racism, and could not understand why it was happening, as Mr Patel was Asian and they thought he would have understood the pain that it caused. The presenting problem was the allegation that one of the Patels' sons had assaulted Mr Braun, who had then taken the Patels, specifically Mrs Patel, to court, to attempt to get her to sign undertakings to stop doing all the alleged things. The Brauns wanted to be able to live their lives in peace, and for their daughters to be able to do their schoolwork and play in the garden without fear of the neighbours.

When the mediators asked more questions about the events behind the bad relationship and the alleged assault, it became clear that the Brauns were very unhappy with the way that the Patels' grandchildren behaved when they came to visit. These children apparently visited on most schooldays and played on the grass at the side of the Patels' house, by the diagonal shared fence. When the Brauns had moved in three years before, this land had been common to both houses, but was then divided between them, and a waist-high diagonal fence was erected. Before the fence was there, the children had played across land the Brauns considered to be their front garden, and they had damaged plants and left litter. Mr Braun tackled the Patels' grandchildren about their behaviour, and this brought him into conflict with the middle generation; the alleged assault occurred after a verbal slanging match over the fence. Because of this assault, the Brauns were not willing to meet with their neighbours, so it was agreed to try shuttle mediation.

The Patels in their turn complained of rubbish, including rubble from a garage, being thrown over the fence, and pieces of broken glass being placed deliberately in the flower beds in their garden. They said that Mr Braun swore at their grandchildren, and that he used a video camera to film them all from the windows at the back of his house. They accused the Brauns of harassing them by continually complaining about them, writing solicitors' letters and taking them to court, forcing them to pay large sums of money for their own solicitors' fees. They perceived this as malicious because the Brauns received legal aid and therefore did not have to pay for their costs, whilst they knew that the Patels could not get this help and had to pay out of their own pockets. The Patels wanted the Brauns to stop harassing them, so that they could live in peace, and so that they could have their grandchildren around without trouble. The picture they gave the mediators was of normal boisterous children, loud but not malicious or rude. They felt it was Mr Braun's intolerance of normal children and his abusive way of speaking to them, that had soured relations between the families and led to the shouting matches and threats surrounding the alleged assault. The Patels were particularly upset that the Brauns were targeting them for things that were the responsibility of their grown-up sons and daughters.

The mediators' second visit to the Brauns was postponed by Mrs Braun going into hospital with high blood pressure, apparently caused by the stress of the dispute. As she was pregnant and worried about the effects of illness on the baby, the Brauns told the mediation service that they would have to suspend participation for a time.

The mediators visited the Patels, and facilitated problem-solving with them, helping them to identify specific and concrete changes they needed from the Brauns, to reach their goal of a peaceful life. These included an end to the video surveillance and the rubbish thrown over the fence, and an agreement that the Brauns would raise any concerns about the children's behaviour with their parents rather than their grandparents. The mediators used the process to maintain a focus on the future, and reframed negative statements into positive ones, checking with the Patels for agreement each time. Thus 'We want them to stop harassing us all the time' became 'You would like to live your life in peace in future. Is that right?' Then concrete steps to achieve this goal were discussed.

The mediators then had to wait for the Brauns to be well enough to return to mediation. It was not clear, however, whether the Brauns were really committed to mediation, for during this period they recommenced court proceedings against the Patels for alleged breaches of some undertakings signed previously. The Patels contacted the mediation service, which then contacted the Brauns to ask if they wanted to resume mediation. The service discovered that the judge had thrown the case out of court for a second time and told the parties to try mediation once again. To safeguard the process, the mediation service asked for an agreement from the parties that no further legal action would be taken during the course of the mediation.

The mediators visited the Brauns for the second time and went through the problem-solving process with them, generating their issues to achieve a peaceful life. These included the Patels' grandchildren keeping away from the fence, not throwing rubbish over, leaving Mr Braun's car alone and no longer abusing the Brauns' children over the back garden fence. The same future focus and reframing skills were used with the Brauns as with the Patels.

However, continued shuttle mediation proved ineffective, as the parties continued to maintain complete denial of the other side's allegations and issues. The Brauns still seemed to hanker after a legal solution, and wanted the Patels to admit their guilt in various matters. The Patels denied that these things were happening, and continued to accuse the Brauns of harassment.

Almost as a metaphor of the conflict, the diagonal wall between the properties was built up from three feet high to six feet in height.

Despite the best efforts of the mediators to reframe issues into positive hopes for the future, neither party could hear the concerns of the other side as anything but accusations to be denied. Accordingly the mediators decided that a face-to-face meeting was the only way to bring about a shift in the parties' positions. They felt that if the four people came face to face, and had the opportunity to listen to one another, to exchange opinions, get angry in a safe context and face their different conceptions of reality, this might shift the process of communication forwards. Both sides had the goal of living a peaceful life in common, and were concerned for the happiness and well-being of their children and grandchildren. If these areas of mutual interest could be recognised, there might be room for transforming the relationship, making it easier to come to agreement about future behaviour. The Patels were very willing to meet, but the Brauns, whom the mediators suspected of stalling, simply never replied to the invitation. Consequently the case was closed.

This case was complicated throughout by its connection with an alleged offence and the desire of one party to use the legal system to punish the other party. The issues of noisy children, verbal abuse and harassment are common enough, and could have been resolved if the parties could have agreed on what reality was in this case. As it was, neither party was prepared to agree that the other had any legitimate concerns, and the issues presented by each party were almost exact mirror images of each other. Perhaps if the mediators had been more proactive in encouraging a face-to-face session, this case might have achieved a growth of understanding and perhaps some agreements on behaviour. Whilst no party should be pressured into meeting, mediators can explore the fears expressed and discuss whether anything can be done to alleviate them, rather than just accepting them as unchangeable.

An unbalanced and unsuccessful mediation

This mediation involved a group of elderly people who, again, were more interested in winning their case than resolving the dispute. The face-to-face meeting was unbalanced in being one neighbour against several others, and this power imbalance encouraged the larger group to concentrate on trying to win.

Background

Mr and Mrs Smith contacted the mediation service over a problem in a cul-de-sac where several elderly people lived. There were similar complaints from two more households, Mrs Thomas and Mr and Mrs Macdonald. They complained that Mrs Ford (who also lived in the cul-de-sac) was making their lives miserable by telling lies, accosting them in the street and harassing them in a number of ways. Mrs Ford was on good terms with the local police officer who (it was alleged) supported her harassment and also made menacing interventions on her behalf. Mrs Macdonald had contacted the local councillor, who seemed to be taking her side, and she had also seen a solicitor and intended to take legal action.

When Mrs Ford was visited, she denied all the allegations and said that Mrs Smith had been a friend, but they had quarrelled over the running of an old people's club, and this was the reason the Smiths were now complaining.

A mediation session was arranged for Mr and Mrs Smith and Mrs Ford to attend, but two days beforehand Mr and Mrs Smith contacted the mediation service co-ordinator to say they would not attend unless the others could come. Eventually, after discussion, they said that they would come if Mrs Ford made a written guarantee that she would meet with each of the other households in turn. The service made it clear that it could not force Mrs Ford to agree to this, and even if she did, it would depend on how this mediation went, whether any others would go ahead. Mrs Ford was contacted and said she wanted to get it over with at one meeting, and was prepared to meet with all of them.

The mediation

The mediation went ahead with Mrs Ford and a friend reiterating to the mediators that they were willing to meet with all the others. It was made clear that both parties would get an equal chance to speak, and that to start with, the three households Smith, Thomas and Macdonald, should have one spokesperson. It was agreed that the Macdonalds' son would also be present at the meeting.

In the face-to-face meeting, it became clear at an early stage that the parties had not come with any intention of moving from their entrenched positions. The complaining parties made a succession of allegations about what Mrs Ford had said and done, all of which were met with an immovable denial. Mrs Macdonald announced that, whatever happened at the meeting, she was taking the matter further – the mediators commented that if she was not prepared to give mediation a chance, it was unclear why she was there.

All the parties were elderly and some were in poor health, and it soon became apparent that progress was unlikely and that the anxiety of the meeting was aggravating their health problems. The mediation was therefore curtailed, with the option of further meetings; these would involve only one of the complaining parties and would require some evidence of change of attitude. The nearest they came to any agreement was the acceptance that if Mrs Ford ceased to do the things which she said she was not doing anyway, there would be no problem! The most constructive summary was made by Mr and Mrs Macdonald's son, who said they were all behaving like children, and he felt very sad that at their age, they were in such a state. When his mother said that Mrs Ford had called him names, he said he had been called many worse things, and had more important worries than that.

Issues for mediation

1   Despite the best efforts of the visiting mediators, the parties did not come with any real understanding of mediation.

2   There was no basis for mediation when there was no common ground of fact, merely a succession of accusations and denials.

3   Although Mrs Ford had expressed the wish to get it over in one meeting, it was inappropriate to have such an unbalanced arrangement; and the service should have refused to change the single-party mediation originally arranged, even though this would probably have resulted in a cancellation.

4   The service was under considerable pressure from other agencies to resolve this long-standing problem, which was causing distress in a community wider than the parties directly involved.

5   The intervention of others, including the local police officer and the local councillor, was too partial to allow parties to change their positions, and gave them false reassurance that by sticking to their guns they would win.

MATTER RESOLVED WITHOUT MEDIATORS

Sometimes talking to mediators is sufficient to empower one party to think creatively and find their own solution. In this case, the first party used a tape-recording of a barking dog to help their neighbours understand the extent of the problem.

The mediation service was contacted by Mr Pearce, an unemployed man living with his retired and widowed mother in a detached bungalow. Next door lived a married couple who owned a dog, which they left locked in their garage all day while they were at work. The dog barked incessantly, causing great distress to Mr Pearce.

The mediators visited Mr Pearce and his mother, who said they had made approaches to the couple, and had been heard sympathetically by the husband but not by his wife. Mr Pearce and his mother believed that, because the dog did not bark while its owners were around, they had no real appreciation of how much of a problem it was, particularly for Mr Pearce, who suffered from a mental condition and found the barking very stressful. Despite his love of animals, Mr Pearce said he sometimes felt like killing the dog – but he did not really want drastic action, just something done about the dog.

The volume of work coming in to the mediation service resulted in a delay in the case being assigned. In the meantime, Mr Pearce made a tape of the dog barking and played it to the couple next door. They realised for the first time the true extent of the problem, and arranged to come home at midday to walk the dog, and since then things had been much better. Mr Pearce and his mother no longer needed mediators, but knew they could contact the service again if the need arose.

SHUTTLE MEDIATION

The bird table

Some disputes involve very particular circumstances and geography of buildings. Mediation can work with these to look for a solution where both parties' needs are satisfied, and a 'win/win' outcome found.

This case involved elderly neighbours living in sheltered housing, Mr and Mrs Calder, in a flat above Mrs Davey on the ground floor (see Figure 9.2 below). Mrs Davey had complained to the local housing office that Mr Calder was being a nuisance and used extremely abusive language to her. The housing office referred the case to the local mediation service.

Figure 9.2: Plan showing positions of the Calders, Mrs Davey and the bird table

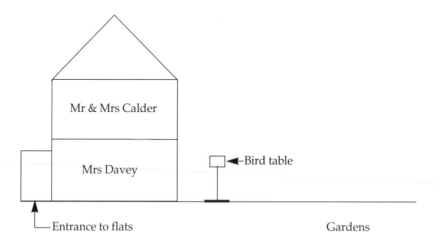

On visiting Mrs Davey, the mediators discovered that the problem revolved around a bird table, on a pole about four to five feet high. Mrs Davey said that Mr Calder fed the birds from his upstairs window, and the seed often missed the bird table, falling on Mrs Davey's garden below. These seeds then sprouted as weeds, and encouraged the attention of birds, which also ate the plant seeds she had sown intentionally. Mrs Davey's main hobby was gardening, and she said Mr Calder had effectively ruined this for her. She was very angry with him, and shouted up at his window, whereupon he became verbally abusive to her. Mrs Davey had been in and out of hospital in the weeks before the mediators called, and attributed her illness and stress to the dispute. She did not want to meet Mr Calder face to face as she was worried about his shouting and abuse.

When the mediators visited Mr Calder, they discovered that he was wheelchair-bound, and caring for his wife, who was bedridden from a stroke. He was a fiercely proud man, who maintained his right to live as he wished, and did not want to accept any help from social services. He fed the birds to please his wife, who had fed them before her stroke had prevented her doing so. She used to go down the stairs, walk along the path round the end of the housing complex, and back down the length of the residents' garden to the bird table, which was just opposite their window. Mr Calder's wheelchair clearly made it impossible for him to do this, so he tried to aim the birdseed at the table from the upstairs window. Mr Calder admitted that he used strong language to Mrs Davey, but claimed he was defending his family's reputation, in response to comments she made about him and his relatives.

The mediators identified several points of potential common ground between Mr Calder and Mrs Davey. Both expressed concern for Mrs Calder, and both wanted to live with each other as neighbours without arguing in the future. Mr Calder recognised that the central issue was the birdseed, and realised himself that the problem lay in his special mobility needs. Mrs Davey had also seen this, and suggested to the mediators that the Calders should apply for a ground-floor flat. The mediators held this suggestion in reserve, thinking that Mr Calder might not respond well to Mrs Davey's ideas, and hoping that he might think of this solution himself. On a second visit, the mediators were pleased to discover that this had happened: by chance the ground-floor flat opposite the bird table had become vacant, and the Calders had applied for it. It was immediately next door to Mrs Davey, and the mediators wondered how Mrs Davey might react, but she too suggested the Calders should apply, and said she was keen to be a helpful neighbour to them.

A follow-up call a few weeks later and a follow-up visit several months later showed that there had been no further problems between the neighbours. The Calders were happy in their new flat and Mrs Davey had begun to enjoy her garden once more. The Calders were able to come out of their back door and across the short stretch of garden to the bird table, or even feed the birds from their own door.

In this case the mediators' role was one of empowerment: hearing the stories of both sides, affirming their concerns, identifying underlying common interests and enabling them to identify ways forwards for themselves. It was sheer good luck that a ground-floor flat became available, and that the Calders were top of the priority list for a transfer into it – this kind of problem-solving can only work if practical solutions are available. This case also shows how mediation can help to find a 'tailor-made' solution to fit the precise circumstances. As with many disputes, the initial 'problem' (the verbal abuse) masked a completely different problem which was then discussed, and in this case, solved to both parties' satisfaction.

Telephone mediation

This case is unusual in being initiated by the person causing the main problem, one of noise. There were different perceptions on each side of the extent and duration of the problem, and a way forward was found when these perceptions were left on one side, and an effort was made to look to the future, and to be more specific about arrangements.

The environmental health department had received a request from Mr Wright for information on the level of noise he was permitted to make when using woodworking machinery in the back garden of his property, and also the length of time and the hours during which he was allowed to carry out such work. A neighbour had made it clear that the noise from Mr Wright's work was disturbing him, but the exchange was confined to an outburst of anger. The properties were bounded by a hedge above head height, so neither party could actually see the other. The environmental health department told Mr Wright that they could do nothing until they received a complaint from his neighbour, and so referred the case to the mediation service.

The mediators visited Mr Wright, who was a joiner, and had lived in the house as its owner for 16 years. About 10 years before, he had built a large shed in the back garden, and had worked in this shed without receiving any complaints. Quite recently he had invested in some new and somewhat noisier machinery. He had also been working more regularly, making a wardrobe for a friend. A few weeks previously, he heard pebbles being thrown at the roof of the shed, and on another occasion a half-brick.

An angry exchange followed between Mr Wright and his neighbour, who threatened to demolish the shed because of the noise. This was the point when Mr Wright contacted the environmental health department to clarify the position, and he had not used the machinery since. He was anxious to resolve the problem, and was willing to meet his neighbours with the mediators to discuss the matter. He was willing to abide by an agreed time for using the machinery and wanted to resolve the problem amicably.

It was agreed that the mediation service would write a letter to the second party proposing a visit. The second party, Mr Musgrove, responded to the letter by telephoning the office to relate his side of the story. As he saw it, the work had been going on for some two years every weekend without a break, every Saturday and Sunday from 9 to 5, as regular as clockwork. As the appointed hour approached, he and his wife braced themselves in readiness for the expected onslaught. The volume and persistence of the noise, as well as its regularity, made it very difficult to live with. He was prepared to accept reasonable amounts of DIY work, but the duration led him to believe that his neighbour must be doing work in connection with his paid employment.

He volunteered that an altercation had taken place but said that it did not involve abusive language or swearing, and he did not mention the throwing of any objects. He thought shouting at his neighbour seemed to have done the trick, as the work had completely stopped.

When the person in the mediation office asked what he wanted, Mr Musgrove said he wanted his neighbour's work to be 'less noisy and less often'.

Although the original intention had been to offer face-to-face mediation, when Mr Wright was contacted, he wanted to sort things out immediately on the telephone. He repeated that Mr Musgrove had been abusive and sworn at him during the altercation mentioned, and had thrown missiles. He disputed the alleged duration and hours of work, as he also had shopping and household chores to do. He maintained that the work was not commercial, but furniture for his home, this being cheaper than purchase.

He also repeated his awareness that the noise he made might disturb others and his willingness to accommodate their needs. However, he felt that if they were not reasonable in turn, he would go ahead and work as he pleased. When asked what 'reasonable' meant to him, he said he needed a whole afternoon, as a couple of hours would not be nearly long enough.

The office then telephoned Mr Musgrove again and told him that Mr Wright understood that his neighbours could be disturbed by the noise, and was willing to accommodate their needs if he knew what they were. The office asked Mr Musgrove again what he wanted, pointing out the vagueness of saying 'less noisy, less often' and encouraging him to be specific. He stated that it would be acceptable for work to begin in the afternoon and to finish around tea time.

A further telephone call was made to Mr Wright, and these points were accepted by him. Each party was told that if further difficulties arose, they could contact the service again.

FACE-TO-FACE MEETINGS

Students and noise

In this case, a face-to-face mediation session changed the perceptions of both parties, so that they saw each other as human beings with similar problems and preoccupations; this in turn made agreement much easier to reach. It was also an opportunity to correct some perceptions of what had happened.

Mr and Mrs Rotblatt contacted the mediation service to request mediation with the group of five students living next door to them. The dispute was about noise from televisions, musical instruments and loud voices.

Mr and Mrs Rotblatt were a young married couple living as owner-occupiers in a Victorian terraced house in a pleasant middle-class area of a large city. He worked in a business and was studying part-time for professional qualifications, she worked as a lecturer and had just finished a part-time higher degree. The students next door were all young, three men and two women. They were studying for first degrees at one of the universities in the city, and had moved into the house three months previously. All of the people involved were very articulate and well-educated.

Two mediators visited the Rotblatts and found that they had been thinking about the dispute for some time. Mr Rotblatt went through a list of incidents of noise that had disturbed them at different times and places, explaining that the main problems for them were the location of the television, which transmitted noise into their front room, and the playing of musical instruments that disturbed them at night and during times when they needed quiet to concentrate on their studies. They explained that they had gone next door on a number of occasions and asked for the noise to be turned down, with some temporary results. Mrs Rotblatt related how she had lost her temper on one occasion because she felt so angry that her husband's work was being disturbed. She admitted that she had been quite rude because she was so worked up. The impression she got from the student who answered the door was that he was uninterested in their problems and was sneering at her. She was uncertain what reception they would give to the idea of mediation.

Both of the Rotblatts were very eager for mediation to work because the problems were causing a good deal of stress and stopping them from enjoying their home life. They had had problems from the previous set of students, and also had a difficult relationship with the landlord of the students' house. This led them to express a considerable amount of sympathy for the students who had to live there. The Rotblatts were also very willing to compromise in order to reach an agreement, and showed considerable interest when the mediators introduced the idea of win/win solutions that were creative and collaborative rather than compromising. They came up with a number of ideas about moving the television, insulating the walls, agreeing timetables and ways of communicating in the future. Both of the Rotblatts were happy to meet the students face to face, and suggested to the mediators that all five students should be there, to ensure that all were committed to any agreement made. Furthermore, they wanted the students to realise that they were not just complainers, and that they could be friendly neighbours.

The mediators asked the intake worker at the office to write to the students requesting a visit, and he did so, specifying that it would be good for all the students to be there. When the mediators visited a few days later, all five students were there, and proved to be as eager to discuss the conflict as their neighbours were. The first complaints about noise had been accepted as reasonable, but the students had become steadily more unhappy as they continued to hear from the Rotblatts. As far as the students were concerned, they had taken steps to deal with the complaints: the TV had been pulled away from the party wall; musical instruments were played in an extension at the back of the house with no common wall with the Rotblatts; an expensive electronic mute had been bought for a trumpet played by one of the students; and instruments were no longer played late at night. Having taken these steps the students felt resentful and angry that their neighbours were still complaining, and were worried that mediation was the first step in a spiral of escalation towards eviction. They thought the Rotblatts' feelings towards their landlord were colouring their attitudes towards the students, and one of the latter wanted the landlord to be involved.

The mediators had to work hard during this visit on issues of trust and impartiality, to help the students feel comfortable and enable them to participate in mediation. The mediators explained that mediation had no legal connections, and that the inequalities of power that worried the students (young and poor students facing older and well-off householders) would have less influence in mediation, not more. The mediators asked questions of the students to draw out and make explicit their fears, and then helped them to problem-solve as a group to discover ways of meeting these fears. The mediators were able to reassure them by explaining how ground rules worked in a face-to-face session, and agreed that they would keep a firm hold on the process to ensure that all had an equal chance to speak and be heard. Two of the students spoke most of all, and noticeable roles emerged during the visit; one took a rational view; another the role of the cynic; a third spoke of fears and emotions. The mediators had to ensure that all five students were given as much attention as each other, and that those who were less vocal were at least given the opportunity to contribute their opinions. Those who wanted to say less were not pressured to speak, but neither were they ignored. It was agreed that the students would like to meet the Rotblatts and that all five would try to come. The mediators discussed possible dates and left to arrange the venue and time.

The mediation service arranged a local venue with a main meeting room and some side rooms in case separate meetings were needed. The mediators met the parties there on a weekday evening, along with an observer from the service who acted as a 'meeter and greeter', as well as being there to stay with one party, if a separate meeting proved necessary. The observer also gave feedback to the mediators after the session to help them to learn from their experience, good or bad. Only three of the students came to the meeting with apologies from the others and a general commitment that they could make agreements for all five.

After welcoming the parties and laying out the ground rules, the face-to-face session began well, with both parties telling their stories with minimal interruptions. The mediators noticed that very constructive language was already being used, despite this being the first opportunity for each party to lay charges and complain. The only interruptions made were far from angry outbursts – instead they were helpful suggestions where the speaker offered to do things differently. The parties were moving into collaborative problem-solving before the issues were even defined and sorted! The mediators could have stuck rigidly to the process, but in such a positive atmosphere this would probably have stifled creativity, so they let the parties continue as long as they were moving forwards. Mrs Rotblatt offered an apology for her outburst on the doorstep, and explained the frustration and upset that lay behind it. In return she learnt that the 'sneering indifference' she had perceived, had in fact been fear of the angry woman facing the young man when he opened the door. The students were able to tell the Rotblatts that they had taken the steps listed above, and the Rotblatts were quite clearly delighted with the positive attitudes they were meeting, and said so to the students. The real power of the face-to-face session is demonstrated when people can see the understanding and recognition unfolding on the faces of their neighbours. The mediators had to keep from smiling too much, but they made sure that both parties were praised for their efforts, and that they realised how well they were doing.

Of course, not everything went smoothly. The students felt they could not make specific promises for the two people who had been unable to come, although they did agree to general undertakings. At one point the discussion about this problem began to weigh down on the agreement achieved so far, so the mediators took more control of the process, asking questions of each party to pin down what would satisfy them, and making sure that the underlying fears and needs beneath the positions of each side were aired. It transpired that the students were afraid that the Rotblatts would begin to bother them again very quickly if they could not get the other two to agree, and the Rotblatts were afraid that the students were just stalling and had no intention of agreeing. Once this was out in the open, the students were able to agree to a number of points in principle, demonstrating their good faith; and the Rotblatts accepted that the students were working on keeping the noise down, and agreed not to complain so quickly. Several mutual interests came out and helped each party to recognise the humanity of the other; Mr Rotblatt also played musical instruments; all of the people involved were students and knew what it was like to have to study; they all found the landlord difficult; and they all wanted to be able to live peacefully as friendly neighbours.

The Rotblatts were able to go home knowing more about the students' timetable, and realised that they were almost always away at weekends. They knew they would have a long stretch of peace over the university holidays, and that the students were taking measures to keep the noise down from their music and television. The students were able to go away to revise for their examinations, knowing that the Rotblatts would not be coming round all the time complaining and shouting at them. The session ended with everyone involved talking and laughing together about the local cats that visited the students' garden, and thanking the mediators for their help. In fact, the mediators had been minimally involved, because the parties had been so positive and eager to reach an agreement, that they had carried the process forwards themselves for most of the session.

A mediator's personal reflections on a mediation meeting

This case study differs from the others in focusing on the mediator's account of the process and his expectations. This first-person account centres round the mediator's belief that letting go of his expectations, while retaining control of the process, was a significant factor in enabling an intractable dispute to be resolved.

Two parties were referred to the mediation service via a housing association. The parties lived a considerable distance from the mediation service, so the case was taken on by a single mediator, a man who worked as a freelance mediator as well as a volunteer mediator with the mediation service. The parties were both men, living in adjacent flats in a block. This account is in the first person, as told by the mediator.

Visit to party A

Having arranged the visit with Mr A, he was not present when I arrived, but his wife and a lodger were there and expecting me. They gave me a lot of information regarding the circumstances of the dispute. Originally, they had all been quite friendly, but this seemed to change when Mr and Mrs A got to know another person in the block of flats.

Mrs A had been and still was very ill, and Mr B had been very supportive during this time, but a change in his behaviour led Mr and Mrs A to feel they were being spied upon. In addition, they felt that Mr B was conspiring with the police to harass them and that he had set his dog on Mr A on one occasion.

It was clear that Mrs A was feeling very stressed about the situation and that she was worried about it damaging her health. Mr A apparently had a potentially violent temper, but was staying with a friend who was having a beneficial effect on his mental health. The relationship between Mr and Mrs A was under strain, and this was another reason for them to live apart.

Mrs A was very clear about the fact that she did not feel able to come to a mediation meeting, but that Mr A would come, if his friend Mr P could also attend with him.

Visit to party B

Mr B lived by himself with a large dog, and had a woman friend who visited occasionally, leading to some issues relating to her car parking.

Mr B felt that his trust had been broken by Mr and Mrs A, and that he had been 'used' by them. He offered a long series of incidents with witnesses and dates to support his grievance. These covered issues relating to noise, reporting of his dog as a dangerous animal, illegal driving by Mr A and a range of other points. By contrast, he felt his own behaviour had been fine. He was willing to come to a mediation meeting, but also wanted a friend to be present. He did not have many expectations regarding any useful outcomes, and in any case thought Mr A was unlikely to turn up.

Phone call to Mr A

I relayed the visit information to Mr A and he confirmed his desire and intent to attend the meeting. He expressed some concerns about both his own and Mr B's potential for physical violence. I set up the mediation meeting so that I could spend some individual time with the two parties, prior to sitting round the table.

Mediation meeting

Both parties and their friends turned up, and I spent about 15 minutes separately with each party. This time was used to address their fears, explain the role of the friends (silent support) and give some information about the mediation process.

The main meeting ran for a total of two and a half hours, including two short breaks for separate meetings. I started with an opening statement and then each party had some uninterrupted time to tell their story. The next stage was an exchange of views and questions, which gave rise to a tremendous amount of high emotion, threats and the need to prove who did what, when and how. There seemed to be great resistance to moving forward into a new type of relationship and there was little 'give' from either party. The process became quite circular, with a lot of energy attached to ideas of right and wrong, and who had the greater number of witnesses to the other party's behaviour.

As mediator I was trying to remain 'future-focused' and ask questions that drew out underlying interests. After about one and a half hours, there were some small areas of agreement, but I did not sense any major change in the disputing behaviour.

At this point, I noticed in myself an attachment to the parties reaching a 'good' agreement. With a conscious effort, I let go of this whilst retaining my belief in the process itself. Within a few minutes of my internal shift, one party said, 'You know, what I would really like ... is if things could be as they were before all this happened'. The other replied with, 'I would really like that as well, and what I need for that to happen is ...'.

Within 30 minutes a clear and exciting agreement had been written, everyone was feeling slightly euphoric, and the parties wanted to shake hands and make a mutual commitment to their future relationship.

I will never know if this change in behaviour was a direct result of my internal realisation, but I know my feelings affect my behaviour and that this is communicated to the parties. As an experienced mediator, this case offered me an important opportunity to notice and remove my own expectations, and open the door to lots of new possibilities.

Children harassing neighbours

Even in some seemingly hopeless situations, mediation may help to improve the situation. This case study describes a dispute involving children who were out of control and harassing neighbours in all sorts of ways, and which was resolved through mediation. It also illustrates the effective contribution of an observer present at the mediation.

On some troubled housing estates, residents feel that there is no help available, and that the rules of law and authority have broken down. Many of those causing the problems for residents are as young as seven or eight and already appear to be out of control. This is an account of such a case. Both parties were directed to mediation by the housing officer of the council housing department.

Mr and Mrs Norman had two boys, nine and eight, who were causing their neighbour, Mr Hallett, a great deal of distress and anger by smashing his hedge, throwing eggs at his door, breaking his windows, scratching his car, uprooting the flowers in his garden and generally destroying and vandalising anything to do with his property. This had been going on for some time, and Mr Hallett was at the end of his tether. He was compiling a record of each occurrence to present to the council, to support his pressing claim to be rehoused elsewhere.

Mr Hallett believed that his neighbours had lost control of their children. Mr and Mrs Norman agreed that there were difficulties living on the estate, and that kids 'got up to all sorts' but that you just learned to live with it, and if you didn't confront the youngsters and kept your head down, they would find someone else to bother and somewhere else to play.

The mediators visited each party three times and made many phone calls in between visits. Their aims with the Normans were to build rapport with the two boys, support the father in his attempts to change his boys' behaviour, and acknowledge the mother's depression and distress. They were encouraged by the father's interaction with the boys and recognised the difficulties the mother had with any kind of communication. They planned beforehand to divide their attention – one would try to build rapport with the boys while the other would listen attentively to the mother's catalogue of despair. She felt listened to and the boys briefly drew and talked.

With Mr Hallett, the mediators' intention was to listen, acknowledge and support him in his desire to maintain some order in what he saw as ever-encroaching chaos. They heard how life and other families' behaviour had deteriorated on the housing estate (where he had been born 60 years before), causing ill health, fear and terrible anger.

This case went to a face-to-face meeting largely because the father was prepared to talk to the older man, to show that he was trying to be a good father despite the circumstances. Mr Hallett was prepared to meet Mr Norman because he wanted him to understand just how appalling this constant battle was for him. If only each of them could see the humanity of the other!

Mr Norman arrived for the meeting without his wife. Mr Hallett brought a colleague, Mr Vowles, since he had been invited to redress the perceived imbalance if Mrs Norman had been there. Mr Vowles was to remain silent. Both parties spoke of their experiences; of the constant harassment, of paint-stripped cars, of smashed greenhouses and gardens laid waste. Mr Hallett was still battling to preserve some kind of order, whereas Mr Norman had only enough strength to try to dilute the activities of his own sons. Insults flew, there were accusations and recriminations. Were the boys out of control? Did Mr Hallett's behaviour make it worse? Why did Mr Hallett write to the council about everything that happened? Why didn't Mr Norman stop his children running riot?

Eventually, after nearly two hours, the mediators established that Mr Norman wanted Mr Hallett to stop writing letters to the council, so that he had a chance to deal with his boys in his own way; if only the man came to him first, he would deal with the boys. Mr Hallett wouldn't budge – he wanted the damage stopped, not a promise that the culprits would be punished afterwards. Then the previously silent witness, Mr Vowles, spoke. He suggested a possible way forward to Mr Hallett, something which would mean a compromise (but would save face), something the mediators had thought of too, separately, but couldn't lead Mr Hallett towards with any subtlety. His colleague ventured where they felt they dared not go. He suggested that Mr Hallett should tell Mr Norman before he reported an incident. Mr Hallett accepted this compromise, they shook hands; the mediators shook hands (very warmly with Mr Vowles!) and they all returned to deal with the youngsters as well as they could.

A follow-up phone call to Mr Norman three months later confirmed that the situation was better, that the boys were out less and that they were in less trouble with the neighbour. Mr Hallett responded similarly, agreeing that the situation had improved and that Mr Norman had kept to the agreement. In a situation like this, it may be too much to expect such an agreement to hold for ever against all the pressures of housing estate life, but mediation certainly enabled some progress where nothing else had succeeded before.

Party wall dispute – building and writing the agreement

A crucial part of the mediation process is building a workable agreement. This case shows one such agreement in detail, steering a course between being precise enough to prevent further misunderstandings, yet flexible enough to cope with unforeseen practicalities.

This case came to the mediation service when Mr A rang the office. The intake worker listened and took down basic details, then allocated the case to two mediators from the service. When the mediators telephoned Mr A, they were invited to come round any evening before it got dark, so that they could see what a dangerous state the party wall was in. When the mediators visited, Mr A vituperated against his neighbours Mr and Mrs B for allowing the garden wall between their houses to collapse through his wire fence into his garden, leaving the remainder in a perilous state. 'A cat could get killed', he said. He was sure it was not his wall, and had repaired the wire fence on his side, so felt the matter was not his responsibility. While standing in Mr A's garden inspecting the wall, the mediators saw Mr and Mrs B's curtains being pulled back, and after conferring with Mr A and each other, they decided to call next door.

Mr B opened the door and launched into, 'What has that old so-and-so been telling you? Who are you anyway, sticking your nose in? You just come inside and I'll tell you the real story' and then 'You are from the council, aren't you?'.

The mediators explained that they were from an independent mediation service and would like to hear Mr B's account of the state of the wall. He said that now seemed as good a time as any, and warned them that his wife was very poorly and couldn't 'take on the worrying'. Throughout the interview she appeared to take very little interest until she suddenly came in with an unrelated story about her relationships with previous neighbours. The mediators learnt to attend to her for a few minutes until she lapsed into silence and ignored everyone again.

Mr B said he had never liked the wall, but couldn't find the money to have it taken away and replaced with a fence. He and his wife were both very frail and never used the garden, so hadn't seen that the wall had collapsed. He suggested, 'Why doesn't Mr A come round now and speak to us?' So the mediators went round to invite Mr A, and he came back with them for a meeting with the Bs.

Mr A and Mr B said they used to be friends in a mild kind of way. They both agreed very quickly that the wall should be rebuilt; it was just a matter of how, and who should pay. The negotiation period that followed required a delicate balance between keeping up the momentum, and having breaks to give the Bs time to recover their strength and continue. If it appeared that progress was slowing down, or Mr B was backpedalling, Mr A became exasperated and started insulting them under his breath. After three half-hour meetings over two days, an agreement was reached, written out and signed by everyone present. It read:

This Agreement between Mr A and Mr and Mrs B is made 18 February in the presence of GP and MW, mediators

The state of the wall between the properties has been discussed and the repairs needed to put each part in reasonable order are agreed as follows:

1. Part near the gate – return of wall to be built to a height of approximately 4 feet to match the pillar. Cost and time to be discussed with Hugh, a stonemason. Mr A, Mr B and Hugh will agree the finer detail on site. Work will go ahead if costs are feasible. Mr B will pay for 4/5 of the work. Mr A will pay 1/5.

2. The end wall facing lane will be tidied up to make it safe but otherwise kept as it is.

3. The lower part of the wall will be capped over, to protect it, in natural-finish cement. It will be made to level off as best as possible.

4. By doing this work to make the wall safer, the Bs have not accepted overall responsibility for the wall, as ownership remains obscure.

5. Before doing any work which involves access via the neighbouring property, Mr B will write a note stating when access is wanted, and deliver it at least a week in advance. If there is no reply, Mr B can assume he may proceed with the work.

In drawing up this agreement, the mediators had to steer a course between being precise where it was possible, to prevent future misunderstandings, and leaving room for on-site decisions where flexibility was needed. Once the work got underway, things went well and the outcome was satisfactory to both parties.

MULTI-PARTY MEDIATIONS

Vandalism and abuse by young people on a housing estate

Mediation principles can also be used to resolve apparently intractable problems involving several individuals, groups and agencies. This can result in huge savings in frustration for the community and long-term costs for local public agencies.

This case was one involving problems within the community rather than a dispute between one resident and another. A number of residents on a housing estate complained about the severely anti-social behaviour of youths on the estate. They complained about vandalism, pelting of houses and residents with bricks and abuse, and threats to worshippers at a local church, by youths aged between 11 and 16. Parents of young people on the estate, on the other hand, stated that the complaints came from a clique of residents who were anti-children. They claimed that their children were subjected to foul-mouthed abuse from these residents, whom they saw as narrow-minded. They complained that their children could not even play football on the estate without receiving abuse. They wanted to campaign for a play area for the children.

The housing department and police had been called in to deal with the dispute, and a 100-name petition had been handed to a councillor. The housing department had responded by writing to five residents asking them to exert greater control over their children. In these letters, the tenants were warned that they were breaching their tenancy conditions and would be served with notices seeking possession of their properties, if they did not comply.

In March, the police and the housing department requested the assistance of the local mediation service. The mediators met with statutory agencies in April and interviewed most of the residents in the area to assess their concerns and problems. It was noted that the young people in the area were not present at these interviews. A meeting was held with the community safety officer and youth workers, to work out how to make contact with the young people. At the same time, one of the mediators made enquiries to the local brewery and planning department about waste land in the area, and a site meeting was held with other agencies to agree a plan of action. Meanwhile, complaints about nuisance from youths were still being made to the police and housing department.

In May, one of the mediators met with the young people in the area and collected their concerns and problems. The young people formed a management committee to liaise with residents and agencies about improving the area. A face-to-face meeting between the young people and the residents was held in June. Although this was poorly attended by residents, there were encouraging reports from them of improvements in the area.

Youth workers continued to work with the young people, and any further problems were addressed by them. One resident, for example, reported to the housing office that the front of her house had been used as a target for throwing mud. This information was relayed to the youth workers and, to the resident's surprise, the young people responsible arrived on her doorstep, apologised, removed all the debris and cleaned the front of her house. Another resident reported to the police that the rear window of his van had been smashed. Because of problems in the past, he blamed the local young people. The young people heard about this and three of them called at the resident's home, but his wife was too frightened to open the door. The same three young people returned later that evening and informed her husband that the person responsible for breaking the van window was an individual who did not live in the street. The resident was extremely grateful and passed the information on to the police. The community safety officer continued to work with residents with a view to holding a planning meeting.

In September, residents reported that, although they had been dreading the summer holidays, they were pleased to report that there had been no major problems. One resident, who had put her house up for sale because of the previous problems, had taken her house off the market as she was happy to stay in the area. There was a meeting with residents and other agencies at which the residents formed a group to plan for the future with young people.

Both groups continue to be supported by youth workers and the community safety officer.

Although the dispute had appeared to be intractable at the outset, the combined efforts of the mediation service, the participants and all the other agencies involved, managed to resolve a difficult set of problems. Not surprisingly, given the intensive involvement on the part of the mediation service, the case proved to be both time-consuming and expensive for them, taking a total of 68.52 hours, at a cost of £842.32. The other agencies involved also incurred costs, although these are more difficult to quantify.[1]

However, it seems indisputable that two agencies in particular – the local housing department and the police – benefited significantly as a result of the outcome. The housing department was spared the direct expense of evicting or moving several residents, and benefited indirectly from the preservation of the reputation and desirability of the estate, through the positive resolution of the dispute. Similarly the police, who had been called out to the estate no fewer than 200 times in the six-month period leading up to the mediation, benefited from the improved state of relations: in the months following the mediation, they were called out to the estate on just two occasions. However, the biggest beneficiaries of all, of course, were the parties themselves.

Generalised feud in sheltered accommodation

This is another example where mediation principles helped to sort out a complex dispute with many strands and many people involved. The added dimension here is the closed residential community, one of the hardest contexts in which to resolve long-standing conflict. The attention to eliciting the concerns of all, coupled with a focus on the future, were keys to resolving the conflict positively.

There were 24 flats in Burgess House, offering sheltered accommodation to elderly residents. A number of them had lived in the village all their lives, but others had come from a distance, to be near sons or daughters who had settled nearby. There was a tendency for them to split into 'natives' and 'incomers'.

The warden-before-last had been wonderful: firm but fair, standing no nonsense, and good at organising social events, accumulating profits to pay for outings from time to time. She was replaced by a warden who – everyone agreed – was a very nice woman, but too soft. Dissension grew, and people started saying about each other, 'If she's going to be there, I'm not coming'. Social events dwindled and finally ceased. A small group of residents still gathered in the common room, however, to gossip and make loud personal

---

1   See Dignan, J, Sorsby, A and Hibbert, J, *Neighbour Disputes: Comparing the Cost-effectiveness of Mediation and Alternative Approaches*, 1996, Sheffield: University of Sheffield.

remarks about anyone who passed through the lobby to or from the front door: 'There she goes again – don't know where she got that coat'.

The warden left and it took time to replace her. Someone came in to clean the corridors, the stairs and the common room, and the emergency call services worked speedily and efficiently; but the residents felt bereft, and fell to wrangling among themselves in a state of general hostility and defeatism. When the Sheltered Housing Officer turned up with a bright smile and two new irons for the laundry room, she was greeted, not with thanks, but with, 'That ironing board's a disgrace'. The newest and youngest resident, who had been a school caretaker and whose chief delight in life was cleaning, took to pursuing his hobby along the corridors and in the common room, but women residents bounced out of their flats to tell him to stop that – he was not allowed to clean. He acquired a letter from the housing officer, licensing him to dust and clean windows (no vacuum cleaning, lest the flex trip someone up), but when he showed it to one of his leading persecutors, her only reply was, 'I'm not interested in bits of paper'.

We (the local mediation service) were asked if we could help. Ten mediators went into Burgess House, to visit each flat (the male mediators were a little shaken to find that only three of the residents were men: it made them reflect on their own mortality). In every case we were given a kindly welcome and offered cups of tea. Each resident was anxiously looking forward to the coming of a new warden ('firm but fair, and no favourites') and to the resumption of social events. Many of them had little faith in the emergency call system ('I could be laid out on that floor for hours'). One thought the place a paradise because she had been institutionalised for more than 40 years and now, for the first time, had her own flat (furnished by local charities), where the social services had visited to teach her how to shop and cook for herself. There was a generalised feud between the upstairs flats and those downstairs, and another between 'natives' and 'incomers'. Madge and Alice, two forceful and outspoken natives, were heartily disliked by many less forceful residents, and Nell, another forceful type who knew exactly how the place should be run, was convinced that nothing could be done to set things right, though she was doing her best by visiting frail residents and giving them their medication.

When the preliminary visits had been completed, we held a conference and then wrote to each resident, saying that we wanted to meet them all together, to discuss with them how things might be improved. We hoped, as we wrote, that most of them would be at the meeting, and in the event they were all in the common room waiting for us when we arrived.

We told them that we had passed on to the Sheltered Housing Officer the concerns they had all expressed about the running of the place and the need for the right kind of warden. Two other areas of unhappiness had been mentioned by a number of them, and we wanted to raise them as topics for discussion. ('I can't hear a word she's saying', said the oldest inhabitant, but her daughter had come in with her, and acted as interpreter for us.)

The first source of concern was the prevalence of gossip and personal remarks. The gossip was especially serious when it went outside Burgess House – like it or not, they were a family, and a good family kept its problems to itself. Did they want to comment on this? There was a silence in which everyone looked shocked, as if gossip was the last thing they would indulge in, and then the woman who had been institutionalised said she hated it and found it hurtful. Others joined in, and it was agreed that everyone would in future resist the temptation to listen when offered some spicy nugget of gossip. Gossip is endemic to any community like theirs, but it had been marked down for disapproval.

We moved on to the absence of social events. Why wait for a new warden to arrive, settle in, get to know the neighbourhood, and then start them up again? They were the generation which had won the Second World War and they had not lost their intelligence and organising skills. Let them now elect a social committee and get things moving.

There was a profound silence, eventually broken by Nell, who said that there was no point in trying anything because it wouldn't work. Not with this lot.

One of the mediators pointed out that wardens came and went, and if they had their own committee, they would not be left high and dry every time a warden left. This thought and a reaction against Nell's defeatism gradually worked on the gathering and, slowly, one by one, they agreed to hold an election. Madge and Alice made tea, and we organised a secret ballot, while the remains of someone's 90th birthday cake were shared out. And people began to talk to one another.

A week later one of the social committee telephoned to say that they had held a coffee morning and made a profit of £4.60. They were to start bingo evenings. A few weeks later, they invited us to a coffee morning and our co-ordinator had the misfortune of winning the raffle. The Sheltered Housing Officer reported that she had found the atmosphere transformed. Everyone seemed much happier, more sociable and more supportive of each other than they had been before our intervention. Not, perhaps, a conventional mediation, but a useful and constructive experience in problem-solving and conflict resolution for us all.

The stolen apples

There is sometimes a fine line between community and criminal justice mediation cases. In this case, victims of a local theft decided to avoid the criminal justice system and try to resolve the theft informally. This had the effect of resolving the matter positively for all concerned. Several young people were involved, and all their parents attended the mediation session as well, so that 15 people (including the mediators) were present.

This case study is unusual in that it has been written from the point of view of one of the disputants. It has been checked with the other parties and the mediation service.

We went camping for a week towards the end of the summer. Before we left we took a look at our six little cordon apple trees lined up along the wall of our small garden behind our terraced house. This particular year they were covered in apples, especially our favourites, the coxes, russets and bramleys. They were organically grown and had a taste quite unlike shop-bought apples, and we looked forward to an autumn of munching home-grown apples.

On our return we saw that the trees had been stripped bare. The apples weren't ripe, so it seemed to us an act of pure vandalism. We were devastated. We suspected some lads in our street, one of whom had previously (but many years ago) taken some apples from us. However, we were reluctant to go to the parents, in case we were wrong in our suspicions, and this then created bad feelings. We thought about reporting the theft to the police, but felt they would not be able to do anything. Furthermore, if it was our neighbour's son, we did not feel very good about him acquiring a criminal conviction.

Then we found out through our daughter and the 'school grapevine' that the apples had indeed been taken by boys in our street (although different stories implicated different boys) – not to eat but to play apple cricket! We worried about the possibility of our daughter being teased or called names if we took any action. We also felt the incident had caused a rift between us and our neighbours, and that we couldn't talk to them or 'look them in the eye' because of our suspicions.

After much thought we decided to ask the local community mediation service to look into the matter, to find out who had taken the apples and, if possible, to arrange a meeting to sort things out.

Two mediators rang and arranged to come round one evening. They listened to our story and also asked our daughter to contribute her views. Then they called on the three neighbours whose sons we suspected of taking the apples. It turned out that they were all involved, although to different degrees. When they heard how upset we were about the apples, they all wanted to apologise.

The mediators shuttled between the four families to arrange a date and time for a meeting. This took place a few days later in a local church hall, and included ourselves and our daughter, and the three boys and their respective parents. Together with the two mediators and a third person from the mediation service, who made coffee and arranged the room, the gathering included 15 people altogether.

The mediators asked us to outline our view, and then asked each boy in turn to say what happened. We could see it wasn't easy for them, as they told us the details and mumbled their apologies. They said they hadn't realised how important and special the apples were for us. We realised they couldn't bring them back, or afford to replace them all, so we asked them to bring us a bag of eating apples and a bag of cooking apples at some point in the autumn. We also asked if they could help clear some undergrowth from the back alley behind our house. This all got included in a written agreement which we all signed.

It turned out that at least one set of the other parents were hurt that we hadn't gone straight to them in the first place, and they asked us to do that if there was ever anything else of a similar nature. We agreed that we would.

The next week was a school half-term holiday, and the boys cleared the back alley as arranged. A few weeks later, first one and then another rang the doorbell to deliver a large bag of apples, before dashing away in embarrassment. It was a great relief to have it all sorted out so that we could put it behind us and get back to the good relationships we had previously enjoyed with our neighbours.

CONCLUSION

These case studies show the wide variety of situations where mediation has a role. They all use the principles of listening to the parties, eliciting their concerns, empowering them and helping them see others as human beings with similar needs to themselves. Once this point has been reached, focusing on the future usually enables the parties themselves to find a way forward.

CHAPTER TEN

EQUAL OPPORTUNITIES AND ANTI-DISCRIMINATORY PRACTICE

John C Patrick

INTRODUCTION

Equal opportunities and anti-discriminatory practice is a subject of great importance, both because of the existence of anti-discriminatory legislation and also in recognition of the multicultural nature of our society. This introduction briefly touches on general issues of equal opportunities as they affect mediation services, including legal obligations, moral aspects and issues concerning effectiveness, accessibility and empowerment.

In the United Kingdom there are several laws designed to prevent discrimination. All organisations need to take into account the Sex Discrimination Acts 1975 and 1986, the Race Relations Act 1976, the Equal Pay Act 1970, the Disability Discrimination Act 1995 and the Rehabilitation of Offenders Act 1974. Northern Ireland has its own legislation on equal pay, sex discrimination and fair employment.

There is also the moral argument that discrimination is wrong and divisive, undermining some people and concentrating power in the hands of selected groups. As organisations aiming to help heal rifts between people, this aspect is seen as very important, and most mediation services have policy statements which develop equal opportunities beyond the essential need to obey the law.

Discrimination impedes effectiveness: the nature of our society is so multi-faceted that any organisation which directly or indirectly discriminates against any group, will be limiting its own effectiveness by not selecting staff, volunteers or customers from as wide a field as possible. Mediation services need to draw on all resources in the community to ensure their effectiveness and to be accessible to all members of that community.

Mediation services aim to empower people to make decisions about their lives more effectively, and therefore need to recognise the disempowering effects of discrimination. Mediators must take account of, and work to balance, power differences between disputants, otherwise mediation can itself become another vehicle of oppression. Staff and volunteers need to understand the issues within their community, including issues of discrimination and oppression, if they are to intervene effectively in individual disputes.

In devising a process for the accreditation of mediation services,[1] MEDIATION UK has rightly laid considerable emphasis on a service's ability to demonstrate good equal opportunity practice. The introduction to its *Training Manual in Community Mediation Skills*[2] also emphasises this, and it is reflected in the training exercises and the programme for an accredited course[3] based on the manual.

ACCESSIBILITY

Every community mediation service needs to be accessible and relevant to the whole community it serves. It therefore needs to be, and be seen to be, open and representative both in its recruitment of staff, committee and volunteers, and in the range of people who seek its services. The make-up of all these groups needs to be monitored and compared with information about the community covered by the service.

The mediation service's policy statements will reflect this concern, so that advertising for workers and promotion of the service to obtain referrals will cover a wide variety of sources including, where appropriate, minority publications. Publicity material needs to be accessible to all who might require the service and may need to use languages other than English. Such material needs to be written so that it is inclusive of all, and does not imply the exclusion of anyone on grounds of disability, sex, race, colour, nationality, ethnic or national origin, class, sexuality, marital status, HIV status, responsibility for dependants, age, trade union activity, unrelated criminal convictions, political or religious beliefs, mental ill health or any other reason not directly related to the subject of the material.[4]

All premises should be accessible to those with mobility or visual impairments, but many mediation services use other organisations' premises and have very limited budgets, so it is often difficult to achieve this. Mediation services may need to book other premises on occasion. In arranging events, services need to be aware of the major festivals and fasting periods of all religions, and provide food and drink which is acceptable across the range of beliefs.

Mediation can involve working with people who have difficulty communicating because they speak different languages. While the vast majority of service users can communicate in English, some may be at a

---

1 MEDIATION UK *Accreditation Pack*, 1994, revised 1996, Bristol: MEDIATION UK.

2 MEDIATION UK *Training Manual in Community Skills*, 1995, Bristol: MEDIATION UK.

3 MEDIATION UK *Handbook for the Training Programme in Community Mediation Skills*, 1996, Bristol: MEDIATION UK.

4 List from MEDIATION UK Equal Opportunities Policy Document 1995.

considerable disadvantage if English is not their first language. Friends and relatives are sometimes available, but it is always difficult to know how accurately they interpret, and how much of their own slant they bring. It is not usually good practice to use anyone as an interpreter who has any relationship with either of the parties, or an indirect involvement in the dispute. Some mediators have language skills and may be able to undertake work in languages other than English, but they may lack the skills of experienced interpreters.

Many areas have interpreters (or signers for the hearing-impaired), who undertake work for statutory and voluntary agencies, and usually have the experience to translate without undermining the mediation process. Working with interpreters requires adjusting to a slower pace of work; many mediators will have little opportunity to gain this experience and will need some training in working with interpreters, just as interpreters will need some training in working with mediators and a basic understanding of the mediation process.

RECRUITMENT

The principle of equal opportunity recruitment is one of 'enlightened self-interest'. Anyone recruiting staff or volunteers wants to appoint the best person for the job, and therefore needs to ensure that the field of selection is as wide as possible, and that all applicants are given the best possible opportunity to demonstrate their ability. Where possible, the interviewing panel and anyone else involved in the selection procedure should reflect as closely as possible the range of candidates, and have some training in the principles of equal opportunity selection.

The basic procedure for all equal opportunity recruitment starts with an analysis of the task to be undertaken by those appointed. This is developed into a job description, which is then used to draw up the person specification, which should include the essential skills, experience and qualities required. It should only include relevant criteria, and should not exclude anyone on grounds which are not directly linked to the task. It will usually contain some elements which are desirable but not regarded as essential. When the selection procedure is competitive, the person specification is applied to each candidate, and is used to eliminate any who lack an essential quality or skill. The shortlist will then be made up of candidates who, on paper at least, are appropriate for the job. Further selection can then be made on the basis of which candidates come nearest to the desirable elements of the person specification.

In interviewing candidates, whether for a competitive situation (such as a paid job) or a non-competitive one (recruitment of volunteer mediators), it is important that each applicant has as similar an experience as possible. It should be clarified what part informal contact plays in the selection process. The formalised interview should cover an agreed set of questions and subjects, with the criteria for selection defined before the interviews.

ISSUES FOR THE MANAGEMENT OF THE SERVICE

A successful equal opportunity recruitment policy will lead to a diverse group of staff and mediators, so mediation services must develop skills in managing differences within those groups. Discriminating against anyone on the grounds listed in the service's equal opportunity statement must be seen to be unacceptable, and management has a responsibility for upholding this principle within the staff and volunteers' group, as well as in the service's dealings with its client group. Complaints and grievance procedures will need to be written with this principle in mind.

Barbara Walker discusses valuing differences [5] and suggests a five-step model for successfully managing a diverse workforce:

1   Stripping away stereotypes;
2   Learning to listen for differences in people's assumptions;
3   Building authentic relationships with people one regards as different;
4   Enhancing personal empowerment;
5   Exploring and identifying group differences.

If those managing a community mediation service can recognise and value the individual differences which contribute to the variety of staff and volunteers, then the self-esteem of those people will be increased. The development of good working relationships and teamwork enhances people's skills, and enables the variety of co-working which is an essential part of the service's operation. Once people feel recognised and empowered, it is possible to explore each other's beliefs without resorting to the dangers inherent in stereotyping.

AWARENESS

Staff, mediators and management committee members need to have an awareness of the nature of oppression and prejudice, and some knowledge of how these operate within the locality of the service. Everyone has his or her

---

5   Walker, BA, in Smith, MA and Johnson SJ (eds), *Valuing Differences in the Workplace*, 1991, Minneapolis: University of Minnesota Press.

own biases and lives with the effects of his or her own upbringing and its cultural assumptions, and all those involved with mediation services need to have some understanding of this. Cultural assumptions about language and non-verbal signals can lead to false impressions of those who do not share the same upbringing.

Differences in assumptions about gender roles and sexual orientation can be a major source of conflict and misunderstanding, and these differences need to be recognised by mediators and those who make decisions about appointments, to ensure that the service operates in an anti-discriminatory manner. In the field of disability, there is the danger of treating all disabled people as if they are the same, or assuming that an impairment indicates that someone is not a capable adult. In many instances, social attitudes and the lack of facilities are a more significant disadvantage than any medical factors present. All people need to be seen as individuals with differing strengths and weaknesses, whatever outward appearances may suggest.

A knowledge of other services and organisations within the area covered by a mediation service is important generally, and services need to work closely with other organisations whose priority is in the field of countering discrimination. Anti-racial-harassment groups, ethnic minority community groups and the local race equality councils are important link organisations for mediation services, to ensure they are addressing the needs of all races and minority groups within their area. Links with organisations particularly concerned with the needs of elderly or young people can be important in ensuring the service is relevant to all age groups.

THE NATURE OF OPPRESSION

Before turning to anti-discriminatory work within mediation, it is necessary to look at the nature of oppression. In an area where different understanding of words and differing assumptions can cause problems, it is important to make clear the assumptions on which this chapter is based. Most people have personal biases and prejudices, and an awareness of these can go some way to counteract their effects, as the biggest danger often comes from people's lack of self-awareness rather than malice. Actions based on prejudice are discriminatory, even if the actor does not realise or intend any discrimination.

The term oppression is used to describe the combined effects of prejudice and power; it is, therefore, primarily an experience of those in a minority or socially weaker position. All of us may find ourselves in this position from time to time but for some groups it is a practical reality of everyday life. Such an experience is deeply disempowering for many, and often leads to internalised assumptions about their lack of power and influence. Cornelius and Faire[6] describe disempowering language typified by such phrases as 'I'm just a housewife', which are often a reflection of the patronising language of the more powerful.

There are three types of oppression which operate in society, and which act as a mechanism for the maintenance of the status quo, in favour of the current holders of power. The first is the personal oppression of individuals, which may be conscious or unconscious, direct or indirect. It is the oppression of individual by individual, and is the one where we can each have an effect to worsen or improve the situation. Our personal prejudices affect the way we relate to others, and we may treat people differently because of how we perceive them rather than because of their behaviour. When we hold a position of power, such as a mediator, this mechanism can operate significantly to some people's disadvantage, if we remain unaware.

Second, there is social oppression, which is the combined effect of cultural and social norms, informal rules of society and structure of groupings within society, and which by default or design disadvantage some groups and favour others. Most organisations and groups inherit images which affect how they are perceived by others. 'Stereotypes' exercises are valuable aids to seeing this: people are asked to note the first word which comes into their head after a category of person is named. For instance, the word 'nurse' usually conjures up an image of a woman and gets high praise for care and dedication, whereas 'company director' conjures up a male image and is associated with more ruthlessness and competitiveness. Our society reflects these differences in socio-economic status, which effectively diminish the power of certain groups within society. Social oppression operates where groups relate to each other, and provides an informal and unstructured way in which groups may be oppressed.

The third form of oppression is institutional oppression, and is the one most people feel least able to affect. Institutional oppression is the result of structures within our society which favour some and disadvantage others. Historically, decisions within our society were taken by a relatively small proportion of the population – predominantly, white male and upper or upper-middle class. The effect of this has been to perpetuate their power, so that social structures built up over centuries are likely to disadvantage black people, women and minority groups.

Oppression is not the monopoly of the malevolent, but an inevitable part of any society, resulting from differences in power between its members. So it is important that community mediation services work to a clear anti-discriminatory policy which involves positively ensuring the service's accessibility and fairness to all sections of the community. It is not enough to

---

6   Cornelius, H and Faire, S, *Everyone Can Win*, 1989, New York and Sydney: Simon & Schuster.

be 'non-discriminatory', which suggests a more passive approach. Mediation has a value base of every person's importance and their need to exercise more power in the decisions that affect their lives. Challenging oppression in all its forms is, therefore, an important issue for all mediators and services; failure to challenge oppression colludes with the oppressor.

EFFECTS OF OPPRESSION

Oppression results in certain groups within society being disadvantaged and this is sometimes a key factor within neighbour disputes. Mediators need to take this into account, to ensure that the service offered does not collude with social oppression. They need to state clearly that oppressive statements are unacceptable within the mediation setting. This may make some disputes inappropriate for mediation, as already discussed in the Chapters 7 and 8. While mediators try to hold an impartial position between disputants, they need to make it clear that they are not neutral on such issues as racism or oppression of any groups within society.

This chapter will not attempt to analyse the general social effects of oppression, but does need to look at the effect of oppression on individuals involved in disputes within their neighbourhood. Andrew Acland[7] describes the negative impact of power as being felt in three ways:

- *Coercion* – implied or actual threat of force or sanctions. This may be felt as a physical threat or the possibility that not accepting a proposal could result in losing more through court action. Some people in conflict act as mental bullies to try to get their own way.

- *Inducement* – while many suggestions are made which seem an equitable compromise, there are times when one party appears to use bribery to get their own way.

- *Persuasion through manipulation* – the inability to make points by assertive communication can often lead people to try to manipulate the situation.

Any agreement reached in such an atmosphere will in itself add to the feelings of oppression for the person, who will already be lacking in self-esteem and feeling disadvantaged in the face-to-face meeting.

POWER AND MEDIATION

Mediation is essentially an empowering activity which aims to help people take decisions about their own lives rather than rely on the arbitration of

---

7   Acland, A, *A Sudden Outbreak of Common Sense*, 1990, London: Hutchinson.

others to resolve disputes. If both parties feel that they are already in a position to make these decisions, then they will negotiate without the need for a third party. We can therefore assume that, if they seek mediation, parties feel they lack power. Parties will, however, have differing abilities and differences of power, and mediation must work on this if it is to be effective in helping sustainable resolution. It is important to analyse power issues in more detail.

Power differences between individuals and parties can come from a number of different sources:

- *Social group differences* – members of socially oppressed groups may feel disadvantaged, particularly when the mediators appear to be members of the group identified with the other party.

- *Economic status* – differences in employment status and financial resources can be an important feature of neighbour conflicts.

- *Knowledge* – while knowledge may not always be power, it can be used as a weapon in power struggles.

- *Personality* – the outgoing and socially able can be seen as a powerful threat, in their ability to get the mediators on their side.

- *Education* – differing educational standards can put some people in a position of disadvantage, and education can be used to put others down. Attempts may also be made to get the mediator to identify with the party whose education and ability to express themselves approaches or exceeds their own.

- *Emotional factors* – conflict is stressful and the ability to appear to cope well with stress can be felt as very powerful in mediation. By contrast, an emotional investment in good relationships by one side can put them at a real disadvantage, if that investment is not shared by the other party. Some people are able to cope well with conflict and seem able to thrive in disputes while others feel paralysed by it.

- *Physiological factors* – physical size can be an obvious difference, giving one party an opportunity to intimidate; people of differing physical or mental abilities can be the source of power differentials.

- *Age* – young people may be seen by older people as threatening, aggressive, able and active, but they can also be patronised by such sayings as 'there's no substitute for experience' and 'you'll learn'.

- *Sex* – the age of the dominant male is far from over.

- *Number of people* – many disputes between neighbours involve different sizes of households, and it is important to maintain a balance in numbers wherever possible. When a couple is in dispute with a single neighbour, the latter will often be invited to bring along a second person to support them.

- *Language* – the disadvantaged position of those for whom English is not their first language has already been mentioned. Even some for whom

English is their first language may be at a disadvantage because of their unfamiliarity with the words used by the other party or the mediators, and may not find it easy to seek clarification.

- *Cultural differences* – some people's cultural background can put them at a disadvantage in the unfamiliarity of a mediation process developed by western nations, and based on familiarity, confrontation and face-to-face working. This will be discussed in more detail later in this chapter.

Any real or perceived power advantage may be used deliberately by parties, either as directly oppressive behaviour, or as a means of establishing to the mediators the rights and wrongs of the situation. Such behaviour may actually break the ground rules set for the face-to-face mediation, or at least bend them. Sometimes power can be used without conscious thought, because of differing attitudes and lifestyles. The man who habitually patronises the women around him may well be quite surprised by the reaction of other women who wish to challenge this behaviour.

A power difference may still disadvantage one party, even if the other party does not attempt to use it, for instance, when there are different numbers present from each party, or where one party has a clear educational or knowledge advantage. In many cases there are different power factors which may work in opposite directions, for example, where a well-educated black woman is in dispute with a larger but less able white man.

BALANCING POWER

Some power imbalance is likely to be present in most disputes which come to mediation, and mediators need to be able to recognise the differences, work to ensure that they are not used inappropriately, and achieve a balance which enables both parties to feel empowered by the process. They also need to be aware of their own biases and how they react to people, especially those with characteristics that remind them of past experiences evoking favourable or unfavourable emotions.

The staged structure of the mediation process (described in Chapter 3) offers several safeguards against a power imbalance which is oppressive to either party. The structure of the session allows all present to contribute fully, and it is important to protect the uninterrupted time, including challenging non-verbal interruptions. The ground rules for each mediation will mention not using offensive language or abuse, and it may sometimes be necessary to emphasise and explain this in more detail at the start of a session. This not only makes clear to the more powerful what behaviour is unacceptable, but also reassures anyone feeling unsafe or uncertain about the process.

Having set the ground rules, it is important that the mediators control the process and maintain those ground rules. Where this does not seem possible, it may be necessary to call for some 'time out' to undertake separate work with the parties. If one or both parties insist on trying to abuse power, then it may be necessary to end the session. It is better to have no agreement than to have an apparent agreement which is the result of coercion by one party. Mediators need to be able to challenge oppressive language and behaviour in an assertive way, and these skills are an important part of any mediation training course, to help mediators balance the power issues.

There are times when the mediators need to check the situation with the parties, either in the joint session or by calling caucuses to explore the feelings of the parties on an individual basis. On occasions, the best way of avoiding a power imbalance is to continue mediating by using shuttle mediation. (Caucuses and shuttle mediation have been discussed in Chapter 3.)

One of the important features of co-mediation is that the mediators themselves can model equality, so it is vital that they work together well and do not get pulled into their own power struggles. This does not imply that mediators need always agree in front of the parties; handling a disagreement constructively can be the best demonstration of good modelling. To discuss a situation openly, listening to and showing respect for each other, can demonstrate an equal relationship offering a better model than the roles of oppressor and victim.

When there are difficulties based on power, the mediators need to ensure that they allow the least powerful to express their views. Seeking suggestions from the party who appears oppressed is as important as challenging the oppressive behaviour. It becomes more difficult to dismiss a person's views, if the mediators are seen to be listening and taking note of what that person is saying.

The structure of the session may also be arranged to help balance power. The addition of a supporter or interpreter may be appropriate. Decisions about who will be asked to speak first and the time for the uninterrupted statements will take power issues into consideration. The seating arrangements can limit opportunities for intimidating behaviour and offer a supportive environment for the less powerful.

MEDIATION AND CULTURE

The nature of mediation, as practised by community mediators in the United Kingdom, developed within the English-speaking countries in the industrialised world, particularly in the UK, the USA, Canada and Australia. These countries have a cultural base in which issues are conventionally resolved through the confrontation of opposing points of view. We work in an adversarial justice system and most political decision-making comes through a primarily two-party system. This cultural climate is not the norm for many peoples, not least the indigenous populations of North America, Australia and New Zealand. The current interest in 'family group conferencing', as a non-adversarial means of dealing with young offenders, is influenced by the norms of the aboriginal peoples of Australia and New Zealand.

David Augsburger[8] describes two models of mediation, the 'North American' model and the 'Traditional Culture' model. These are characterised as follows:

Figure 10.1: Two models of mediation.

North American model	*Traditional Culture model*
Mediation is formal, structured and undertaken by specialists.	Mediation is a communal process involving trusted leadership or elders.
Direct confrontation and communication are considered desirable. Rules are established for the running of the session.	Indirect go-between processes are considered desirable to save face, balance power and reduce threat.
Time is controlled and issues dealt with in order.	Issues are interwoven, time schedules and issues are secondary to relationships and communal concerns.
Process is task-centred and goal-directed. Autonomy and the disputants' individual choices are central.	Process is directed towards resolving community tensions. The responsibility of disputants to their wider context is central.
Mediators are present as technical specialists and involved only in the process of dispute resolution.	Mediators are recognised and trusted within their community. They are part of the community network and continue in this relationship after any resolution of the dispute.

---

8   Augsburger, D, *Conflict Mediation Across Cultures*, 1992, Louisville, Kentucky: Westminster/John Knox Press.

Even within those countries which work to the 'North American' model, the more geographically stable populations often resolve conflict and tolerate differences in ways more related to the norms of the traditional culture model. All community mediation services in the UK operate in a multicultural environment, and need to recognise that some cultures do not favour confrontational face-to-face meetings, so that another way needs to be found.

CROSS-CULTURAL MEDIATION

Differences in predominant attitudes, styles of communication, feelings about conflict and norms of behaviour will therefore vary considerably, and mediators need to recognise this. Of course, mediators also need to recognise their own cultural norms, and accept the limitations of these. Assumptions that our attitudes are shared by others is dangerous, as is the process of making assumptions about others based on limited knowledge of their culture. Within all cultural groups there are those who will not conform to our expectations of that group; many have a large variety of subcultures; and all have their non-conformists and rebels.

No mediator can have a detailed knowledge of all the cultural norms of possible disputants coming to the service, although a basic knowledge of the main groups in the service's area is helpful. It is more important for mediators to understand which of their own assumptions are based on cultural factors, and to be open to differences with others.

Few, if any, non-verbal signals are universal; for example, in some Eastern European cultures a nod of the head means 'no' and a shake of the head 'yes'. Avoidance of eye contact, often interpreted in western cultures as indicating shiftiness or deceit, is a sign of politeness or deference in many other cultures. For some peoples, close personal space is uncomfortable and may be felt as aggressive, whereas for others it is the normal means of conveying friendliness. Bodily contact such as shaking hands may not be acceptable in certain cultures, particularly between those of different sexes, so that the avoidance of a hand proffered in friendliness can be misinterpreted and offence taken. Differences in styles of communication are the result of both cultural and individual backgrounds.

Differences in verbal communication will also need to be taken into account. Familiarity with spoken English does not mean there are no linguistic differences in the use of common expressions. 'Yes' for many people might be assumed to be agreement, but for others it may be a polite response indicating that the point has been heard, without any implication of agreement. As with non-verbal signals, it is important for mediators to check whether their understanding of a disputant's meaning is correct. They also need to ensure that the communication between disputants is clarified.

In addition, cultural differences may occur in the understanding of the concepts used. Confidentiality may have different connotations, and simply accepting that parties have the same understanding as the mediator or each other can lead to difficulties. The ideas of autonomy and self-determination implicit in much of the work of the mediator may not be shared by someone from a 'traditional culture' background. If mediators just assume this is a shared goal for all involved in the mediation, that person will feel uncomfortable and disadvantaged.

The MEDIATION UK *Training Manual in Community Mediation Skills*[9] suggests a three-step process for dealing with difficulties in cross-cultural communication. The first is to step back mentally, to attempt to understand better what is going on. This can lead to a recognition that the difficulties in communication may be the result of cultural differences, and the discomfort of the mediator may be the result of her or his own cultural biases. To do this successfully, mediators needs to know what makes them feel uncertain or uncomfortable, so that they do not interpret someone's reaction to them as personal.

The second step is to avoid snap judgments or jumping to conclusions. Mediators need to be able to bring communications out into the open and raise questions with participants about their view of what is happening, to help them recognise that differences do not imply rightness or wrongness. Openness based on knowledge rather than assumptions is the key to helping cross-cultural communication work better.

The third step is to move forward, to be open and honest about what is wanted from the situation. Mediators need to seek understanding and then identify common ground and interests which overlap. They need to show that they recognise and value those differences which may at first seem to be a barrier, and then help each party do the same. Where mediators find particular difficulties, they need to look at their own behaviour, assumptions and value systems, and if necessary re-evaluate them with a view to change.

Much of this is good mediation practice, and the development of this will generally coincide with the development of good equal opportunity and anti-discriminatory practice. Cross-cultural mediation is a particular challenge, but the skills required of mediators are those that are fundamental to the work generally. The mediation process, flexibly applied, offers an effective basis for resolving differences between people from different cultures.

---

9   *Op cit*, see footnote 2 for details.

SUMMARY

Throughout this chapter we have looked at the nature of oppression, power and difference, and these can be the basis of many conflicts. They tend to disempower the people affected and it is important for community mediation services to address these issues. As a community-based organisation, a community mediation service must be seen to reflect the needs of all within that community. As a service that aims to take a neutral stance between the parties in a conflict, it needs to work to equalise the situation and be clear that the value of all people is recognised. Mediation can only work to empower people to take decisions about their own lives if it works to counteract the disempowering effect of discrimination and oppression.

CHAPTER ELEVEN

STANDARDS AND ACCREDITATION

May Curtis

INTRODUCTION

The expansion of interest in mediation services in the UK comes at a time when the issue of standards of service and quality of delivery are priorities for government and employers, and also important for 'customers'. Quality systems (eg BS 5750),[1] Investors in People, National Vocational Qualifications and National Education Attainment Targets are all examples of government-led 'quality initiatives' being promoted. Professional bodies are also concerned to define 'client charters' and codes of conduct. Contractors of services are increasingly asking for evidence of quality assurance.

This strong external imperative is matched by commitment from within the mediation field. For MEDIATION UK and its membership, standards of practice, both for services and for practitioners, have been a prime concern for many years. MEDIATION UK'S Accreditation Committee has already formalised codes of practice and standards for service delivery, and provides accreditation for community mediation services. It is now also working on a process for accrediting individual mediators.

Other mediation organisations are also concerned with standards and accreditation, such as the family mediation organisations National Family Mediation and Family Mediators Association, and the commercial dispute resolution organisations CEDR (Centre for Dispute Resolution) and ADR Group, which has recently published its own policy document *Assuring Competence and Quality in Mediation*.[2] In the field of family mediation, the UK College of Family Mediators (which brings together National Family Mediation, Family Mediators Association and Family Mediation Scotland for the purposes of standards) has published standards[3] and provides a mechanism for the approval of bodies providing training for family mediators.

---

1   BS 5750 – a British Standard for Total Quality Assurance. This provides a framework of standards against which to carry out an audit of all aspects of an organisation, whether manufacturing or service oriented. It looks at all the organisation's systems and assesses their effective operation in practice from everyone's point of view: employer, employee, customer, supplier and relating organisations. It was the first to be introduced and is a model for many other subsequent quality frameworks.

2   Fraley, A, Temple, E and Paton, A, *Assuring Competence and Quality in Mediation*, a policy document, 1996, Bristol: ADR Group.

3   UK College of Family Mediators, *Standards*, 1997, London: UK College of Family Mediators. See Chapter 2 for more information on Family Mediation.

MEDIATION UK sees quality as central to its mission,[4] with one of its tenets to '... promote constructive ways of resolving conflicts, in particular mediation, and to ensure that everyone has access to quality mediation services in their local communities', with a strategic aim to 'ensure the highest possible standard of mediation'.

This chapter describes the accreditation initiatives undertaken by MEDIATION UK and traces their development; explores the issues concerning standards and accreditation; and looks into the immediate future from a community mediation perspective.

THE HISTORY

The innovative nature of Alternative Dispute Resolution and mediation has been recognised since the early days of FIRM (Forum for Initiatives in Reparation and Mediation), which became MEDIATION UK in 1991.[5] A body of knowledge, understanding and skills, specific to experience in the UK and derived from practice, has been assembled over the years, offering guidelines for good practice. These were drawn together in 1989,[6] in consultation with members, and revised in 1993, to form the *MEDIATION UK Practice Standards*.[7] This document describes core values and principles, and sets out standards for mediators, mediation services (including guidelines for managers of projects) and a clients' charter.

The same year, an Accreditation Committee, drawn from the membership, was set up to consider how these practice standards might be applied, and produced an *Accreditation Pack*[8] to facilitate the accreditation of mediation services. Then the committee developed an accredited training programme and started work on the accreditation of mediators and trainers. These four aspects – accreditation of mediation services, mediators, training courses and trainers – came to be seen as the 'pieces of a jigsaw' making up a picture of quality services – the rightful expectation of all clients and users of mediation services.

4   MEDIATION UK, *MEDIATION UK into the Millennium: Strategic Plan 1997–2000*, 1997, Bristol: MEDIATION UK. This document sets out the vision, mission and aims for MEDIATION UK over the next three years. It identifies the promotion of quality mediation as a core aim, and the facilitation of accrediting systems as a key role for the future.

5   See MEDIATION UK, *Mediation Takes a FIRM Hold*, 1995, Bristol: MEDIATION UK, for the history of the first 10 years.

6   Marshall, T, 'Values and Principles in Mediation – A FIRM View of Practice Standards' (1989) *MEDIATION* Vol 6 No 1.

7   MEDIATION UK, *MEDIATION UK Practice Standards*, 1993, being revised 1997, Bristol: MEDIATION UK.

8   MEDIATION UK, *Accreditation Pack*, 1994, revised 1996, Bristol: MEDIATION UK.

MEDIATION UK is a 'grass-roots' organisation, working with and through its membership. The work of the Accreditation Committee was therefore guided by six key principles:

1   The setting of standards should be a shared responsibility of practitioners and services and their associations.

2   The setting of standards should be informed by the users of the services – clients, local authorities, legislators and other bodies.

3   The processes and systems must incorporate ongoing review, evaluation and revision.

4   Processes must enable access to accreditation – not discriminate unfairly or be exclusive.

5   Standards must take account of, reflect and encourage the variety of contexts and settings in which mediation takes place.

6   Accreditation should recognise, value, encourage and expand the many varied 'routes' to becoming a competent and skilled mediator.

MEDIATION UK's Accreditation Committee continues its work, which now includes managing the accreditation scheme it formulated for services. In 1996 MEDIATION UK secured funding from a number of charitable trusts to employ an Accreditation Co-ordinator to take this work forward at a faster pace. The co-ordinator is responsible to the Accreditation Committee for the day-to-day management of the scheme and for the development of all other aspects of accreditation. The funding is short term – for three days per week for two and a half years.

In 1995 MEDIATION UK published its *Training Manual in Community Mediation Skills*,[9] compiled by a working group of MEDIATION UK members. The Accreditation Committee, in partnership with members of training manual group, designed a training course for community mediators, based on material in the training manual. That course – the *MEDIATION UK Training Programme in Community Mediation Skills*[10] – gained endorsement from the National Open College Network in May 1996.

Good quality training is part of the strategy for achieving quality mediation. However, the committee recognised that training input alone is not a guarantee of competent and skilled performance. There needs to be a system for the assessment of a mediator's practice and the underpinning knowledge and understanding. The committee therefore fully supported the writing of

---

9   MEDIATION UK, *Training Manual in Community Mediation Skills*, 1995, Bristol: MEDIATION UK.

10 Published as: MEDIATION UK, *Handbook for the Training Programme in Community Mediation Skills*, 1996, Bristol: MEDIATION UK.

National Standards for Mediation and the development of a Scottish/National Vocational Qualification (S/NVQ).[11]

The development of S/NVQs has been a government-inspired initiative aimed at rationalising all vocational qualifications and building them into a framework of comparable levels. This is part of the National Development Agenda for vocational education and training, as set out in *Prosperity through Skills*.[12]

The Accreditation Co-ordinator represents MEDIATION UK on the Lead Body (AGC&PLB – Advice, Guidance, Counselling & Psychotherapy Lead Body)[13] which is responsible for developing and eventually implementing the qualification for mediators. MEDIATION UK, along with other mediation organisations, is at the leading edge of these developments.

The Accreditation Committee, and MEDIATION UK generally, keeps in touch with developments in other mediation agencies. MEDIATION UK is represented on the Advisory Board of the UK College of Family Mediators, and seeks to keep up to date with developments and quality initiatives in all kinds of mediation across the globe.

---

11 S/NVQ – shorthand for SVQs and NVQs, standing for Scottish Vocational Qualifications and National Vocational Qualifications, the latter being offered in England, Wales and Northern Ireland. This separation recognises a separate and differently organised education system in Scotland. However, there are reciprocal arrangements whereby each Vocational Qualification is recognised simultaneously across the whole of the UK irrespective of its origin. Thus qualifications developed in England will be submitted to both NCVQ (National Council for Vocational Qualifications) and SCOTVEC (Scottish Vocational Education Council) and have equal status. So all that applies to NVQs also applies to SVQs, and for the rest of this chapter, NVQ will be used to stand for both. The publication of the *New Training Initiative* in 1981 set the scene for training based on national standards of competence, and NVQs were introduced in 1986. The *Review of Vocational Qualifications* in 1996 called for a coherent national framework of qualifications, and NCVQ was set up to rationalise the plethora of vocational qualifications that had developed over decades. Other key purposes for the development of NVQs include: comparability with European vocational qualifications; a change of emphasis from 'can know' to 'can do' outcomes; the development of standards and qualification specifications that are employer-led rather than education-led; a system which is not tied to a particular learning mode and which offers very wide access.

12 Department of Employment, *Prosperity through Skills: The National Development Agenda*, 1993, London: Department of Employment.

13 AGC&PLB – Advice, Guidance, Counselling and Psychotherapy Lead Body. A Lead Body is an organisation given the task by NCVQ to map occupations, produce standards for those occupations, and develop a range of qualifications that reflect the needs of those occupational areas. It must have overwhelming support and input from employer organisations in order to qualify as a Lead Body, although education, training and union organisations also participate. AGC&PLB was deemed the most appropriate 'home' for the development of mediation qualifications.

ACCREDITATION SCHEME FOR COMMUNITY MEDIATION SERVICES IN THE UK

Ensuring quality is unquestionably good, and for mediation services, as for other public services, it is essential. However, without explicit, commonly held standards, evaluation may be facile and subjective, resulting in little useful information to help improvement. The opposite danger is of very high and unrealistic expectations which are impossible to maintain and may lead to discouragement. Clearly, without standards, there is unlikely to be consistency of quality in service delivery across the country. Defining standards for practice, covering processes and procedures as well as end results, provides a sound basis for evaluation and external accreditation. Thus, accreditation means that clients, users, contracting agencies and mediators can be confident they are dealing with a quality service.

'Is this a MEDIATION UK-approved service?' is a question being asked by funding agencies and contractors. An accreditation scheme provides the way of saying 'Yes!'

The standards

The standards that currently underpin the MEDIATION UK Accreditation Scheme are the *Practice Standards*, mentioned above.[14] In the light of experience and use, consideration is being given to a further revision. The core values remain unchanged, but there is a need to review the language, and to present the standards in a more coherent format. Also, more specific guidance is needed on the evidence required to demonstrate that the standards have been met. Neither the standards nor the process of accreditation are set in stone. This is a dynamic process, which members are continually seeking to improve. One proposal is that we should aim for a 'working draft' rather than 'the final set of standards', to acknowledge the fact that there is always room to improve and that, with the expanding contexts for mediation, there are new insights into 'What is quality?'

The current *Practice Standards* include:

- values and principles;
- the management and operation of a mediation service;
- a client's charter;
- mediation practice.

Each of these is described briefly below.

---

14   See footnote 7 above.

Values and principles

These are concerned with: a common belief in non-violent, socially constructive approaches to conflict; a commitment to treating people with equal respect, without violence and without judgment; a recognition of the importance of openness, self-determination, collaboration and flexibility in the mediation process; upholding the tenets of voluntary participation, confidentiality, impartiality, fairness and empowerment.

The management and operation of a mediation service

This is concerned with the qualities of a good organisation such as – soundly constituted, well managed, having efficient systems, working within a good policy framework and supportive of all the people involved with the service. The standards also emphasise involvement in and responsibility to the community; responsibility to the clients; and responsibility to all staff (paid or unpaid). The independence of services is seen as important in preserving the principle of neutrality.

A client's charter

This explains what can be expected by clients of the service and of mediation.

Mediation practice

This includes standards for mediators. These contain detailed guidance on the behaviour of mediators in relation to ensuring quality, impartiality, a professional approach, setting ground rules, voluntary participation, fairness, ensuring viability of agreements, and following up the mediation as is appropriate. The responsibility of mediators to maintain personal effectiveness and be committed to ongoing development is also included.

MEDIATION UK's Accreditation Scheme for mediation services requires the *Practice Standards* to be applied to the systems and processes of the service, its policies, its value base, its management and the quality of its mediation services to clients. The criteria are:

- Membership of MEDIATION UK.
- Commitment to the aims of MEDIATION UK.
- At least 18 months to two years in operation to provide sufficient evidence of:
  - working to a sound governing document;
  - working to agreed aims and objectives;
  - working to policies and codes of practice covering all aspects of service delivery, including equal opportunities, health and safety, recruitment and selection, and training;

○ at least one annual general meeting and an annual report which includes audited accounts;

○ monitoring/record systems and their effective use;

○ a large enough caseload from which to evaluate the effectiveness of quality assurance systems;

○ the generation of information from which to assess cost/time/effort;

○ sound initial and ongoing training for mediators;

○ strategic planning, including plans for financial viability for at least five years.

These criteria, along with information in the *Accreditation Pack* and the *Guide to Starting a Community Mediation Service*,[15] help mediation services to gather evidence about their systems, procedures and operational practices. When a service judges itself ready for accreditation, the next stage is registration for formal external assessment.

The procedure

The accreditation procedure consists of:

- *An application questionnaire* which demonstrates that the organisation of the service is sound, that the service is working in accordance with its governing document and within the requirements of the Charities Act 1992/93, and that its practice is compatible with MEDIATION UK'S philosophy and *Practice Standards*. As soon as the application is received, a member of the Accreditation Committee is appointed as a MEDIATION UK representative to oversee the procedure and support the assessors (see below).

- *Assessment of the mediation service's working practices* by two appointed assessors. The assessors examine the application form and all accompanying documents, and then visit the service to gather direct evidence of its working practices.

- *Moderation by an external moderator* to ensure that the assessment is fair and consistent with other assessments, and that there is sufficient evidence to support the recommendation for accreditation.

A pool of assessors has been recruited from the membership of MEDIATION UK and selected against criteria which ensure experience in the field of mediation and preferably in the management of a service. These assessors are given initial and ongoing training. Regular recruitment drives ensure that the pool of assessors is large enough and contains an appropriate range of

---

15 MEDIATION UK, *Guide to Starting a Community Mediation Service*, 1993, revised 1996, Bristol: MEDIATION UK.

experience to meet the needs of the scheme. This means covering the range of contexts of mediation services supported by MEDIATION UK, including neighbour, victim/offender and schools/peer mediation; and the management of independent services as well as those run by public services such as housing, probation or environmental health. The appropriate assessors are chosen for each application by the Accreditation Committee with the accreditation co-ordinator.

The accreditation procedure is not a search for perfection or uniformity, but rather the assurance that this is a sound, well-managed, self-evaluating, learning and developing organisation. There must be clear evidence of the core values described in the *Practice Standards* and systems for the service to identify its strengths and weaknesses. The whole process is a co-operative one between the service and MEDIATION UK, whose representative liaises between all the parties at every stage.

The outcome of the procedure may be:

(a) unconditional accreditation valid for five years;

    or

(b) conditional accreditation – with an opportunity to discuss areas of concern and a time frame for review or re-assessment;

    or

(c) non-accreditation for the time being – with clear reasons stated in the report.

Responsibility for according or withholding accreditation rests with MEDIATION UK.

To maintain valid accreditation, a service is required to complete an annual return, confirming the information in the original application. If this information shows significant changes in the organisation, an interim visit may be judged necessary by the MEDIATION UK representative (the same person as before, if possible). Or the representative may ask questions about the changes but take no action. After five years a full questionnaire and a visit to the service by assessors will be required to renew the accreditation. Currently, the average cost per accreditation is £400, of which half is found by the service and half is grant-aided by MEDIATION UK.

Quality assurance

Quality assurance of the Accreditation Scheme is addressed through:

- the moderators;
- selection and training of assessors;
- continuous monitoring and review of the scheme via evaluation forms received from all parties involved. This has led to the development of

support material for assessors and to the current rewriting of the *Practice Standards*.

Further developments are always being considered, such as a regular performance review of assessors. Another suggestion is random, unannounced visits to accredited services, to ensure that standards are being maintained.

ACCREDITATION OF MEDIATORS

Doctors, solicitors, teachers and social workers all require qualifications to practise their professions. Currently there is no formal qualification for mediators in the UK. Individual organisations such as the FMA and CEDR have their own accreditation, based on evidence of prior educational achievement – usually at degree or professional level – combined with attendance at their own training programmes, followed by supervised practice. This follows the traditional educational route, which may be exclusive at the point of entry and miss out on the wider potential that exists.

Experience in community mediation has shown that people from varied educational backgrounds and life experience, possess or can learn the skills, understanding and competence required to be a good mediator. Indeed, it is essential that a community mediation service has access to this variety, to meet the needs of that community. The challenge in taking this inclusive approach, is to ensure that the highest standards of training, supervision and assessment of practice are offered to new mediators. Then we shall resist the sort of 'professionalisation' that 'digs moats around its members and pours hot oil on those who dare to scale the ramparts'.[16]

The first step is to have clarity about the standards required to be a 'professional' mediator. We need to know:

- What is it that mediators do?
- Under what conditions and in what contexts?
- How would we distinguish between good and bad mediation?
- What ethical codes and values would we expect a mediator to follow?
- What personal and interpersonal skills are needed?
- What breadth and depth of knowledge and understanding will be required of a mediator?
- What range of experience is required to be able to infer a competent and professional mediator?

---

16 Davis, A, 'Ensuring High Quality Mediation: The Issue of Credentialing' (Summer 1992) *MCS (Mennonite Conciliation Service) Conciliation Quarterly*, pp 2, 3, 11.

Once answers to these questions have been formulated and generally agreed, the next step is to decide how the knowledge and practice of an individual can be tested and judged in order to offer accreditation.

The National Vocational Qualifications (NVQs) answer this need, and offer a systematic approach that provides the means to assess competence. This includes:

- explicit statements of WHAT a skilled mediator does;
- performance criteria by which to judge the QUALITY of performance;
- range statements that describe the range of CONDITIONS under which a skilled and competent practitioner would be expected to perform;
- the range of underpinning KNOWLEDGE and UNDERSTANDING that is required to sustain competent performance under a wide range of conditions;
- evidence requirements for each aspect of the work.

In addition, after the qualification has been accredited by NCVQ (National Council for Vocational Qualifications),[17] the Awarding Bodies[18] prepare detailed information about appropriate evidence and guidance to ensure that assessment is fair and reliable.

To achieve an NVQ, a candidate is required to produce evidence of competence in the performance of an occupation – ie demonstrate both skill and understanding. The skills and understanding may be acquired in a variety of ways: through experience in doing the job; on training programmes; in supervision; or a mixture of these. The routes will vary but the performance criteria and required evidence of competence are the same for everyone.

It is expected that the standards will be available at the end of 1997 and the national mediation qualification in spring 1998. However, the mediation organisations in the UK will decide what they require to recognise a mediator as accredited, and whether this will be a licence to practise. The achievement of all or part of the NVQ could be the sole requirement for accreditation, or there might be a need to stipulate a certain amount of experience as well.

The principal tension is between maintaining rigour in standards and the costs of accreditation. An accreditation process must have credibility, but it must also be accessible to competent mediators. Experience in other fields has shown that the achievement of NVQs is an expensive business, especially in

---

17 NCVQ – A regulatory body overseeing the development of vocational qualifications, accrediting qualifications and commissioning approved bodies to do the development work (SCOTVEC in Scotland).

18 Awarding Bodies are independent commercial organisations which confer the awards once the standards and qualification specifications have been accredited by NCVQ and SCOTVEC. Awarding Bodies are responsible for setting up the assessment and verification systems required in the delivery of awards. They are accountable to NCVQ for the quality of these systems.

establishing new qualifications. However, NCVQ has addressed this in the *Beaumont Report*, and is currently acting on recommendations to reduce costs.[19]

It is unlikely that there will be only one form of accreditation for all mediators across all contexts. The needs of the different mediation providers vary and will therefore demand different areas and levels of knowledge. However, we will have clarity about the core skills of mediation and its underpinning body of knowledge, as an absolute requirement of all mediators. There will also be a mechanism for the rigorous assessment of practice. This will provide confidence in a mediator's ability in core skills, and clarity about the further learning and development needed for the different settings where mediation is used – whether in community, family, commercial or industrial contexts.

The core activities, applicable to all, will include:

- establishing contact with clients;
- assisting clients to identify the potential of mediation;
- developing and maintaining interaction with clients;
- preparing and setting up mediation;
- staging the mediation process;
- facilitating the process of mediation;
- evaluating and developing own work;
- working within an ethical code.

Each of these activities will have performance criteria against which to make judgments about the quality of the practice.

National standards can be used in many ways: in the selection and training of mediators; for informing clients what they can expect from the mediation process, the mediators and the service; in assuring users of the service that what is contracted can be delivered; for evaluating the quality and effectiveness of mediation; and providing a basis for performance reviews and supervision. Also, standards provide clarity about what is expected of potential new mediators and what they in turn can expect from mediation. National standards also offer assessment of practice that can be translated into qualifications.

National standards for mediation provide the means to measure the skills and understanding developed by a mediator through experience. Thus an

---

19 Beaumont, G, Beaumont Report: Review of 100 NVQs and SVQs, 1995, London: Department for Education and Employment. This report contains the recommendations of the Evaluation Advisory Group, chaired by Gordon Beaumont, following a review of 100 of the most-used NVQs and SVQs. The findings reveal widespread support for the concept of NVQs, but makes clear recommendations about quality of assessment, reducing costs, access to qualifications for those not yet working, reduction in bureaucracy, provision of information, marketing and developing a culture of excellence.

experienced mediator is able to gain affirmation and recognition for professional practice. Conversely, practice that falls short of quality mediation can be identified, and areas for improvement highlighted.

As suggested above, the attainment of these standards alone may not be sufficient to achieve 'Accredited Mediator' status, as defined by the various mediation bodies. It is likely that other criteria may be required, such as evidence of a given level of experience (eg number and/or range of cases) and a commitment to regular supervision.

A system for accrediting competent mediators will in turn provide reliable information for a national register of mediators, should this be considered desirable. The options for such a scheme have yet to be costed, but this could offer a way of protecting both clients and mediation services.

ENDORSEMENT AND ACCREDITATION OF TRAINING PROGRAMMES

Training for mediators, both initial and ongoing, is a key activity examined by MEDIATION UK during accreditation of a service. A service must demonstrate that new mediators have sound basic training; that they are fully supported in their early days as practitioners (often by pairing with an experienced mediator); and that there is ongoing training and development. A service may have the resources and the expertise to offer this training in-house or it may secure training from another mediation service, a further education college or freelance trainers.

Experience over many years saw the evolution of a generally accepted basic training for new mediators. This covered: an introduction to mediation; preparing for mediation; conducting mediation; and evaluation. However, the question remained, how could mediation services and mediators be confident that the training covered all essential skills and knowledge, and was of good quality? Also, new mediation services were seeking advice and guidance about training, and asking for materials to support their programmes; they needed a national resource to avoid having to contact many other services to obtain the information.

In response to this need, a national training manual was compiled with the generous co-operation and collaboration of many experienced trainers from all parts of the UK, to be a resource for future training programmes. The manual was published by MEDIATION UK in 1995.[20] The format of the manual follows a logical progression through the mediation process. It also

---

20 MEDIATION UK, *Training Manual in Community Mediation Skills*, 1995, Bristol: MEDIATION UK.

reflects the participative style of training which has proved to be a sound basis for the development of competent mediators.

Mediation services were beginning to look for some form of certification for mediators who had completed the training, and one or two services had produced courses accredited by their local Open College Network (OCN). The National Open College Network (NOCN)[21] provided an opportunity of gaining national accreditation for a course based on the manual. Successful accreditation for the training programme would provide mediators with a way of achieving a nationally recognised vocational qualification.

A member of the accreditation committee who had already worked with the South West Access Federation, a local branch of the Open College Network, started the process, which required first local accreditation and then simultaneous recognition at the national level with NOCN. The training programme was recast in terms of the expected learning outcomes, which were grouped in coherent units, with the addition of criteria and methods for assessment. It was important to secure consistency in the training if the programme was to have national recognition.

The process towards accreditation of the training programme proved arduous and lengthy. However, the *Training Programme for Community Mediation Skills*[22] was given endorsement by NOCN, with simultaneous recognition across England and Wales, in May 1996 and as such, achieved the status of a DfEE (Department for Education and Employment) approved programme, eligible for central government funding through the Further Education Funding Council (FEFC).[23] It is now recognised as a vocational training programme, with the potential to offer a pathway into mediation, but also a means of progression into other associated occupations or higher education.

The learning outcomes have been given OCN rating at both levels 2 and 3 for the first three units, and level 3 only for the fourth. Level 2 requires competence through understanding of the information provided on the training course, and an appreciation of how it relates to practice. This includes experience of using skills under guidance, and competence in some core skills. At level 3, the expectation is of a deeper understanding of the information provided on the training course, and some independent exploration of the

---

21 OCN and NOCN – Open College Networks are consortia of local organisations concerned with education and training opportunities for adults. They provide a quality assurance and accreditation service for a wide range of education and training, and issue credits to learners. The National Open College Network is the national body which links all OCNs. In Scotland, SCOTVEC takes on this role, as there is no such network. The role of the OCN is to validate training courses which meet its specific criteria.

22 MEDIATION UK, *Handbook for the Training Programme in Community Mediation Skills*, 1996, Bristol: MEDIATION UK.

23 FEFC – Further Education Funding Council is a governmental body responsible for the funding of post-16 tertiary education in England and Wales.

principles and ideas involved. This is related to practice and competence, with learners able to reflect on their experience and improve their own performance. The target for new mediators would be to achieve level 3, with level 2 for those not intending to practise as mediators at this stage (although they may want to do so at a later date, or move into other areas of learning).

What can be confidently predicted from this NOCN-accredited training programme?

First, there is consistency of input. NOCN has its own quality indicators. These are concerned with the preparation, planning and delivery of the whole programme, with particular reference to the care and guidance given to learners at each stage: pre-entry, during the programme and post-programme. So clarity about target group, recruitment, guidance and equal opportunities will be important. Other important aspects of an NOCN-accredited programme are the explicit learning outcomes and the assessment of achievement.

There are four units to the programme:

Unit One – An Introduction to Mediation.

Unit Two – Mediation in Practice: Preparing for Mediation.

Unit Three – Mediation in Practice: Managing a Mediation Session.

Unit Four – Mediation in Practice: Working as a Community Mediator.

Second, there is assessment of output in the learning outcomes, including competent performance in mediation. There are 51 learning outcomes, 18 in Unit 1, 11 in Unit 2, 15 in Unit 3, 7 in Unit 4, to be assessed for certification. The *Handbook*[24] offers a range of exercises and activities (taken from the *Training Manual in Community Mediation Skills*),[25] through which the assessment might be accomplished. The aim of the programme is to ensure that new mediators have the skills, knowledge, understanding and confidence to mediate alongside an experienced mediator, and so build up a body of personal experience and become competent mediators. The assessor must be a skilled and experienced mediator.

Third, a moderator will monitor the programme to ensure that all requirements are met and that it is delivered in accordance with the original submission. The moderator also samples assessments, and on this basis NOCN will award certificates and unit credits to learners for successful completion of the programme.

---

24 See footnote 22.
25 See footnote 20.

Where does the NVQ framework fit with OCN?

The NOCN framework has a focus on both inputs (facilitating the acquisition of knowledge and skills) and outputs (assessment that skills and knowledge have been acquired) and these are linked within the programme. By contrast, NVQs are about outputs only, and specifically in the context of performance within the work situation of a mediator. The focus in NVQs is exclusively on assessment of evidence of competence (detailed guidance on evidence requirements is given). In this context, competence implies that the mediator has a thorough understanding of the theory and knowledge underpinning mediation, possesses the skills required to mediate, and is able to operate as a skilled mediator. How that knowledge and skill has been gained is of no concern, and there is no formal link with any particular training programme. NVQs are therefore concerned with the assessment and accreditation of mediators rather than with the quality of training input.

Nevertheless, it makes sense that MEDIATION UK's *Training Programme in Community Mediation Skills* should lead to the achievement of the standards described in the Mediation NVQ. It is also in the learners' interest that the knowledge and skills gained during their training should be recognised, assessed and gathered in a portfolio of evidence, which can also be submitted towards the NVQ. Analysis of the learning outcomes in the current *Training Programme* indicates that it could provide up to 75% of the required evidence for the NVQ .

Moreover, the NVQ standards provide essential information to guide the content of individual training courses. They provide a benchmark for reviewing students' learning and help to identify gaps that need to be addressed during the training. This could be helpful in deciding what weighting to give to particular topics with each group of trainees.

Thus there is a close relationship between the accredited *Training Programme* and the achievement of the NVQ, particularly as the *Training Programme* focuses on the application of knowledge and skills, and has an experiential, performance orientation. On the other hand, training programmes that concentrate on the acquisition of knowledge alone – what might be called 'mediation education' – would provide more limited evidence of mediation competence.

One of the greatest benefits of this NOCN-accredited training programme over other training courses is that, if delivered in partnership with a further education college, it can now attract FEFC funding as a vocational course.

MEDIATION UK's *Training Programme in Community Mediation Skills* is unique amongst mediation organisations' training in having accreditation from an *external* national, validating body. Quality assurance for all other mediation training is 'in-house': in the hands of individual mediation organisations. For example, National Family Mediation accredits eligible training bodies through the UK College of Family Mediators, and the Centre for Dispute Resolution (CEDR) has its own prescribed and centrally controlled training programmes.

For an organisation such as MEDIATION UK, with its ever-expanding membership and complex training needs, it will be important to achieve a system for accrediting all mediation training, both for initial training and continuing professional development. One option would be to work on a range of NOCN-accredited programmes, written up, published and delivered to a similar format across the UK. Another option might be to focus on a framework for quality training which could be assessed and accredited, leaving the style, format and content free to respond to local needs and different contexts. The latter would mirror the approach used for the accreditation of services, and would reflect more appropriately the diversity of community mediation services.

In the longer term, CAMPAG (Counselling, Advice, Mediation, Psychotherapy and Guidance), which is due to replace AGC&PLB, and become one of the new National Training Organisations (NTOs), may well become the appropriate source of external endorsement for training programmes.[26]

ACCREDITATION OF TRAINERS

Many people and organisations in the UK have expressed a need for accreditation of mediation trainers and training agencies. These include new services seeking good quality training at a reasonable cost; established mediation trainers on their own competing with training agencies with more resources to promote and sell their 'product'; services which have had experiences of poor training in the past; and colleges wanting to run an accredited course which requires accredited trainers.

Over the past 10 years mediation has 'grown' its own trainers and teachers. Experienced trainers have added an understanding of mediation to their skills; and skilled mediators have learned and developed training skills. In this process, a curriculum for training has developed, along with a style of learning and teaching. The *Training Manual in Community Mediation Skills* and the *Training Programme in Community Mediation Skills* are testimony to this.

---

26 NTO – National Training Organisations: Created to rationalise the many and disparate bodies involved with the development of standards and vocational qualifications and with the provision of employment training, such as Industrial Training Organisations, Lead Bodies and Occupational Standards Councils. The purpose of this development is to seek a more coherent and strategic approach to standards and vocational qualification, identification of skills gaps and the provision of training within specific occupational groupings. The Advice, Guidance, Counselling and Psychotherapy Lead Body made its submission to become a NTO in May 1996.

Accreditation for mediation trainers would acknowledge these achievements, and also offer affirmation to individual trainers, some of whom have no formal training qualifications. Many of these trainers have given of their time freely both to deliver training and to write up and develop courses.

The higher profile of mediation and the increasing demand for mediation training has led to many more trainers and training organisations offering mediation training, sometimes for high fees. Larger commercial training organisations see mediation as a growing area of activity, and move in to add mediation as a new 'product' in their portfolios. Mediation is also being included in higher education fields such as law, environmental studies, local government, peace studies and so on. There is little evidence that experienced mediation trainers are being sought to deliver this explosion of provision, except in peace studies, where experienced international and community mediators have always done the teaching. Often expertise in allied fields, such as counselling, guidance, team building and problem-solving, rather than mediation itself, is deemed sufficient to deliver mediation training. There is an urgent need to recognise and accredit quality trainers – for the sake of trainee mediators, mediation clients, trainers, organisations looking for trainers, and the general credibility of mediation as a definite skill.

MEDIATION UK is therefore working towards accrediting trainers. As a first step, the publication of a *Directory of Trainers in Mediation and Conflict Resolution*[27] is planned, initially without any attempt at endorsing or regulating the contributors. It will provide much fuller information than has hitherto been available, give wider options to those who need trainers, and be a platform for the full range of mediation training providers. However, it will still be a case of 'buyer beware', and the directory will include guidance for organisations seeking trainers, to help them ask the right questions. The next stage will be to agree criteria for making judgments about the quality of a trainer, and then to provide a way of assessing trainers seeking accreditation.

There are already national standards for training and development, and awards and NVQs are available to trainers.[28] These comprehensive standards cover the gamut of functions and practice in the training and development field at all levels. There are standards for training practitioners, managers of training, designers of training materials, assessors, verifiers and so on. There is no need to reinvent this wheel: the standards are there to be used in whatever way is desirable. For MEDIATION UK, the challenge is to decide which to use and in what way, and then to devise a scheme which can be operated effectively.

---

27 It is hoped this will be published by MEDIATION UK early in 1998, and thereafter updated annually.

28 Training and Development Lead Body (TDLB) – The TDLB developed standards for all aspects of training and development. This body was subsequently brought together with other associated organisations concerned with personnel and human resources, and is now the EOSC – the Employment Occupational Standards Council.

KEEPING A BALANCE

The need for quality and competence in mediation has been well-recognised, but the issue of 'qualifications', 'professionalisation', or, as Albie Davis called it, 'credentialing', has fuelled a debate about the danger of creating an expert elite and shutting the door to the 'home-grown' community mediator. These concerns are illustrated by the following list of questions gathered from various meetings, workshops and letters in the UK over recent years.

Why define standards and offer accreditation? Definitions result in reducing the process, and precludes the creativity of the process. There is a danger of defining out important aspects of mediation.

Can the work of mediation be subjected to this mechanistic dissecting process and still retain its subtle nuances? Can the quality of the process be measured?

What is to be measured? Will it be concerned only with the outcomes of a mediation? What about the transforming nature of the mediation process? How will that be measured?

This is a professional activity – the notion of mere competence/vocational qualification reduces its credibility and standing.

Qualification/accreditation is not appropriate for voluntary activity – it will put people off. Volunteers will be unwilling to submit to accreditation.

Once you 'professionalise' mediation, it becomes an elite activity. Good volunteer mediators will be driven out. Mediation will become expensive – out of reach of those who need it.

There is a danger of requiring services to fit rigid strait-jackets, and this would prevent creative responses to local need.

On the other hand, there are many people who see the benefits of accreditation, and say such things as:

I have undertaken a training course and developed many skills – how can I have this acknowledged and certificated?

We want to ensure that mediation is recognised as a distinct method of dispute resolution with its own body of knowledge, skills and processes.

We need to convey to users and funders that we offer a quality service which is value for money.

We need bench marks against which to carry out our own audit.

Anyone can set up as a mediator. How do I know this person is qualified to do this?

We need to be able to recognise performance that falls short of best practice and be able to give precise feedback to the mediator.

We need to know which are approved services.

A framework provides for consistency of quality, not uniformity

Both positions have something to offer in the quest for quality and accreditation. There is a groundswell of opinion that desires it, giving clear motivation for making progress. On the other hand, there are views that warn caution and remind us that the processes and underpinning values of mediation must not be lost. It is possible to meet the interests of both.

All the national mediation umbrella organisations have been working independently, but also collectively with NVQs, towards ensuring competence and quality. As intimated earlier, it is unlikely and probably undesirable to have a single, uniform framework to accredit all mediation activity. What is important is that mediation, in all its manifestations, has credibility as a mainstream option in dispute resolution, so that policy-makers and clients have confidence to use it, and mediation becomes accessible to those who wish to take up the option. It is also important that the competence of a mediator can be recognised across the range of mediation services, and that mediators are able to operate in different settings, if they wish. Accreditation based on explicit standards would facilitate this.

THE FUTURE FOR MEDIATION UK

MEDIATION UK is currently very involved in accreditation issues, and will remain so for the immediate future. Ideally member mediation services will continue to move voluntarily towards achieving accredited status after operating for two years, seeing the benefits of being an 'approved service'. The option for new services to be recognised as 'working towards accreditation' is also a possible development in the Accreditation Scheme. Continuous improvement and expansion of the scheme will come about through systematic evaluation. The current review and rewriting of the *MEDIATION UK Practice Standards* is one example of this.

We hope that mediators will also aim to achieve accredited status, not just as a 'licence to practice', but as a mark of commitment to the quality service that clients should expect. MEDIATION UK intends to provide the means of achieving this, by setting clear criteria and perhaps by becoming an Awarding Body itself. In the meantime, MEDIATION UK is working closely with the Lead Body to ensure that the concerns mentioned above are met, by enshrining key principles in the materials for NVQs. For example, a group is working on a community mediation evidence route which contextualises the mediation qualification for those working in community mediation.

MEDIATION UK also has a key role to play in ensuring that quality training and trainers are available, both for its membership and others with an interest in mediation. Again, this is likely to happen through providing the lead in setting standards and defining the ways in which the standards can be demonstrated.

There is a cost in all this aspiration for quality and standards – in time, effort and money. For most voluntary organisations (the majority of community mediation services), this poses a huge funding problem. However, a commitment to quality services in the form of quality assurance systems is now expected by most funding agencies, and in the long run this can only increase the credibility of mediation.

As always with a 'grass-roots' organisation, these goals can only be achieved in concert with the membership. The 'four pieces of the puzzle' for standards and accreditation will only come together with the support and collaboration of all involved. This has been the history of community mediation thus far and there is no reason to believe it will not continue.

CHAPTER TWELVE

EVALUATING COMMUNITY AND NEIGHBOUR MEDIATION

Jim Dignan

INTRODUCTION

This chapter will commence with a brief introduction to the field of evaluation research, which will also set out to answer the questions why, and for whom, such research is important. Evaluation research is far from being unique to the field of community mediation although, as we shall see, it raises a number of issues that are of special importance to those engaged in this work. For this reason the chapter will also set out a typology of evaluative approaches, which seeks to identify the range of issues specific to community mediation that evaluation research might be capable of addressing. This is followed by a very brief history of evaluation research in the field of community mediation.

The rest of the chapter draws extensively on the findings of a recently completed evaluation study which set out to compare the impact of mediation with alternative, more traditional methods of dealing with neighbour disputes, focusing particularly on the role of local authority housing and environmental health service departments. The detailed findings of this study have been written up elsewhere,[1] but for the purposes of this exercise a much more selective approach has been adopted. This involves the identification and more detailed consideration of a number of key policy themes which specifically relate to the typology referred to above. The chapter concludes with a discussion of the issues that still need to be addressed by means of evaluation research, and offers a blueprint for the projected next main phase in the evaluation process.[2]

---

1   Dignan, J, Sorsby, A and Hibbert, J, *Neighbour Disputes: Comparing the Cost-effectiveness of Mediation and Alternative Approaches*, 1996, Sheffield: University of Sheffield. The study and its findings will be referred to hereafter as the 'Neighbour Dispute project' and 'Neighbour Dispute report' respectively.

2   A small pilot evaluative project is currently under way involving a single community mediation service. It is hoped that this will form the precursor for a much more intensive follow-up study focusing on the comparative effectiveness and quality of different approaches as perceived by neighbour disputants themselves.

WHAT IS EVALUATION RESEARCH?
WHY (AND FOR WHOM) DOES IT MATTER?

Evaluation research can take a number of different forms and serves a variety of purposes. In essence, it involves the use of standard research techniques to collect and systematically analyse information about the characteristics, activities and outcomes of different social processes or programmes. These include the provision of mediation services by either voluntary organisations or statutory agencies.

The data and analysis that are derived from evaluation research can be used by the agencies concerned as a kind of quality audit, to assess and improve the quality of service they deliver. Alternatively, and increasingly, evaluation research is used by policy-makers and planners at both central and local government level as an aid to strategic decision-making, particularly where important choices have to be made regarding the allocation of public funding. In recent years there has been a tendency for both civil[3] and criminal justice systems[4] to be (re)assessed in terms of their effectiveness and value for money, and this a tendency that is likely to continue for the foreseeable future.

Evaluation research, and the findings of evaluation research, are thus of growing importance to policy-makers and funders, to those engaged in the provision of a wide range of social services, including the use of mediation as an alternative form of dispute resolution, and to the users and potential users of such services; indeed to everyone with an interest in improving people's access to justice and developing more effective ways of resolving a wide range of disputes. This shared concern on the part of voluntary agencies, social reform organisations and government departments was reflected in the commissioning in 1995 of a jointly funded project to examine the way neighbour disputes were dealt with, and to compare the approaches and outcomes associated with mediation and more traditional approaches.[5] Before we turn to the findings of this project, however, it is important to be aware of the different types of evaluation research and their application to the field of community mediation.

---

3 See, for example, Lord Woolf's review of the civil justice system: Lord Woolf, *Inquiry into Civil Justice: Access to Justice*, 1995 and 1996 (Woolf Inquiry Team's interim and final reports respectively).

4 See, for example, Audit Commission, *Misspent Youth: Young People and Crime*, 1996, London: Audit Commission; also Shapland, J et al, *Milton Keynes Criminal Justice Audit*, 1995, Sheffield: University of Sheffield.

5 See p 225 for a more detailed account of the way these different organisations came together to fund the Neighbour Dispute project which is discussed in more detail below.

TYPOLOGY OF EVALUATION RESEARCH APPROACHES AND THEIR APPLICABILITY TO COMMUNITY MEDIATION

Much has been written about the aims and methods associated with evaluation research, though this often tends to be specific to the kinds of programme being evaluated.[6] Nevertheless, it is possible to identify the following three main types of evaluation research,[7] each of which has an important role to play in the assessment of community and neighbour mediation projects:

- programme effectiveness analysis;
- comparative impact analysis;
- value-for-money or cost-benefit analysis.

Programme effectiveness analysis is chiefly concerned with the extent to which a given programme – for example, a newly established mediation service – succeeds in achieving its aims and objectives. Consequently, the focus is often confined to a specific service; the assessment criteria are likely to be heavily influenced (if not exclusively defined) by the providers of the service; and the main aim of the research is to monitor the performance of the service and provide feedback. This may be used by the providers of the service either to assist its development and improve the quality of the services on offer, or to generate financial and other support. This approach is probably the least demanding, both in terms of the data required to undertake the analysis and the research techniques involved. Most of the studies that have been undertaken to date provide descriptions of project caseloads, referral sources, procedures and (recorded) outcomes. Some also examine client feedback, average time per case, average cost per case and other performance-related data. Since the assumptions on which these are based are far from uniform, however, it is usually difficult, if not impossible, to compare one effectiveness analysis study with another.

Comparative impact analysis seeks to answer the question whether a given programme or type of programme makes a difference to those at whom it is aimed, either in comparison with an alternative service (or range of services) or compared with no provision of any kind. For example, one of the crucial issues for mediation services is how their interventions compare (in terms of

---

6   Readers wishing to explore this topic further may wish to consult Schalock, RL, *Outcome-based Evaluation*, 1995, New York: Plenum Press. Although much of Schalock's work has involved the evaluation of programmes designed to improve the quality of life of those suffering from various forms of mental retardation, much of what he has to say on the subject of outcome-based evaluation is of much wider interest. Indeed, the following attempt to articulate an evaluative framework for the assessment of community mediation services has been strongly influenced by the approach proposed by Schalock.

7   Although presented as discrete approaches, in practice evaluation research projects often incorporate elements of more than one approach.

quality of process, outcome etc) with those associated with alternative service providers such as local authority housing and environmental service departments.

Here, the focus of the evaluation is likely to be much broader in two important respects than is the case with programme effectiveness analysis. First, it is less likely to be confined to a single community mediation service. As was the case with the Neighbour Dispute project, the aim may be to compare the effectiveness of mediation as a process with that of its alternatives (which might include taking no action). And second, as we shall see, the evaluation criteria are likely to encompass a much broader range of concerns than the relatively straightforward question of the extent to which a service or programme is achieving its stated aims and objectives.

This kind of evaluation is as likely to be of interest to policy-makers and alternative service providers as it is to those offering mediation services. However, comparative impact analysis is much less easy to undertake in this field than are single-service effectiveness studies. One reason for this is that there are likely to be serious problems when seeking to obtain the data that is required to complete the analysis. Before the Neighbour Dispute project was undertaken, for example, there was little standardisation in the kind of data compiled by the growing number of community mediation services. And since no attempt had been made to compile a uniform database, there were no sufficiently reliable, comprehensive or comparable statistics on which to undertake even a comparative analysis involving different mediation services, let alone a comparison between mediation and other kinds of services offered to those involved in neighbour disputes.

Not surprisingly, the data collection problems are compounded when seeking to compare the process of mediation with the often fundamentally different range of interventions associated with local authority housing and environmental service departments. As far as housing departments are concerned, much of the data that is required to undertake this kind of analysis may simply not be compiled at all by hard-pressed local housing officers, for whom dealing with neighbour disputes may rank as a relatively minor, if increasingly frustrating, part of their overall responsibilities. In the case of environmental services, the position is not quite so bad, since environmental health officers do have statutory responsibilities for recording and investigating noise nuisance complaints; but even here their records tend to concentrate on the outcomes associated with formal as opposed to informal interventions. Consequently, there is a serious dearth of accessible, reliable and comparable data relating even to such basic matters as the number and types of neighbour disputes dealt with by the various statutory agencies, and the way these are classified and processed.

Moreover, these data-collection problems are compounded still further by the serious methodological difficulties involved in seeking to compare two sets of processes that differ quite fundamentally in terms of their aims, objectives, methods, approaches and also the outcomes they strive for. The apparent incommensurability between mediation, on the one hand, and the variety of alternative interventions adopted by local authority housing and environmental health officers, on the other hand, poses a major challenge for those engaged in comparative impact analysis. Another challenge is presented by the cross-sectoral nature of the comparisons involved, since mediation services are largely (though not exclusively) confined to the *voluntary* sector, whereas most other forms of intervention in the field of neighbour disputes involve *statutory* agencies operating in the public sector. Once again, there are considerable differences between these two sectors in terms of ethos, as well as the institutional and financial contexts in which they operate.

Value-for-money or cost-benefit analysis is a methodologically complex and often controversial form of evaluation research, though the main question it seeks to address is straightforward enough: do the benefits that accrue from a service or range of services justify the expenditure that is involved? Very often the question may be posed simply in respect of a particular service or programme, such as a given community mediation service, in which case the approach may be thought of as a rather specialised form of programme effectiveness analysis. However, it is also possible to adopt a much broader focus, for example, by posing the question whether an increase in funding for community mediation services in general might be justified by the benefits that could be expected from this additional expenditure. In practice, this would be likely to involve a detailed comparison of the relative costs and benefits associated with spending more money on mediation as opposed to more traditional ways of dealing with neighbour disputes. Where this is the case, the value-for-money evaluation would share many of the characteristics (and problems) that are associated with comparative impact analysis, as we saw above.

However, the application of cost-benefit analysis to activities in the statutory and voluntary sectors also raises additional difficulties, stemming from the fact that normally such activities do not produce any saleable output. Moreover, most of the benefits that may be produced are likely to be of a non-monetary kind,[8] and are therefore difficult to quantify, let alone compare across the different sectors. In the past, cost-benefit analysis has been heavily criticised for not paying sufficient regard to these non-monetary benefits, and for focusing too exclusively on the costs incurred by the producers (or funders) of a service without taking into account the benefits enjoyed by its

---

8   One of the few direct monetary benefits that mediation services might in principle be capable of delivering is a saving in the costs that might otherwise be incurred as a result of more formal methods of intervention (for example involving court action of various kinds). However, even these benefits are difficult to measure, since it is impossible to be sure whether mediation might have successfully resolved the problem at an earlier stage in the history of the dispute.

users or consumers. However, as we shall see, it should in principle be possible to adapt the methodology involved, to devise a broader form of 'value-for-money analysis' which is sensitive to issues of effectiveness, quality and consumer satisfaction, while treating the relative costs involved as just one factor in the equation.[9]

Compared with more traditional forms of cost-benefit analysis, this broader perspective relies on a more qualitative approach and does not set out to deliver a precise 'balance sheet' assessment. However, by identifying the range of criteria by which different programmes and processes may fairly be evaluated and compared, and by indicating how these findings can be related to the costs involved, such an approach may be more helpful (and intellectually honest) in formulating and sharpening up the policy issues that may have to be addressed – for example, when determining whether a given process or programme such as mediation in the field of neighbour disputes really does offer sufficient 'value for money' to justify the costs involved in funding it.

There are some additional problems that are likely to be encountered when attempting to conduct value-for-money comparisons involving mediation and alternative ways of dealing with neighbour disputes. Some of these problems also have to do with the above-mentioned fact that these different processes are mainly conducted in different sectors of the economy. The difficulty here is to establish a reasonably 'level playing field', to minimise any in-built cost advantage or disadvantage between the two sectors. This is a largely technical problem and is not insurmountable, at least in principle.[10]

One final difficulty relates to the acute sensitivity surrounding some of the financial information required in order to conduct a thorough value-for-money analysis. In the wake of the government's compulsory competitive tendering requirements, those local authority departments that have to put their services (including housing) out to tender, are, not surprisingly, increasingly viewing such data as highly commercially sensitive. Ironically, therefore, even some of the more reliable and comparable data recorded by housing departments is in practice very difficult to obtain, because of these understandable concerns about its confidentiality.

Given its highly strategic focus, it is not at all surprising that cost-benefit or value-for-money analysis should be strongly favoured by policy-makers and planners. As we shall see in the next section, however, mediators themselves are also becoming increasingly interested in this kind of evaluation as a means of demonstrating the value of the service they provide, and thereby strengthening the case for additional funding.

---

9   See also Schalock, *op cit*, pp 76ff for further discussion of the way cost-benefit techniques can be modified to meet these and other concerns.

10 See Dignan *et al*, *op cit*, Chapter 9 for a detailed account of the way this was done in relation to the Neighbour Dispute project.

THE HISTORY OF EVALUATION RESEARCH IN THE FIELD OF COMMUNITY MEDIATION

The evaluation of community and neighbour mediation is still in its infancy, though the pace of development has quickened considerably over the last few years, especially in the UK. Some of the earliest evaluations carried out in the field of community mediation[11] set out to examine the effectiveness of specific community mediation services. Richard Young's evaluation of Sandwell Mediation Service[12] in its early days is a good example of this type of programme effectiveness analysis. The study was based on a series of interviews with clients of the service, in which they were asked about their expectations, their degree of commitment towards the process as a method of resolving their dispute, and also their assessment of its effectiveness. No attempt was made to conduct any comparative impact assessment[13] involving other ways of dealing with neighbour disputes; nor was cost-effectiveness an issue. Examples of this type of evaluation can also be found in other jurisdictions from around the same period.[14]

One of the earliest examples of a comparative impact analysis was an American attempt[15] to compare the effectiveness of citizen dispute hearings in Florida with a sample of complainants whose complaint had not resulted in a hearing, and to analyse the impact of the citizen dispute settlement project on the local criminal justice system. In another early comparative impact study,[16]

---

11 At first most research attention was focused on the use of mediation in the criminal justice system. See, for example, Blagg, H, 'Reparation and justice for juveniles' (1985) 25 British Journal of Criminology 267–79; Smith, D, Blagg, H and Derricourt, N, 'Does mediation work in practice?' (1985) 32 Probation Journal 135; Davis, G, Boucherat, J and Watson, D, 'Reparation in the Service of Diversion: the subordination of a good idea' (1988) 27 Howard Journal of Criminal Justice 127–34 and Dignan, J, 'Repairing the Damage: Can Reparation be made to work in the Service of Diversion?' (1992) 32 British Journal of Criminology 453–72.

12 See Young, R, 'Neighbour Dispute Mediation: Theory and Practice' (1989) 8 Civil Justice Quarterly 319–28. See also the Evaluation Study on the work of Southwark Mediation Centre conducted by the Grubb Institute: Quine, C, Hutton, J and Reed, B, *Community Mediation of Disputes between Neighbours*, 1990, London: The Grubb Institute.

13 The following remarks are not intended to be critical of the approach adopted or the methods used. There is a clearly a place for tightly focused studies of this kind, particularly in the early days of an initiative, since feedback about the extent to which it is (or is not) achieving its objectives, can be invaluable in improving the service as it develops.

14 See, for example, Cameron, J, 'Community Mediation in New Zealand: A Pilot Project' (1988) Journal of Social Welfare Law 284–99. Although the focus was somewhat broader and more policy-oriented than Young's evaluation it, too, made no attempt to conduct a comparative impact or value-for-money analysis. Similar evaluations were pioneered in the USA a few years earlier. See, for example Cook, RF, Roehl, JA and Sheppard, DI, *Neighbourhood Justice Centres Field Test*, 1980, Washington DC: US Department of Justice.

15 See Conner, RF and Surette, R, 'Processing Citizens' Disputes Outside the Courts: A Quasi-Experimental Evaluation' (1980) 4 Evaluation Review 739–68.

16 See Davis, RC, 'Mediation: the Brooklyn Experiment', Chapter 8 in Tomasic, R and Feeley, MM (eds) *Neighbourhood Justice: Assessment of an Emerging Idea*, 1982, New York: Longman.

also carried out in the United States, the question posed was whether the level of satisfaction experienced by disputants whose conflict resulted in a felony case, was higher when the case was dealt with by mediation than when the case was dealt with in the normal way in the criminal courts. However, such studies are only marginally relevant in an English context since comparatively few interpersonal disputes get as far as the courts.[17]

Prior to the Neighbour Dispute project, there were no systematic attempts to undertake a comparative impact analysis of the way neighbour disputes were dealt with in the UK, though some very useful preparatory work had been undertaken by Karn et al,[18] who both set out the legal context and described the various administrative procedures and legal remedies available to local authority housing and environmental health officers when dealing with neighbour disputes. The process of mediation was also described, and its potential advantages spelt out. These alternative approaches to the problem of neighbour disputes were assessed in the light of information obtained mainly from interviews with tenants who had complained to their local authority, and from case studies involving nine social landlords, with reference also to other sources.

The position was very similar in relation to the third main type of evaluation based on value-for-money analysis. A number of cost-benefit evaluations had been conducted in the USA, but these had almost invariably sought to compare the cost of mediation with court costs.[19] Once again, there were no comparable studies in the UK prior to the Neighbour Dispute project, though Karn et al[20] did identify many of the factors that would need to be taken into account in such an analysis, and sketched out a very helpful method of assessing those costs. Apart from these highly tentative steps, the most thorough attempts to investigate the cost-effectiveness of mediation in the United Kingdom had been conducted in relation to family disputes, though here again the main aim was to compare the relative costs and effectiveness of different types of family conciliation schemes with

---

17 The difference between the two jurisdictions may be due in part to differences in the level of litigiousness, but another factor is the major differences in the structure and role of local government institutions.

18 Karn, V, Lickiss, R, Hughes, D and Crawley, J, *Neighbour Disputes: Responses by Social Landlords*, 1993, Coventry: Institute of Housing. See also Crawley, J, Neighbours, *Nuisance and Mediation*, 1994, Odsey, Herts: Conflict Management Plus, who conducted a study to establish whether there was an unmet need for a neighbour dispute mediation service in Hackney.

19 In one such study, an attempt was made to estimate the costs that the district court in Dorchester, Massachusetts would have incurred but for the mediation project, though no attempt was made to assess the comparative benefits of mediation and conventional court processing. See Felstiner, WLF and Williams, LA, 'Community Mediation in Dorchester, Massachusetts', Chapter 7 in Tomasic, R and Feeley, MM (eds) *Neighbourhood Justice: Assessment of an Emerging Idea*, 1982, New York: Longman.

20 See note 18 above, pp 71ff.

adjudication.[21] This is the background against which the Neighbour Dispute report came to be commissioned.

By 1993 MEDIATION UK, the umbrella organisation representing the great majority of community mediation services, was becoming increasingly uncomfortable at being unable to respond to requests from journalists, politicians and others for basic information about the numbers of cases handled by mediation services across the country, the process by which they were dealt with and the outcomes achieved. At the same time, MEDIATION UK was actively seeking additional funding for mediation, and had concluded that, in addition to this basic factual information, the case for increased resources could only be made on the basis of a rigorous value-for-money assessment. The Neighbour Dispute project was born out of these twin concerns, which also helped to shape the research specification itself, once joint funding for the project was obtained from the Lankelly Foundation[22] and the Department of the Environment.

AIMS AND APPROACH
OF THE NEIGHBOUR DISPUTE PROJECT

The first aim of the project was to compile a national database that would present basic information about the work of all affiliated community mediation services, in a format that would enable generalisations to be made about the overall process of mediation, and allow reliable comparisons to be drawn between the different mediation services. An auxiliary aim was to devise a standard data-collection system that would enable such information to be regularly updated. This part of the project was undertaken principally by means of a national postal survey of mediation services, followed by a consultation exercise, and was completed by November 1995.[23]

A reliable (and updatable) database of this kind is an essential prerequisite for undertaking the kind of comparative impact study or value-for-money analysis that might inform future policy decisions about the level of funding and other forms of support for community mediation. Indeed, the second main element of the research specification was to undertake the first British study to investigate the cost-effectiveness of mediation compared with

---

21 See Robinson, *Report of the Inter-Departmental Committee on Conciliation*, 1983, London: HMSO; Conciliation Project Unit, *Report to the Chancellor on the Costs and Effectiveness of Conciliation in England and Wales*, 1989, Newcastle: Conciliation Project Unit.

22 The Lankelly Foundation is a charitable organisation which supports other registered charities working in the field of social welfare.

23 This aspect of the survey was written up separately as an interim report and did not feature in the Neighbour Dispute report itself: Dignan, J and Sorsby, A (1995) 'Towards a National Database for Mediation Services', unpublished. Copies of the report may be obtained from MEDIATION UK, under the title *Community Mediation General Survey 1995*.

conventional methods of dealing with neighbour disputes. However, in terms of the classification described earlier (see pp 219–22 above), the project is perhaps best thought of as a combined comparative impact assessment and value-for-money analysis. It was certainly never intended to apply a strict cost-benefit approach in analysing the data, since there are so many non-monetary benefits to take into account that any attempt to arrive at a simple ratio of benefits to cost would almost certainly have been doomed to failure. The approach was based instead on a broader 'value-for-money' perspective, incorporating a much more qualitative analysis of the available data, and in which the emphasis was at least as much on the potential quality of the service provided[24] as its monetary cost.

This part of the project involved a national questionnaire survey of local authority housing and environmental service departments,[25] the aim of which was to provide an up-to-date overview of their work in relation to neighbour disputes, including their caseloads and responses, the costs involved[26] (including human and social costs as well as purely monetary costs) and to assess the potential scope for increasing the proportion of cases dealt with by mediation. In addition to the survey data, a small number of detailed case studies were undertaken, involving three contrasting mediation services and a similar number of housing departments,[27] together with one environmental service department. Here, the aim was to develop a method of identifying and reliably comparing the costs and outcomes associated with such different types of processes, operating in different sectors of the economy; and to apply this methodology to the data obtained, to enable comparisons to be made and conclusions drawn, about the effectiveness of mediation compared with alternative methods of handling neighbour disputes.

---

24 At least insofar as this could be measured without directly investigating the perceptions of those who make use of mediation and the alternative interventions available for dealing with neighbour disputes. Unfortunately this dimension lay beyond the scope and resources of this particular project, though it is hoped that a 'consumer satisfaction' survey will be conducted as part of a follow-up investigation.

25 Postal questionnaires were sent out to a roughly one-in-seven sample of local authorities, selected on the basis of two matched groups: first, those authorities which had access to a community mediation service; and a second group of broadly comparable councils (in terms of council type, population size, approximate geographical location and level of poll tax levied) which lacked access to such services. Slightly different versions of the questionnaire were sent to housing and environmental health service departments.

26 These include the costs incurred (principally by the disputants themselves) as a result of unresolved neighbour disputes, together with those incurred by social landlords when seeking to deal with them. See the Neighbour Dispute report, especially Chapters 5–7, for further details of this aspect of the study.

27 Because of the concerns referred to above (see p 222) over the sensitivity of the financial information we requested, it was not possible to adopt a research design involving 'twin' housing department and mediation services. Instead, the choice of housing department was constrained entirely by the willingness of individual departments to co-operate with the project in this way, and even where such co-operation was forthcoming, it was only provided (for obvious reasons) on the basis of absolute confidentiality.

The detailed methods and findings of the project have been written up elsewhere.[28] In the final report of the project, the emphasis was mainly on the comparative costs involved, and the potential scope for financial savings to be made, where mediation can be used instead of the generally much more expensive court-based approaches used for particularly intractable disputes. In the following section, the emphasis is more on the qualitative aspects of the findings, which are presented in terms of a comparative impact analysis. Here the aim is to consider some of the main differences between the two sets of processes that are potentially likely to affect the clients themselves, rather than concentrating on the agency perspective as in the final report. Both dimensions are important in undertaking a value-for-money assessment. However, before any final conclusions can be drawn, it will clearly be necessary to undertake a thorough 'consumer satisfaction survey' comparing the views of those who experience for themselves the different forms of intervention. In the final section some suggestions will be presented for a projected follow-up study that will seek to combine a client-focused comparative impact assessment with the kind of value-for-money analysis that has been developed in the course of the Neighbour Dispute project.

NEIGHBOUR DISPUTE STRATEGIES: TOWARDS AN EVALUATIVE FRAMEWORK

In comparing the impact of mediation and the various alternative legal and administrative procedures that are available to local authority housing and environmental health officers, the aim should be to identify and evaluate the main differences in the way neighbour disputes are likely to be dealt with, from the standpoint of the disputants themselves rather than the agencies involved. Although, as we have seen, it was not possible to undertake a direct assessment of disputants' views and perceptions as part of the Neighbour Dispute project, a number of inferences can nevertheless be drawn from the agency data we obtained, about the comparative impact likely to be associated with the different processes we examined. This differential impact potential[29] is assessed in the next section in terms of the following four sets of criteria:

- access to justice issues;
- quality of process issues;
- quality of outcome issues;
- value-for-money issues.

---

28 See the report of the Neighbour Dispute project referred to in footnote 1 above.

29 The inferences outlined below may be thought of as a checklist of potential differences between the alternative ways of handling neighbour disputes, which would need to be assessed in any follow-up consumer satisfaction survey.

The first three of these are largely client-centred, while the fourth is more agency-focused. As we shall see, any attempt to compare different approaches in terms of their effectiveness, needs to devise a workable method of combining appropriate and reliable cost-benefit measures with quantifiable measures relating to each of the three non-monetary criteria.

NEIGHBOUR DISPUTE STRATEGIES: FINDINGS OF A COMPARATIVE IMPACT ANALYSIS

Access to justice issues[30]

One of the most important issues to consider in any comparison between different sets of dispute settlement processes is their availability to those who might wish to have recourse to them. Accessibility is influenced by a number of considerations, the most important of which, normally, are the scope of any criteria for intervention on the part of the dispute settlement process; the existence of any thresholds or restrictions limiting the range of otherwise eligible disputes that might be accepted by the process; and the cost of intervention[31] (either to the parties or to the agencies involved).

An additional factor that until recently has limited the availability of mediation as a form of intervention has been the limited number and restricted distribution of community mediation services. The position is changing rapidly as a result of the dramatic expansion in the number of services over the last few years,[32] though there is still a considerable way to go before the optimum density is achieved of one service for each population centre of 50,000 – 100,000.[33] Although this represents a serious restriction on

---

30 Access to justice can be evaluated both subjectively, from the standpoint of the disputants themselves, and also objectively with reference to the existence of formal or operational criteria, that either facilitate or impede access to the particular dispute settlement process. Here we concentrate on these objective factors, though the perceptions of the disputants themselves will also need to be assessed before reaching any final conclusions.

31 None of the three agencies normally charges directly for the services they provide. As we shall see, however, the high costs of some of the more formal legal and administrative remedies associated with local authority housing and environmental service departments may limit the number of cases in which the agencies are prepared to invoke them. In addition, we are aware of at least one mediation service that operates an advisory charge for self-referral cases, at least where parties can afford to pay. However, this service is somewhat unusual (though not unique) in making use of paid mediators.

32 At the start of the Neighbour Dispute project in the spring of 1995, there were just 36 operational services in the UK and a further 11 still at the planning stage. By the end of the project, the total number of operational or incipient services had increased to 65 (MEDIATION UK (1996) 3 Mediation Digest 1) and since then it has risen to 97 (see Chapter 14 and Appendix 1).

33 MEDIATION UK, *Guide to Starting a Community Mediation Service*, 1993, updated 1996, Bristol: MEDIATION UK.

the availability of mediation in practice, it is of less relevance when considering the potential impact of mediation compared with other dispute settlement processes. Here a much more significant consideration is the existence and extent of any formal eligibility criteria that might be applied to aspiring users of the relevant services.

Access to dispute settlement processes may be subject to a variety of criteria, the most important of which are likely to relate to the category or status of the disputants, and the nature of the dispute. Here it is necessary to differentiate not only between mediation and the legal or administrative processes that are open to local authorities, but also between the different council departments with responsibilities relating to neighbour disputes, since the legal duties of housing and environmental health service departments are not the same.

The most restrictive of all the services with a role in resolving neighbour disputes[34] are local authority housing departments, since their willingness to intervene in a neighbour dispute is likely to be strongly influenced by the tenure of the parties to the dispute. Indeed, their involvement in neighbour disputes is likely to arise as a direct consequence of their responsibilities as social landlords,[35] which include the enforcement of tenancy conditions, such as those prohibiting various forms of nuisance affecting their neighbours. As landlords, they also have a direct stake in the successful resolution of neighbour disputes, since the cost of failure can be considerable for them.[36] However, they may be less willing to accept responsibility where the complainant is an owner-occupier. Similarly, housing departments may feel unable to become involved where tenants complain against neighbouring owner-occupiers. These 'grey areas'[37] are becoming ever more problematic as a result of the increasingly complex tenure mix in many former areas of social housing. Moreover, the proportion of the population that is eligible to seek intervention from council housing officers has diminished dramatically in recent years as a result of the Conservative government's 'Right to Buy' legislation.

Local authority environmental service departments do not discriminate between different categories of complainant and, in this sense at least, are much less restrictive than their housing department counterparts, since they

---

34 The police are also frequently called upon to deal with neighbour disputes, but apart from a brief mention in the Neighbour Dispute report, their involvement lay outside the scope of the study. See, however, Kemp, C, Norris, C and Fielding, NG, *Negotiating Nothing: Police Decision-making in Disputes*, 1992, Aldershot: Avebury.

35 A term which includes both local authority housing departments, and also Housing Associations, which perform a similar role in some parts of the country.

36 They include the cost of repairing damage to property, securing 'void' premises and loss of rental income in areas that are particularly affected by anti-social conduct on the part of neighbours. See Neighbour Dispute report, Chapter 6, for details.

37 As they were described by Aldbourne Associates, *Managing Neighbour Complaints in Social Housing: A Handbook for Practitioners*, 1993, Aldbourne: Aldbourne Associates.

have a statutory duty to investigate a wide range of neighbour nuisance complaints, including noise, which is the most frequent source of neighbour friction.[38] Although the responsibilities of environmental health officers cover a wide variety of other nuisances that might give rise to neighbour disputes,[39] not all neighbour nuisance complaints necessarily fall within their jurisdiction. Disputes over boundaries, for example, are excluded, as are many of those animated by prejudice or personal animosity, unless they are accompanied by behaviour that constitutes a statutory or common law nuisance.

Because of their independent status and lack of uniformity, it is more difficult to generalise about the formal eligibility criteria operated by community mediation services, though in general these appear to be much less restrictive than those associated with either of the statutory agencies we have just been considering.[40] Thus, unlike local authority housing departments, community mediation services do not exclude cases on the grounds of tenure; nor, unlike environmental service departments, do they confine themselves to cases amounting to a legal nuisance. Community mediation services would therefore seem to be much less restrictive than either of these other two agencies in terms of their eligibility criteria, which suggests that they are potentially capable of conferring access to a dispute settlement procedure on a much broader range of neighbour disputants.

As we have seen, the eligibility criteria that are applied by dispute settlement agencies delineate the types of conflict (or disputants) they cater for in principle. Beyond these 'formal criteria', however, there may be additional 'operational criteria' that determine which of the potentially eligible disputes are deemed appropriate for intervention by the agency concerned. For example, intervention by the agency may be limited to cases of a given level of seriousness. By adjusting the relevant 'thresholds for intervention', access to the dispute settlement process may be made more or less restrictive.

In the Neighbour Dispute project we found that both local authority housing and environmental service departments make relatively little use of their formal legal and administrative powers.[41] In the case of housing departments, their powers to arrange tenancy transfers, seek evictions or

---

38 For details, see the Neighbour Dispute report, Chapter 2, which was based on statistics compiled by the Chartered Institute of Environmental Health. These are published annually by the Department of the Environment in the Digest of Environmental Statistics.

39 These include the burning or dumping of rubbish, dog fouling and the conduct of any activity likely to cause injury to another's health.

40 The eligibility criteria applied by community mediation services when considering cases for acceptance are set out in the Neighbour Dispute report, Appendix 1. A minority of services (five of the 31 supplying information) exclude cases involving people with a history of violence; four exclude cases with court proceedings or legal action in process; three take mental health factors into account and two do not accept cases involving racial harassment. In some of the more recently established services, the criteria for acceptance are still under consideration.

41 See Chapters 3 and 9 of the Neighbour Dispute report for details. Some of the reasons why they may be reluctant to act are explained in Karn *et al*, *op cit*, footnote 18, pp 107ff.

enforce compliance with tenancy conditions by means of injunctions are used very sparingly, and tend to be reserved for cases involving only the most blatant breaches. A number of recent legislative changes have been introduced[42] in an attempt to strengthen the enforcement powers of social landlords, but the expense and legal uncertainties involved in pursuing these remedies will almost certainly continue to limit their availability.

Similarly, environmental health officers appear reluctant to invoke their ostensibly wide powers to require those responsible to abate an alleged nuisance, seize equipment or bring criminal proceedings in all but the most blatant of cases. In practice, therefore, access to the kind of justice that is administered by formal court proceedings (or even the threat of such proceedings) is restricted to a tiny minority of neighbour disputants who can satisfy the extremely stringent 'seriousness threshold' that is usually applied. The need for such a threshold is based partly on the legal requirements that have to be satisfied in order to obtain a remedy successfully, and partly on the expense that is involved.

Most mediation services do not operate a threshold based on the seriousness of the dispute,[43] so the access they offer to their dispute settlement process is potentially far less restrictive than in the case of the two statutory agencies just considered. Access is not totally unrestricted, since a majority of services will only accept cases on referral where at least one (and often both) parties are willing to participate in the process of mediation. But as mediation is most unlikely to succeed unless parties are prepared to work at reaching a settlement, rather than having one imposed on them, this stipulation is at least a functional restriction. As mediation becomes better known, it is possible that services will find it difficult to meet the increased demand, in which case they, too, might feel the need to 'ration' access to the service. However, although we came across one or two services which felt it necessary to operate a 'waiting list' in order to cope with demand, this does not at present appear to pose a major restriction on the availability of mediation.

The difference between these three sets of agencies in terms of the extent to which they afford access to their dispute settlement processes, is also reflected in their respective 'intervention rates' and the nature of any intervention made. In the case of environmental health services, for example, the national survey undertaken as part of the Neighbour Dispute project revealed that formal legal powers[44] were invoked in just over 5% of cases dealt with, while

---

42 See the Neighbour Dispute report pp 17ff for details, including consideration of the remaining limitations that are likely to restrict their effectiveness.

43 As we have seen, a minority of services may refuse to take on certain cases on the grounds that they are *too* serious, either because they involve violent individuals, racial conflict or a power imbalance between the parties, or because the case is already the subject of legal proceedings.

44 Abatement notices were served in just 5.7% of cases, while prosecutions for non-compliance were launched in less than 1% of cases.

fewer than 2% of cases were referred to mediation. The most frequent course of action[45] was to send an advisory letter to the complainant (often containing diary sheets). In many cases this was the only response. (In one environmental health department we examined, 87% of all complaints went no further than the sending of an advisory letter; though this may have been exceptional.) For the rest, complainants were visited in just 56% of cases, and those whose behaviour was the subject of a complaint were visited in 48% of cases. Warning letters were sent in 41% of cases.

In the case of housing departments, fewer than 10% of cases resulted in 'formal' legal action, and in about 3% of cases the matter was dealt with by transferring one of the disputants. Here there did appear to be a greater willingness to refer neighbour dispute cases for mediation (15% of cases); and the proportion of cases involving visits to one or both parties was also somewhat higher.[46] But once again the tendency was for the matter to be dealt with informally rather than through the exercise of formal legal or administrative remedies.

As far as community mediation services are concerned, among the established services (those which had been in operation for two years or more), the proportion of referred cases accepted for an attempt at mediation was over 75%.[47] Just over one quarter (27%) of these were dealt with by bringing both parties together in a face-to-face meeting (direct mediation); 40% involved a process of indirect negotiation or shuttle diplomacy, in which the mediators acted as go-betweens; and 27% involved work with one party only.

Perhaps we can summarise the position by saying that for housing and environmental health departments, the tendency is for them to deal with a comparatively *high volume* of cases, but in the great majority of these their input will be relatively limited. Whereas for community mediation services, their throughput at present is comparatively small, but both the acceptance rate and the amount of effort that is expended in seeking a resolution of the dispute are relatively high. This was borne out by the Neighbour Dispute project, which calculated that the average time expended per neighbour dispute case by two of the case study community mediation services was 8.8 hours and 10.4 hours respectively, whereas the average time spent on such cases by housing officers over a 12-month period, in one of the case study areas investigated, was only 1.75 hours.[48]

---

45 Over two-thirds of complaints (69%) elicited this response.
46 Complainants were visited in 42% of cases, and the person whose behaviour was the subject of a complaint was visited in 59% of cases.
47 Neighbour Dispute report, p 25.
48 Neighbour Dispute report, pp 45 and 76.

Access to mediation in areas served by a community mediation service, as we have seen, is much less restricted than access to the formal legal (or administrative) remedies associated with housing and environmental health officers. Not all neighbour disputes are amenable to mediation, of course, particularly where one of the parties refuses to participate, attitudes have become too entrenched, there is a gross power imbalance between the parties, or there is a need for either a declaratory legal ruling or the power of enforcement that accompanies a legal sanction. However, such cases are probably relatively infrequent in the field of neighbour disputes. In most other cases, those seeking assistance in resolving a neighbour dispute are more likely to receive it from community mediation services than from hard-pressed housing or environmental health officers, for whom the settlement of disputes is not normally their paramount concern. However, the nature and degree of any intervention is likely to depend considerably on the attitudes of the other party involved in the dispute, as we shall see in the next section.

Quality of process issues

Dispute settlement processes differ not only in terms of the level of 'access to justice' for those seeking help with a dispute, but also in relation to the quality of service they provide. Quality in relation to process issues can be evaluated both subjectively (for example, in terms of the perceived fairness of the dispute settlement procedures and the extent to which they meet the aspirations of the disputants) and also objectively.[49] In this section I will concentrate on the following sets of issues:

- functionality of dispute settlement procedure;
- presence or absence of appropriate procedural safeguards for the disputants;
- degree of empowerment associated with the dispute settlement process.

The functionality of dispute settlement procedures needs to be assessed in relation to the different purposes they might be expected to serve.[50] The most important of these are the resolution of current conflict, the prevention of future friction and the protection of legitimate interests. The different agencies

---

49 As we have seen, the remit of the Neighbour Dispute project did not extend to the conduct of a consumer survey, so the present evaluation is confined to more objective measures of quality.

50 The purposes identified here relate to two essential functions of law identified by the American jurist Karl Llewellyn as part of his 'law jobs' theory. The first of these is dispute settlement, which might involve attempts to reduce friction between parties (for example by negotiating a compromise settlement) or an authoritative pronouncement in favour of one party or the other (for example by an adjudicator or arbitrator). The second consists of preventive channelling whereby behaviour or expectations are adjusted to reduce the risk of future conflict. See Llewellyn, K, 'The Normative, the Legal, and the Law Jobs: the Problem of Juristic Method' (1940) 49 Yale Law Journal 1355.

called on to deal with neighbour disputes differ considerably in their aims and objectives, the approaches and methods they adopt and, consequently, in their effectiveness in dealing with different kinds of disputes.

In the case of local authority environmental health officers, their primary aim is *not* to resolve conflict between neighbours but to enforce the law relating to statutory nuisance. By discharging their legal duty to investigate breaches of the statutory nuisance controls and to secure compliance with the existing legislation, they may help to protect the legitimate interests of those who are affected by the nuisance; for example, by securing a pronouncement that the behaviour complained of is unacceptable. It is also possible (though by no means certain)[51] that the application of sanctions will moderate the offending party's behaviour in the future. However, such measures are highly unlikely to reduce the friction between the disputing parties (since this is not their primary intention) and could even make it worse in some instances.

As far as local authority housing officers are concerned, their legal responsibilities in relation to neighbour disputes are somewhat less clearly defined. They have the power to take various forms of legal action[52] in order to secure compliance with (or deal with breaches of) tenancy agreements or restrictive covenants, if they choose to exercise these. They also have an interest, as landlords, in ensuring that relations between tenants don't deteriorate too drastically, since they may themselves stand to lose out where this does happen.[53] However, these measures are expensive to pursue, involve difficult evidential issues[54] (including a reluctance on the part of some complainants to be witnesses, for fear of retaliation), and tend to be unpredictable in outcome because of the very high levels of proof involved. Moreover, the enforcement of tenancy obligations on behalf of other tenants is only one, relatively minor, aspect of the landlord's role; and has to be balanced against a variety of other considerations including their duty to house increasing numbers of vulnerable people. These include not only some of the poorest and most deprived households – elderly people, ethnic minority families, single parents with small children, homeless people and those discharged from institutions into local authority care under the government's 'Care in the Community' policies – but also some of those whose behaviour is most likely to give offence to others.

---

51 In the course of the Neighbour Dispute study, we came across a number of cases where recourse to legal sanctions failed to moderate the offending behaviour. They included the only two prosecutions for noise nuisance, pursued by one particular (very large) environmental health department in the course of a year. See Neighbour Dispute report, pp 73ff.

52 Including applications for injunctions or possession proceedings.

53 See footnote 36 above, and also Neighbour Dispute report, Chapter 6, for further details.

54 In spite of recent attempts to strengthen the position of social landlords, for example under the Housing Act 1996. See Neighbour Dispute report, Chapter 3, for details.

Social landlords also have the option of arranging the transfer of one of the parties to a dispute. In view of the problems involved with an eviction, this is most likely to happen as a result of an application, normally by the complainant. However, this option is not without its own costs[55] for social landlords, in addition to which their room for manoeuvre is becoming increasingly restricted as a result of the 'Right to Buy' legislation and the considerably increased tenure mix that has resulted from this. While they do have an interest in preventing or reducing friction between tenants, therefore, the settlement of disputes between their tenants is understandably not a primary aim for the majority of social landlords, even if they had the resources and skills to undertake this role.

Of the agencies we have been considering, only community mediation services have as their primary aim the settlement of disputes between neighbours. For them alone it is their core function. Moreover it is a service they provide irrespective of whether a party's behaviour might constitute a statutory nuisance or a serious breach of their tenancy obligations. As we shall see, this marked contrast between the basic aims associated with mediation, and those associated with more formal conventional processes, is also reflected in the way the different agencies approach the problem of neighbour disputes and the methods they use.

Both housing and environmental health officers have a range of legal measures they can call upon, when dealing with neighbour nuisance complaints, and the current tendency is for these to be strengthened in various ways. However, these are mainly fault-based remedies, in the sense that they generally require one of the parties to have acted extremely unreasonably before any formal enforcement action will be taken. This necessarily involves a high standard of proof, especially since many of these sanctions, such as eviction, have extremely drastic consequences. They are also expensive and success is by no means guaranteed. Consequently they are rarely used.

Nevertheless, the need for hard evidence before invoking the various legal powers that exist calls for a much more judgmental approach on the part of housing and environmental health officers, which in turn encourages all concerned to adopt a quasi-legalistic approach to the problem, even though the vast majority of neighbour disputes are never aired in court. Disputants may initially have unrealistic expectations about the extent of housing and environmental health officers' powers and their willingness to invoke them, while officials may unwittingly encourage the adoption of a more adversarial approach by issuing complainants with diary sheets at an early stage in the dispute, as a means of obtaining and assessing the evidence that might later be required to justify the use of these powers.

---

55   See Neighbour Dispute report, pp 18 and 57ff.

The need for procedural safeguards to be observed, and for officials to err on the side of caution, is understandable in view of the drastic consequences when legal sanctions are invoked. However, this legalistic approach is unlikely to be conducive to the reduction and resolution of conflict between neighbours. In cases that do not warrant formal intervention, officials may feel powerless to act. This means that the council may find itself receiving complaints, because it is not perceived to be taking effective action to deal with grievances.[56]

One of the main differences between mediation and the kind of interventions associated with most housing and environmental health officers, is that mediation seeks to be non-judgmental in its approach. This is symbolised in its rejection of the terms 'complainant' and 'perpetrator'; which is partly an acknowledgment that there are two sides to most disputes, but also reflects a recognition that even where one party appears to be acting totally unreasonably, this may often be symptomatic of more fundamental problems that may need to be addressed if harmony is to be restored. Mediation is based on a constructive, problem-solving approach to conflict, in which one of the main skills is to identify obstacles to successful negotiation and to help the disputants overcome them.[57] While such an approach will not always be successful, it does offer a potentially more constructive method of controlling or reducing friction than the adversarial methods associated with more conventional approaches.

Another important difference between mediation and more adversarial approaches to dispute settlement, as we have seen, is that the latter appear to be much more concerned about the need to observe procedural safeguards, based on the idea of 'due process' and the requirements of natural justice. Indeed, this is one of the reasons for the reluctance of housing and environmental health officers to initiate formal legal proceedings, unless the behaviour in question is in clear breach of the applicable rules, and there is sufficient compelling evidence to prove this in court. Some lawyers may feel uncomfortable with the apparent lack of procedural formalities surrounding the process of mediation, since one of its main aims is to facilitate communication between the parties without being too circumscribed by the formal legal issues involved. In fact mediators do also apply some basic

---

56 We came across a number of examples, when conducting our case studies for the Neighbour Dispute project, of complaints being made to senior departmental officers, and ultimately to the local government ombudsman, alleging maladministration on the part of the council, in handling a complaint that was originally directed against another neighbour.

57 See Acland, AF, *Resolving Disputes Without Going to Court: A consumer guide to Alternative Dispute Resolution*, 1995, London: Century Business Books, Chapter 4; and Karn, V *et al*, *Neighbour Disputes: Responses by Social Landlords*, 1993, Coventry: Institute of Housing, Chapter 5.

ground rules[58] to ensure that both parties are able to present their case, while keeping the confrontation within acceptable limits. However, the need for formal procedural safeguards is arguably much less pressing in the absence of coercive sanctions of the kind associated with formal legal processes.[59]

Finally, mediation is also distinctive in seeking to vest control over, and responsibility for, the dispute and its settlement firmly in the hands of the parties themselves rather than professional experts. Not only is the job of the mediator to help parties come to their own decisions and negotiate their own agreements but, in contrast with most other dispute settlement processes, mediation does not require the parties to a dispute to couch their problems within a particular conceptual or linguistic framework; nor are they required to focus only on selected aspects of the conflict to the exclusion of others, as is often the case in a court of law.

Once again, therefore, mediation appears to offer several advantages in terms of the quality of the dispute settlement process, with regard both to its functionality in actually attending to the causes of the conflict, and also in terms of the degree of empowerment it appears to confer on the disputants. The one ground on which it appears to compare less favourably with more formal dispute settlement processes relates to its more relaxed attitude towards procedural safeguards. It might be argued that such safeguards are less necessary, in the absence of coercive sanctions or a pronounced imbalance of power between the parties. However, a final verdict on this issue will have to be deferred until we have more reliable data from those who have direct experience of the different approaches.

Indeed, we need to be clear that so far we have been comparing the potential differences between mediation and more conventional approaches to the problem of neighbour disputes, based solely on the data that is compiled by the agencies concerned. It remains to be seen whether the potential advantage in favour of mediation which we have identified is sustained after conducting a rigorous consumer satisfaction survey. Moreover, the need for such a survey is even greater when comparing the different processes in terms of their outcomes.

Quality of outcome issues

One of the most difficult and sensitive issues that needs to be addressed in any comparative impact analysis concerns the way outcomes are assessed. The difficulties relate both to the measures that are used to evaluate particular

---

58 See the MEDIATION UK *Training Manual in Community Mediation Skills*, available from MEDIATION UK. See also Chapter 3 in this book, p 50.

59 And assuming approximate parity between the disputants; also that neither side poses a threat to the other's basic rights, such as the right to personal safety.

outcomes, and also to the availability and reliability of the data needed to make any assessment. Once again, the fact that the agencies responsible for dealing with neighbour disputes differ so profoundly in terms of their aims, approach and methods (including their record-keeping practices) poses a major challenge for anyone seeking to devise a suitable basis on which to compare outcomes. Nevertheless, it should in principle be possible to overcome both sets of difficulties by undertaking a follow-up study which adopts a client-centred approach to complement the agency-centred approach used in the original Neighbour Dispute project.

We have already established that neighbour disputes can have a variety of adverse consequences for those involved, and have illustrated some of the human and financial costs.[60] However, because we were unable to elicit the views of disputants themselves, we were unable to quantify these costs. And because we were restricted to outcome records provided by the agencies themselves, which are compiled for very different purposes, it was only possible to make the most tentative comparisons between the outcomes achieved by the two sets of agencies.[61]

The most straightforward way of comparing different dispute-settlement processes in terms of their outcomes in any follow-up study, would be to investigate the extent to which they are capable of improving the 'quality of life' for a representative sample of those seeking assistance from each of the agencies concerned. In trying to measure such improvements, it would be important to concentrate on changes that could be attributed to the dispute settlement process itself. If successful, this might be expected to secure one or more of the following types of outcome:

- an end to the source of antagonism between the parties;
- an improvement in relations between the protagonists;
- an enhancement in the 'coping skills' of one or more of the parties.

Most disputes involve behaviour that is felt to be unacceptable, and very often there will be mutual recriminations. The termination or moderation of behaviour which causes offence is thus one possible measure of success. Sometimes this might result from an explicit agreement between the parties, and many mediation services view such agreements as an important indicator of success. However, the crucial issue that needs to be addressed is whether the parties themselves are satisfied that the source of antagonism has ended, or at least has moderated either in frequency or intensity; though it would also be important to establish that any improvement in outcome is attributable to

---

60 See Neighbour Dispute report, Chapter 5, for details.
61 See Neighbour Dispute report, especially Figures 4.7 and 9.1, and accompanying discussion, for details.

the dispute settlement process itself.[62] Moreover, some forms of intervention (for example tenancy transfers) may provide relief for the original complainant, but unless the issues giving rise to the complaint are addressed, there is a danger that the problem will resurface with a new set of neighbours.

A second possible measure of success has to do with the state of relations between the parties, and the extent to which these are felt to have improved, irrespective of any behavioural changes that might have taken place. If relations have improved, this could range from a willingness to engage in (or resume) dialogue over the dispute, at one end of the spectrum, to full reconciliation at the other.

A third possible measure of success relates to possible improvements in the abilities of parties to cope with the conflict or their neighbours, as a result of any assistance they receive. Again, it is possible to imagine a continuum of improvements, ranging from increased levels of tolerance towards anti-social behaviour, at one end of the spectrum, to the development of conflict resolution skills that might help prevent future disputes from arising, at the other. Indeed, while collecting data for the Neighbour Dispute study, we came across a case in which a community mediation service client decided to become a volunteer mediator herself, as a direct result of her experience.[63]

The measures outlined above have been deliberately defined in very broad terms, since they will need to be equally applicable to the different outcomes associated with the different neighbour dispute-settlement techniques likely to feature in a comparative impact study. Another important dimension that needs to be addressed, in relation to each of the above measures, concerns the durability of any improvements. Moreover, in evaluating the different ways of dealing with neighbour disputes, it might also be important to take into account a variety of other considerations, including the duration and intensity of a dispute, and also the attitudes and expectations of the parties concerned, since these are all factors which could influence the success of any outcome. Finally, although it is extremely difficult to make generalisations about the costs and benefits associated with neighbour disputes, the above measures should make it possible to quantify the extent of any improvements brought about as a result of different dispute settlement approaches. This is particularly important if, as is hoped, the next phase of research makes it

---

62 In the Neighbour Dispute survey, we came across an apparently successful intervention by one of our case study housing departments, which involved the issuing of a Notice of Intent to Seek Possession. However, notes in the file made it clear that the apparent improvement in a tenant's behaviour was the result of arrest and detention on unrelated charges, and not the action taken by the council.

63 This example suggests another possible measure of success, which concerns the extent to which different dispute settlement processes might contribute to enhanced levels of community integration. Indeed, some programme effectiveness studies (see p 223 above) have specifically included this aim among the objectives they have evaluated; see Cameron, footnote 14 above.

possible to combine a client-centred comparative impact analysis with a value-for-money assessment.

Value-for-money issues

The Neighbour Dispute survey demonstrated first that, in spite of the methodological and practical problems involved, it is possible to devise a reasonably fair and reliable method[64] for comparing the costs of mediation with at least the direct costs that are likely to be associated with more conventional ways of dealing with neighbour disputes; and second that it is possible to use this approach to make comparisons on both a 'global' and also a 'unit cost' basis. The approach is based on an assessment of the 'resource costs' that are involved, and enables comparisons to be made both in terms of the amount of effort expended by a given agency in relation to a given dispute or set of disputes; and also (in principle) in terms of the quality of outcome. As we have seen, however, it was only possible to draw limited inferences from the initial study in relation to the latter aspect, in the absence of any opportunity to speak directly with disputants who might have had experience of the different approaches.

Assuming that it is possible to devise appropriate measures of outcome effectiveness along the lines suggested above, it should then be possible to calculate the unit costs involved in respect of the different dispute settlement techniques, which would then enable dependable judgments to be made concerning the value for money they offer. In particular, it should enable conclusions to be reached about which approach provides the most effective (and durable) outcomes for a given level of cost and, conversely, what the minimum cost might be in order to achieve a given level of effectiveness. It should also be possible to compare the level of satisfaction recorded by disputants with regard to the dispute settlement process itself (as opposed to the outcome) as part of the overall 'value-for-money' assessment. It would be difficult to exaggerate the importance of this next phase of the evaluation process. For without such comparisons, it is almost impossible to say whether the relatively intensive (and therefore comparatively costly) process of mediation really does provide better value for money than the relatively high volume, low intensity, informal interventions that are most frequently employed by local authority housing and environmental health officers; or indeed with the even more expensive formal legal remedies that tend only to be invoked as a last resort.

---

64   See Neighbour Dispute report, especially Chapters 1 and 9, for details.

CONCLUSION

Evaluation research is a continuous process. In this chapter we have examined the different kinds of evaluation research, and have noted the progress that has been made, and also the work that is still outstanding, in the field of community mediation.

Evaluation research is never straightforward and, particularly in relation to comparative impact studies and value-for-money analyses, it involves numerous methodological and practical challenges. Nevertheless, many of these have now been overcome, and the next major questions that have to be addressed concern the quality of the mediation process and its outcomes, in the eyes of those who have experienced it. Once again the comparative dimension is crucial. Based on the findings of the Neighbour Dispute study, mediation appears to offer a number of potential advantages compared with alternative approaches: particularly extending access to justice, and also the quality of both process and outcome. However, the acid test is whether these potential advantages are achieved in practice, and it would be impossible to draw firm conclusions, in the absence of a rigorously conducted comparative impact study, involving disputants with experience of all the main dispute settlement approaches.

In addition, the value-for-money issue is likely to be of equal importance, particularly in the eyes of policy makers and potential funders. They may need to be convinced not only that mediation can be more effective than alternative ways of dealing with the problem of neighbour disputes, but also that it represents a more cost-effective way of deploying scarce resources. This question can only be addressed by attempting to combine a comparative impact study with appropriate forms of cost-benefit techniques.

Finally, evaluation research will not automatically elicit a change in policies or even a change of attitudes towards community mediation; still less will it automatically unlock resources, however favourable its findings might be. Nevertheless, evaluation research may still perform a valuable role in questioning traditional assumptions about whether established approaches to the problem of neighbour disputes are performing satisfactorily; and, in that sense, it may contribute to a perception that appropriate changes might be desirable. Moreover, it should also provide a much more informed basis on which arguments for and against change can then be joined. In short, evaluation research has much to offer in the field of community and neighbour mediation, both internally as a technique for assessing and improving performance, and also externally in the continuing quest for recognition and support.

CHAPTER THIRTEEN

THEORY AND ETHICS
IN COMMUNITY MEDIATION

Gavin R Beckett

INTRODUCTION

For most people, including many mediators, theory is a word that very quickly stops them from reading on. If you are one of these people, it is important that you read this chapter. I want to put across a view of theory as something that must concern us all. My concern here is to argue that we cannot divide theory and practice as simply as people often do. I will use the word theory to mean the mass of values, assumptions, beliefs and systematic arguments about the social world and politics that all of us hold, more or less consciously, and more or less coherently. These thoughts and ways of thinking guide us in our everyday lives in an implicit way. They are not some kind of rulebook that we consult for every action. But they do give us frameworks to interpret the world, and help us decide what is possible and desirable to do. We are moral creatures and we are reasoning creatures, and in almost everything that we choose to do or not do, we base our actions on our personal social, political and ethical theories. And these theories are also affected by the way that we live our lives; we incorporate this into our theories, justified and explained after the fact.

If you accept this view of the relationship between theory and practice, I hope it is also reasonable to conclude that to ignore theory in favour of an exclusive focus on practice – techniques and skills – is to shut off some very important questions about why we do what we do; and whether what we do – mediation – actually gets results that fit in with our ethics and theories. By ethics, I mean those ways of thinking and acting that are directly linked to the consideration of the question 'What *should* one do?' We are thinking and acting ethically whenever we get into situations involving judgments about what ought to happen, and what ought to be. As mediators, we are constantly concerned with what should be done in relation to conflicts. In this chapter I will make explicit some of the values, assumptions and beliefs held by mediators about people, mediation, society, and what *should* be done with conflicts. I am doing this from the dual position of an academic peace researcher, and a community mediator/trainer. I have a great deal of respect for people from both communities, and have experienced the broader perspective open to those people who combine the two fields.

In this chapter I will look at a number of different theoretical debates relevant to community mediation. I begin with two sections that consider recent work by US academics, who are supportive of mediation as a process, but critical of some of the developments. First I discuss Bush and Folger's work, which surveys the different perspectives on mediation in the USA, and the values and assumptions that lie behind them. Second, I look at Scimecca's critique of the Alternative Dispute Resolution movement in the USA, focusing on the lack of theory in the field. I draw links between the conclusions of these authors and the situation of community mediation in the UK, arguing that we too must take heed of the dangers pointed out by them. Finally, I refer back to Chapter 7 on Dispute Analysis, and discuss the implications for developing theory about community mediation. I argue that we must see mediation as one possibility in a range of different interventions, that is used when the circumstances of the conflict make it appropriate, and in such a way that it supports and is supported by other interventions used before, during and after it.

WHAT SHOULD MEDIATION BE?

Mediation in the UK began with considerable influences from the USA, amongst other places, but it has developed in a different way and is still far less institutionalised.[1] Bush and Folger have recently argued that mediation in the USA has become dominated by an outcome-based perspective, in which the production of a mutually-agreed settlement between the parties is the most important aspect of the process.[2] They express their concern that mediation's potential for transforming the individual and social relations is often lost. They outline four different perspectives, based on different ethical standpoints and different ways of describing the US situation. In my experience, these perspectives have also been central to the UK mediation movement, although the boundaries between them are less clear-cut. Bush and Folger call these perspectives 'stories', meaning constructed views of the world, involving assumptions about reality and ethics. They are alternatives to one another, but none of them is 'true' in any ultimate, once-and-for-all sense.

Bush and Folger identify four different stories: the 'satisfaction story', the 'social justice story', the 'oppression story' and the 'transformation story'.

The 'satisfaction story' sees mediation as a tool for satisfying human needs. The strategies and techniques of the mediators are all designed and used to maximise the possibility of a creative, win-win outcome to the dispute.

---

1   For more details, see Chapter 2.
2   Bush, RAB and Folger, JP, *The Promise of Mediation. Responding to Conflict Through Empowerment and Recognition*, 1994, San Francisco: Jossey-Bass.

The 'social justice story' sees mediation more as a tool for building communities, enabling individuals to organise together against social injustices. Neighbours are helped to see that they have common interests and mutual, external enemies.

The 'transformation story' sees mediation as a tool in the transformation of individuals and society, providing the former with opportunities to take control of their lives and recognise the other as important. Neighbours are enabled to become more powerful and at the same time to extend their understanding of each other.

The 'oppression story' is a critical view of mediation as a tool for the strong to use against the weak, because it has inadequate checks on power imbalances and mediator bias. It also criticises mediation for dealing with cases as isolated instances of conflict, thus diffusing the potential impetus for change that mass disaffection and conflict may create.[3]

The ethos of mediation in the UK has incorporated elements from both 'satisfaction' and 'transformation' stories, and arguably also the 'social justice/oppression' stories too. Chapter 2 describes the development of these different strands of the movement here, and Chapter 4 also touches upon it. The dominant 'satisfaction story' has certainly influenced mediation in the UK. I would say that part of Bush and Folger's description could be applied directly.

> The mediation process is a powerful tool for satisfying the genuine human needs of parties to individual disputes. Because of its flexibility, informality, and consensuality, mediation can open up the full dimensions of the problem facing the parties. Not limited by legal categories or rules, it can help reframe a contentious dispute as a mutual problem. Also because of mediators' skills in dealing with power imbalances, mediation can reduce strategic maneuvering and overreaching. As a result of these different features, mediation can facilitate collaborative, integrative problem solving rather than adversarial, distributive bargaining. It can thereby produce creative, win-win outcomes that reach beyond formal rights to solve problems and satisfy parties' genuine needs in a particular situation.[4]

Certainly parts of this story have come to the fore in the UK, in the focus on money-saving aspects of mediation, in the attempt to secure its long-term financial future (see discussion in Chapter 12). Yet mediation in the UK has also contained central elements of the 'transformation story' in equal measures.

> Because of its informality and consensuality, mediation can allow parties to define problems and goals in their own terms, thus validating the importance of those problems and goals in the parties' lives. Further, mediation can

---

3   *Ibid*, pp 16–24 for full descriptions of the four stories.
4   *Ibid*, p 16.

support the parties' exercise of self-determination in deciding how, or even whether, to settle a dispute, and it can help the parties mobilise their own resources to address problems and achieve their goals ... Participants in mediation have gained a greater sense of self-respect, self-reliance, and self-confidence. This has been called the *empowerment* dimension of the mediation process. In addition, the private, non-judgmental character of mediation can provide disputants a non-threatening opportunity to explain and humanise themselves to one another ... Parties often discover that they can feel and express some degree of understanding and concern for one another despite their disagreement ... Mediation has thus engendered, even between parties who start out as fierce adversaries, acknowledgment and concern for each other as fellow human beings. This has been called the *recognition* dimension of the mediation process.[5]

Transformative elements can be seen in UK mediation at points where current practice diverges from the model originally taken from US mediation. Over time UK mediation services have developed the practice of mediation beyond the face-to-face mediation session where all parties meet together in a room. UK mediation services have come to see mediation as the entire process, from first contact with the first party, through to any face-to-face meeting with both sides. This places considerable importance on the early stages of the process, where important conflict resolution work may be done with either party on their own, regardless of whether the process results in a meeting or an agreement. Furthermore, many mediation services offer one-party conflict resolution work in cases where the second party refuses to become involved. Both of these practices suggest that the mediation services are more interested in the potential for transforming individuals and their relationships than with producing a settlement. This may be attributable to the historic tendency for mediators in the UK to be people who are concerned with interpersonal relations, social change and progressive activism. Many mediation services began from Quaker roots, and many others also involved in the peace movement and non-violent direct action have been influential in them.

With the institutionalisation of the field and the concomitant need for funding, we may see the growth of a 'satisfaction-oriented' approach to mediation. Chapter 4 discusses the differences between services focused on dealing with cases as effectively as possible and those concerned with community development and empowerment, and this dichotomy has obvious echoes of the 'satisfaction' versus 'transformation' situation. We in the UK should take heed of Bush and Folger's cautions about the satisfaction story. Their description of the increased acceptance of the right of the mediator to judge what 'the best solution' is, and to intervene directively in the framing of the issues and the choice of which ones to discuss, should ring alarm bells for mediators in the UK. I will look at the idea of mediator neutrality in more

5   *Ibid.*

detail later in the chapter, but for now I want to flag up the danger that such directive interventions are more likely to produce solutions that parties accept without feeling satisfied than ones that truly meet their needs.[6]

CRITICISMS OF MEDIATION

Joseph Scimecca, professor of sociology at George Mason University and a long-standing analyst of conflict and conflict resolution, accuses Alternative Dispute Resolution (ADR) in the USA of lacking a theoretical grounding, thus leaving itself open to charges of being a tool for social control.[7] As with Bush and Folger's reflections, I want to look at these criticisms in relation to community mediation in the UK.

Scimecca summarises six criticisms of ADR in America:

1   ADR is not based on a broad theoretical concept of conflict. Instead it relies on the experience of individual practitioners and sets of processes that are thought to work well.

2   ADR works from a philosophy of individualism. The idea of individual responsibility for conflicts, and the assumption that rational individuals can solve their own conflicts, both hide the way that structured inequalities play a part in causing conflict. The social structure of the society is seldom questioned.

3   The role of the third party in ADR, helping to conduct discussions and facilitate communication, trades on the underlying assumption that the parties involved know how to solve their dispute and only need a framework for this insight to come out. However, clear communication will not help where people simply hold opposing beliefs and views on how things should be.

4   Third parties in ADR have emphasised their neutrality. This neutrality, in situations that are frequently power-laden and unequal, simply enables the status quo to be reproduced.

5   ADR has moved away from its original concern for those with an unequal access to justice, and is now concerned with organisational expansion and the creation of new jobs for new professionals.

6   Linked to the last point, ADR has developed into a new profession, and in doing so, has failed to maintain any organic link to the community it serves. Its original goal of offering communities justice and ways of

---

6   *Ibid*, pp 68–75.

7   Scimecca, JA, 'Theory and Alternative Dispute Resolution: A Contradiction in Terms' in Sandole, DJD and Van Der Merwe, H (eds) *Conflict Resolution Theory and Practice. Integration and Application*, 1993, Manchester: Manchester University Press, pp 211–21.

dealing with conflicts, through the work of trained people from within those communities, has been left behind.[8]

I will now look at each of these criticisms in detail, and see how far it applies to community mediation in the UK.

Mediation is not based on an explicit theory of conflict

I want to begin by looking at why we choose mediation as a method of dealing with conflicts. Even if Scimecca is right that mediators do not work from explicit theories of conflict and conflict resolution, I think most mediators have their own social theories about the causes of conflict and how it can be dealt with. These theories are constructed from our general beliefs about the world, the basic introduction to conflict usually included in mediation training, and mediators' observations of what happens in their cases. Preceding these ideas is usually the notion that there is something wrong with our present ways of dealing with disputes. This feeling that all is not well with the law, or with the procedures of local housing authorities and environmental health departments, and that conflicts between neighbours are often made worse by these adversarial processes, motivates many of the people who become mediators. Mediation training builds upon this with the principle that conflict can be useful and positive, that it is an opportunity for creative action, and that it is only some ways of dealing with it that are destructive and negative. Mediators are not aiming to do away with conflict, they are judging some ways of dealing with it to be more effective, and better. Non-violence is introduced as a core value of mediators, and is a principle against which other methods of dealing with disputes can be judged.

Many mediators to whom I have spoken resist the idea of justifying mediation by reference to the successful outcomes that it can produce. Partly this seems to be an adherence to the principle of neutrality – mediators do not attempt to suggest the contents of any agreement between the parties. The word 'outcome' is being interpreted as meaning the same as 'agreement'. However, this resistance can also go further to encompass a general antipathy to looking for measurable results of the mediation process. Mediators make the point that going through the process has intangible benefits that cannot easily be captured by the tick-boxes of traditional assessment procedures, and there are more cogent reasons for arguing that mediation is a powerful and fruitful process. These include the positive effects of venting long-suppressed emotions and seeing the other party hearing and understanding them; the changes in self-esteem and personal power from taking control of the conflict through mediation; and the moral growth that Bush and Folger argue comes from transformative mediation.[9]

8   *Ibid*, pp 216–19.
9   *Op cit*, Bush and Folger, pp 82–83.

A big problem with providing a unified theory for mediators to work from, when dealing with conflicts, is that it is not clear that any such unified theory of conflict exists in the social and political sciences. Scimecca puts forward a theory based on Max Weber's sociology and claims that it can provide us with a single overarching framework in which to place our practice. However, many other theorists have challenged this view, and there is no agreement even amongst academics who have spent their entire working lives studying these theories. There are many different theorists who can contribute to our understanding of different dimensions of the social and political world.

Even if there is no one undisputed grand theory for mediators to learn and use, there are several theories which may be useful in developing and extending our practice. The question is, how could complex academic theories be incorporated into basic or advanced mediator training, in the context of the community mediation movement as it now is in the UK, composed largely of volunteers? In this situation, there are important ethical considerations against becoming an overly professionalised field that demands degree-level qualifications. Perhaps one way would be for mediation services to incorporate some academic study in their ongoing training programmes, so that debate and discussion about social, psychological and political theories becomes part of the ethos of the services. I know that there are many mediators who would be uninterested in this idea and contest its relevance, but I also know many mediators who have begun degree courses in psychology, sociology and politics as a result of, or at the same time as, being mediators. So another way would be for mediation services to encourage mediators to enrol on degree or diploma courses in conflict resolution and mediation, as they become more available in the UK.[10]

Mediation is based on a philosophy of individualism

If Scimecca is right that ADR is based on an essentially individualistic social philosophy that is blind to structured social inequalities, then mediators can be accused of failing to expose the problems of the status quo, and thereby protecting those people in responsible positions, who have the power to do something about the social inequalities that are causes of conflict. This criticism is along the same lines as the criticism of counsellors as people who patch up the victims of our society, so that they can go back out there to be victimised again. Activists in other fields accuse mediators of needing disputes more than disputes need mediators. This accusation is at the heart of

---

10 Such courses have been run on and off for several years by the Department of Peace Studies, University of Bradford, and a new course in Mediation Studies has been developed at the University of Derby.

what Bush and Folger have called the 'oppression story'. Critics of mediation have accused it of being:

> a dangerous instrument for increasing the power of the strong to take advantage of the weak. Because of the informality and consensuality of the process, and hence the absence of both procedural and substantive rules, mediation can magnify power imbalances and open the door to coercion and manipulation by the stronger party ... since mediation handles disputes without reference to other, similar cases and without reference to the public interest, it results in the 'dis-aggregation' and privatisation of class and public interest problems.[11]

Scimecca argues that conflict resolution can be 'a viable mechanism for social change' if it is based around the idea of empowerment.[12] This would mean that mediators would not be strictly neutral, because they would seek to promote the empowerment of the less powerful party. I shall look at the question of neutrality in more detail shortly. Scimecca argues that if mediators work from a conception of conflict resolution that involves empowerment before mediation is attempted, 'the conflict manager is offering an education in sociological analysis ... he or she is showing that conflicts are rarely individual problems but are instead structural ... Conflict resolution based on empowerment can help people to turn around and shape both their lives and the history of their society.'[13] Interestingly, Scimecca calls for more professionalisation of the field of conflict intervention, because rigorous and extensive training is necessary for mediators to understand the theoretical basis of conflict in modern societies. Professionalisation is not only invoked in the entrenchment of the 'satisfaction story'.

It is beyond the scope of this chapter to establish whether the majority of mediators working in the UK have an understanding of structured social inequalities, or whether they are individualists. Instead, towards the end of this chapter, I will outline an understanding of mediation that recognises the structural causes of disputes, and accepts that mediation is only of use in certain circumstances. Mediation is not the only method of dealing with disputes, and may not be helpful in dealing with problems of social and political inequality. The key questions here are whether people can get what they want or need through mediation; what other methods exist; and whether mediation can bring about significant transformation in personal and social relationships. This implies a further question about the interests of the State (national/local government, judiciary, police) in the outcomes of mediation. As mediators, are we delivering 'quick fixes' for the State, and thereby letting

---

11 *Op cit*, Scimecca, pp 22–23.

12 Scimecca, JA, 'Conflict Resolution: the Basis for Social Control or Social Change?' in Sandole, DJD and Sandole-Staroste, I (eds) *Conflict Management and Problem Solving: Interpersonal to International Applications*, 1987, London: Frances Pinter, p 30.

13 *Ibid*, p 32.

it off the hook? Or are we genuinely doing something that the State cannot do, that has a real benefit for people in conflict and perhaps society in general?

Mediation assumes that parties know how to solve their own disputes

Scimecca points out that ADR relies on a model of miscommunication as the primary cause of conflict. The mediation process aims to provide a structure for communication, to enable disputants to hear and understand their neighbours, in the belief that once they have done this, it will be possible for them to come to agreements over the issues. However, this model breaks down where parties hold opposing viewpoints, or have deep-rooted interests that simply cannot be satisfied at the same time. Conflicts caused by structured social inequalities cannot simply be communicated away. Again, the question of power and empowerment comes up here. Whether neighbour conflicts in the UK fall into this type is a matter for investigation. Certainly there are structural causes for some sorts of neighbour conflict that lie outside the control of the individuals involved, and that bring political issues into the frame.[14]

Mediators need to be aware that some problems cannot be resolved using problem-solving by the disputants. Mediation may still be extremely helpful for transforming the relationship between neighbours, enabling them to focus on the problem together, rather than fighting each other about who is to blame. It may turn out that the fabric of the buildings involved is defective, and both parties may end up working together to effect change in the physical situation. In a dispute between neighbours, one above the other in a block of flats, mediation helped them to identify that noise from a washing machine was actually travelling through pipes which ran down through all of the flats. The washing machine was actually in a third flat, unsuspected by either neighbour, and they were able to jointly contact the landlord about the problem of the pipes conducting sound.

Mediator neutrality reproduces the status quo

Scimecca's argument here raises questions for us all in community mediation. In fact, there have been a number of very well-argued defences of non-neutrality of mediators. I believe that it is very important for mediators to be aware of the precise boundaries of the idea of neutrality. As Keith Webb puts it, 'The act of mediation is not a neutral act; it is a moral and political act undertaken by the mediator to achieve desired ends. The mediator may claim

14   These are discussed in Chapter 7 .

to be neutral with respect to the values and claims of the combatants, but the activity of mediating is still a declaration of values held by the mediator.'[15] My whole thrust in this chapter has been to argue that, as mediators, we are doing what we do because we believe our actions to be of value in achieving positive goals, and I have suggested that the goals of 'satisfaction' and 'transformation', identified by Bush and Folger, are both important to the mediation movement in the UK. As James Laue says, 'There is a range of orientations that one could take toward a conflict – ignore, study, agitate, regulate, manage, instigate, repress, or forget it. Conflict resolution is only one approach, representing a value position – not a neutral stance – on how one will approach conflict.'[16]

We can differentiate between this value position on conflict, and partiality for one or the other party, by distinguishing, as Laue does, between three types of advocacy. Some third parties are party advocates, that is, they argue for one party's interests. Other third parties are outcome advocates who pursue a particular outcome to a situation. Mediators are a third type, process advocates – they do not base themselves in one party or the other, nor do they have a view on what the specific outcome should be, instead they advocate the use of a particular type of process. This gives us a better framework for thinking about our role in conflicts. We are part of the conflict, third parties perhaps, but still parties to it. We can claim impartiality concerning the outcome of the dispute, and explain that we stand between the two primary parties, but we must be clear that we are asking people to try out our way of dealing with conflicts. Mediators may actually ask plainly for permission to have control of the process. They then have the option to intervene in ways that balance power, and enable all sides to speak and be heard. Mediators have a choice when faced with the use of power, including agreements that are the product of the unjust use of power. They can act neutrally and allow the parties to come to an agreement, they can intervene and criticise the agreement, or they can walk out of the process. Many mediators would go through all of these strategies, first giving parties time to recognise that their interests are being neglected, then raising their awareness to the power abuse going on, and finally choosing to end the process if they felt that their own values were being badly undermined.

---

15 Webb, K, 'The Morality of Mediation' in Mitchell, CR and Webb, K, *New Approaches To International Mediation*, 1988, Westport: Greenwood Press, p 16.

16 Laue, JH, 'The Emergence and Institutionalisation of Third Party Roles in Conflict', in Sandole, DJD and Sandole-Staroste, I (eds) *Conflict Management and Problem Solving: Interpersonal to International Applications*, 1987, London: Frances Pinter, p 19.

The mediation movement values organisational expansion over dealing with social inequality

The community mediation movement in the UK is at a stage where it is expanding extensively with many new services, and intensively with new levels of national and regional structures.[17] It would be foolish for any movement to ignore important questions of institutional survival; if mediation is important, organisations are needed to push it forward both locally and nationally. However, most community mediation services are charities providing a free service to their communities, and any funding follows expressed need rather than organisational expansion for the sake of it. Moreover, the mediation movement in the UK is still sufficiently small and diverse that it can be decentralised and democratic, with policy and publications developed by working groups composed of ordinary members, who are working mediators and trainers. These people still mostly see themselves as activists, and their influence maintains the value base of the movement.

Scimecca's point is worth noting. If services and the national organisation become more concerned with their own expansion, for the sake of their financial and corporate interests, then mediation will surely suffer, and this means that people in conflict will suffer. However, in a situation where the national office of MEDIATION UK has only seven staff (two full-time, five part-time), and most community mediation services have between one and four paid staff (mostly part-time and often on short-term contracts), any organisational expansion is more beneficial than sinister, enabling more conflicts to be dealt with, more people to be trained and the message of mediation to be spread more widely.

Mediators have become professionals with no organic link to the community they serve

There is considerable movement towards 'professional practice' in the UK, led by MEDIATION UK, and focused on improving standards of best practice, to ensure that mediation services work as effectively as possible. 'Professional practice' – good practice, seen as unequivocally desirable – is distinguished from professionalisation, the provision of paid career posts in mediation. At the time of writing, it is still not possible to follow a professional career in community mediation in the UK. The only paid people working in community mediation are co-ordinators/administrators of services, freelance consultants who run their own businesses offering training consultancy (and some mediation), and a handful of paid mediators (usually part-time). Not all

---

17   See Chapter 2 for discussion of these changes.

of the services have paid staff. Almost all community mediators are volunteers in the UK, with only a few services employing mediators on a sessional or full-time basis. There is no clear hierarchy of grades, no career path to progress along, and certainly no salary scale!

Mediation certainly has a strong base amongst middle-class professionals, but people from all backgrounds, and from many sections of the community, volunteer and work as mediators, especially in the services based in the larger, more socially mixed cities. The strong commitment to equal opportunities in mediation means that community mediation services aim to recruit from all sections of the community, as discussed in Chapters 6 and 10. However, it is fair to say that many local communities are resistant to the idea of mediation. On one housing estate of some 3,000 households, a recent training course only received one or two applicants. These communities are affected by very high unemployment, social exclusion and poverty, and most people do not have the time or energy to volunteer. In addition, residents may believe in strongly hierarchical authority systems, and this causes difficulties in trying to persuade them to become involved in mediation.[18]

This is not to say that Scimecca's picture could not develop in community mediation. Family mediation in the UK is already very different. Mediators are mostly qualified social workers, counsellors or lawyers. Fees are charged, mostly on a sliding scale, and mediation is becoming an institutionalised part of the legal divorce process through the Family Law Act 1996. (There is more on this subject in Chapter 2.)

Scimecca's arguments have some bite in the UK as well as in the USA. As mediators, we must be concerned with the role of power, the interplay between individuals and social institutions, and the differences between impartiality and neutrality. I offer no easy answers or ready-made theories, only the conviction that these questions need to be considered by practising mediators and the services they work for. Otherwise we run the risk of finding ourselves co-opted by a mainstream that resists the transformative aspects of mediation, in favour of the technical production of satisfaction.

CONTINGENCY IN SOCIAL CONFLICTS

In Chapter 7, I described how conflicts are complex social processes, involving a multitude of causal factors, both structural and psychological. Recognising this requires us to analyse the conflicts where we are called to intervene, to try to understand them, so that we can choose how to act. We may be able to identify particular approaches that deal better with some elements of a conflict

---

18 Legg, H, 'The Clash of Cultures. The Immobile and Mobile – Certainty and Uncertainty', *Mediation*, 11, pp 14–15.

than others, and it would make sense to tailor our use of intervention methods on the basis of such understanding. This general approach has been called the 'contingency approach', because the choice of method of intervention is dependent, or contingent, on the circumstances of the conflict in question. Mediation may well be appropriate for many disputes, but there will be others whose characteristics make them unsuitable for mediation, and more suitable for intervention by an authority, or a one-party intervention like counselling. Knowing which approach to use relies on a body of knowledgeable people, who can analyse conflicts and ways of dealing with them, and match elements of conflict with different forms of intervention.

Contingency models used in relation to international conflict have been based on an analysis of conflict as composed of four stages of escalation. The focus on differences through time, where each stage of escalation has a defining central characteristic that can be matched to a particular form of intervention, has been shown to be too limiting for use in real conflicts.[19] Instead it makes sense to analyse conflicts in terms of their structure, as discussed in Chapter 7. International conflicts need to be analysed using different frameworks from social conflicts, because different elements are involved. Where international conflict involves nationalism, relations between states and large-scale political structures, a conflict between neighbours is likely to involve structural elements concerning housing conditions and their socio-economic context; and psychological elements concerning communication, emotions, perceptions, beliefs and prejudices. Whilst mediation may be able to deal with many of the latter, it is unlikely to be able to affect the former. Thus the potential for conflict will remain, although the parties may be able to manage it more effectively in future, if the relationship between them has been transformed.

So contingency comes into play in community mediation when mediators spend time during the first meetings with the parties to the conflict, analysing its causes – establishing how the parties feel, what the issues are for them, and what the context of the conflict is. In this process, mediators have to decide whether the conflict is mediable, that is, whether mediation is appropriate. This decision is made using several 'rules of thumb' about which issues and contexts are suitable for mediation and which are not (see also discussion in Chapter 8). I see this as an implicit acceptance of the contingency model. Mediators make their decision by considering the characteristics of the conflict. In cases where there are large power imbalances, or judgments are

---

19 For the original statement of the model in relation to international conflict, see Fisher, RJ and Keashly, L, 'The Potential Complementarity of Mediation and Consultation within a Contingency Model of Third Party Intervention' (1991) 28, 1 The Journal of Peace Research 29–42; for the critique of the model see also Bloomfield, D, 'Towards Complementarity in Conflict Management: Resolution and Settlement in Northern Ireland' (1995) 32, 2 Journal of Peace Research 151–64, and Beckett, GR 1996, 'Constructing Peace in Croatia. Complementarity and the Transformation of Conflict', unpublished PhD thesis, University of Bradford.

required, or legal action is being taken, or basic rights are at stake and personal safety is at risk, mediation is usually judged inappropriate.[20] Where ongoing relationships are important, or the parties want to retain control of the outcome but do not feel able to negotiate directly, or confidentiality is important, or communication is difficult, and there are specific issues that need to be dealt with, mediation is frequently a successful method of handling the conflict.[21]

COMPLEMENTARITY IN SOCIAL CONFLICTS

Following the logic of the previous section, dealing with all the characteristics of a conflict requires several different types of intervention. This has been called 'complementarity' because each different intervention used on each different element of the conflict complements the work of other interventions. Collectively they may enable the comprehensive transformation of the conflict. Currently in our society we have a wide range of agencies involved in conflict management, although they may not be described as such. The main agencies likely to be involved in a neighbour dispute are the police, the environmental health and housing departments of the local authority, social services, the local health services, solicitors, local MPs and councillors, Citizens Advice Bureaux and the community mediation service. At present, with mediation a relatively unknown and new option, these agencies are as likely to impede the transformation of conflict as promote it, but the potential exists for them to work in a complementary way.

For example, in one of the cases described in Chapter 9 (see pp 164–66), the conflict involved neighbours who lived in sheltered accommodation, in flats above and below one another. The conflict had arisen over the attempts of the person living upstairs to feed birds out of the window. Bird seed falling on the garden below was sprouting as weeds and attracting birds that ate the flower seeds too. The owner of the garden became abusive, and the conflict was characterised by a high degree of verbal abuse from both parties as a result. The mediators in the case discovered that the people upstairs had mobility needs preventing them from walking downstairs and around the long housing block to the bird table. As a result, they had no option but to try to throw the seeds to the bird table from their window. The mediators were able to help the parties clarify the exact cause of the conflict, and as a result the upstairs tenants were able to identify the action needed to transform the conflict. But the mediators had no power to affect the housing situation. The housing department, which had the power to allocate a ground-floor flat to

---

20 MEDIATION UK, *Training Manual in Community Mediation Skills*, 1995, Bristol: MEDIATION UK, p 56.

21 *Loc cit.*

these people, was thus able to intervene in a complementary way. There is a similar situation if noise is the problem and better soundproofing is an answer.

At present, in the context of poorly-resourced local government, the flexibility needed for agencies to take a proactive role in the management of conflict, is very limited. In the example above, had a ground-floor flat not become available quite coincidentally, the problem might have persisted for some time, whilst waiting for a suitable property. Similarly, the ability to rectify problems of soundproofing quickly will often be beyond the resources of local housing departments. In these circumstances, local authorities' involvement in disputes, like that of the police and lawyers, is generally of a punitive nature. Injunctions for people who cause noise pollution, threats of possession against people who transgress tenancy agreements, and other legal threats, are used in an attempt to push people into changing their behaviour. Such methods may work in some situations. However, they do not deal with the roots of conflicts, only symptoms, and if they are used immediately before or during a mediation (usually inadvertently due to a lack of co-ordination), they generally predispose people against co-operation and the idea of talking through the situation.

In an ideal world, one we might aim to achieve in the future, these agencies could work together in a complementary way. At the first point of call for a person involved in a neighbour dispute, whether a solicitor or a local authority department, the conflict would be analysed by an appropriately skilled person, and a suitable first course of action agreed with the person in conflict. Often there are no legal grounds for intervention in disputes: for instance, boundaries have to be over a certain height before they need planning permission, and noise has to be of a certain level and duration; but even lower fences and quiet intermittent noises can be real issues for neighbours. Perhaps an interagency conference would take place, or at the least a report sent to all agencies, so that it is clear where first responsibility lies, what action is to be taken, and what actions must not be taken. If mediation is the first intervention, nothing else would be done during the process. If structural causes are identified which are outside the scope of mediation, the appropriate agencies would be informed, and would be responsible for making the necessary changes. If mediation is inappropriate, perhaps due to unacceptable racist behaviour constituting harassment, the appropriate agency would take on responsibility for the case.

CONCLUSION

The critical perspectives on mediation that I have been considering, have all begun with the assumption that mediation is an effective and important process, which can have powerful social and personal effects on conflicts between individuals. All the criticisms were originally made in an attempt to make mediators think more clearly about their practice, and therefore deliver a better service to people in conflict. They make us aware that there are larger questions surrounding our individual cases and local community mediation services, and this awareness gives us the opportunity to deal with them. At present mediators in the UK do not spend enough time considering why they do what they do, and whether their results are truly what mediation is capable of. The growth of regional networks, regional and national conferences, and training events, where ordinary mediators are exposed to the diverse ways of organising mediation services in the UK, is one way of ensuring that mediators look outwards. We need to develop others.

A positive view of the underlying values of community mediation in the UK has been implicit in much of the discussion in this chapter. I believe that a productive synthesis has been created from the best elements of the various 'stories' from the USA. The ethos of the mediation movement, embodied in MEDIATION UK, the Community Mediation Network and the MEDIATION UK publications (collated from materials from many services across the country), is one of voluntary participation, empowerment and creativity. This is important because it provides a central and influential force that pushes against the danger of mediation in the UK becoming more outcome-focused, coercive and manipulative. Bush and Folger's description of the 'satisfaction story' is a possible future for mediation in the UK; we cannot deny that there are elements of it in our practice. Mediators from Bristol to Bradford, Cambridge to Cardiff, London to Edinburgh, are all concerned with enabling people in conflict to reach mutually satisfactory agreements. However, the training materials and 'best practice' guidelines of these services and of MEDIATION UK still emphasise that 'mediation provides for participation, the parties retain control over the decision-making', that facing conflict as a shared problem helps the parties to 'build, rather than destroy, a relationship', and that 'mediation empowers people'.[22] This is the language of transformation, married to elements of satisfaction.

Most mediators in the UK want to contribute to the growth of positive and collaborative ways of dealing with conflict in local communities. If mediation were to develop into a coercive option for the poor (on grounds of cheapness), most mediators would regard this as a betrayal of mediation's promise. By enabling neighbours to deal more constructively with conflicts, making communities more peaceful and future-focused, mediation is not simply ameliorating symptoms of deeper social injustices. Indeed, if neighbour conflicts are often caused in part by large scale structural factors, as I have argued in Chapter 7, then offering neighbours a constructive process to settle their differences enables them to turn their energies towards the more important causes of their problems. Mediation aims to introduce collaboration

22 *Ibid.*

and co-operation into systems of conflict and competition. If it can help to break the escalatory spirals of conflict between neighbours, mediation will release energy spent fighting with neighbours to be better used fighting for more resources and developing community power.

CHAPTER FOURTEEN

LOOKING FORWARD

Marian Liebmann

INTRODUCTION

Neighbour disputes have become a 'hot topic' of discussion over recent years, with many radio and television programmes devoted to it. A recent survey[1] explored people's attitudes towards their neighbours, to see how far 'neighbourliness' exists in modern-day Britain. During September and October 1995 1,062 interviews were conducted, with set quotas to ensure the sample was representative of the British population. The survey showed that, on the whole, good relations existed between neighbours, but the incidence of 'rows over the fence' was higher than might be expected, with 20% admitting having let conflict turn into a heated exchange of words.

Mediation is one – very timely – response to these concerns. In this chapter I will try to draw the threads together and comment on current developments in the rapidly changing picture of community mediation. I will also summarise some of the parallel developments in research and evaluation in this field. Many questions remain to be answered and I will try to highlight the main areas where discussion is focused, and where there are divergent possibilities for the future.[2]

DEVELOPMENTS IN COMMUNITY MEDIATION

The number of community mediation services continues to grow apace. At the last count, there were 97 community mediation services in the UK, of which 27 started within the last 18 months. A complete list is given in Appendix 1. Every week the MEDIATION UK national office hears of new mediation services in the planning stages. It is quite a job to keep lists updated so that telephone callers experiencing disputes can be put in touch with their most local service! Whereas only a couple of years ago, there was a fairly slim chance that there would be a local service, and the office had to send self-help leaflets or listen to long and terrible tales of woe, now most callers can be directed immediately to a local service providing the practical help needed.

---

1   Opinion Research Business, *Good Neighbours Survey*, 1995, Perth: General Accident.

2   I would like to acknowledge the particular help received from Carey Haslam and Tony Billinghurst, current Chair and Director of MEDIATION UK respectively, in updating this chapter.

Much of this expansion has happened because local authorities have become convinced about the value of community mediation, as has been described in Chapter 2. The Department of the Environment booklet *Mediation: Benefits and Practice* (produced with help from MEDIATION UK, following a joint noise mediation seminar), circulated in November 1994,[3] was very influential in this respect: although the Department of the Environment did not promise any funds for local mediation services, it gave the concept its blessing and encouraged local authorities to support or develop local initiatives. Local authorities pay keen attention to government circulars, and this gave many of them the 'green light' to go ahead.

As community mediation becomes established, experienced community mediation services start to think of using community mediation as a platform for developing other kinds of mediation. Often the first extra service is schools work, because of the potential for educating children and young people in constructive ways of handling conflict. The current concern over bullying also provides a strong incentive for this work. Other community mediation services move into victim/offender mediation and form links with police, probation and social services. Some community mediation services work with police on conflict resolution, and one works with other agencies on domestic violence. Others have taken on medical mediation and one has become involved in family mediation for divorce and separation.

In addition, community mediation services have inspired variations in the services, extending mediation and its contexts in several ways. Some mediation services have undertaken more proactive work on high-crime housing estates, bringing together residents and agencies to discuss long-term objectives for handling endemic conflict. Others have developed expertise in holding multi-party mediations involving whole streets, or situations of conflict involving several groups, such as young people and older people. A new African-Caribbean project is developing mediation in the context of conflict involving children, parents and schools, especially where children are likely to be excluded from school; another project for children and parents has similar aims. A new service for young homeless people in London is mediating between them and their families, using trained volunteer mediators drawn from London community mediation services. Another service for homeless young people in a small country town aims to provide accommodation, work and activities to integrate the young people into the community – and has appointed a mediation worker to undertake the latter. Many of these developments enlarge the concept of mediation from a service focused on neighbour problems to one encompassing whole communities.

---

3   Department of the Environment, *Mediation: Benefits and Practice*, 1994, London: Department of the Environment.

There are several large, established community mediation services which have thus become 'multi-mediation' centres, and this could be a model for the future. Many mediation centres in the USA operate in this way – whatever contract comes their way, they do it. This has implications for training: usually volunteer mediators undertake a basic mediation training and then further specialist training in the area of mediation where they choose to work.

In the UK, family, commercial, environmental and medical mediation are usually organised separately by the different professional groups. However, because MEDIATION UK has always had members working in community, victim/offender and schools mediation, there has been encouragement for cross-fertilisation and extending principles of mediation across the borders from one kind of mediation to another. It will be interesting to see whether the different strands of community, victim/offender and schools work will, in the long term, go their separate ways – or whether their close proximity will continue to enrich each other and promote mediation as the central focus rather than the particular context. Many people hope they will stay together, as they have a common bond in being based in the community, rather than the more private domain of other kinds of mediation.

This could be particularly appropriate for rural centres, as mentioned in Chapter 4. In rural settings with sparse population, there may not be enough referrals for one particular kind of mediation to make a specialist mediation service viable. This raises questions about training and compatibility between organisations which now operate separately (mainly for historical reasons, having developed at different stages). For instance, National Family Mediation has a centralised structure for training, whereas MEDIATION UK has chosen to leave training to local services, to allow for the diverse nature of communities; this means that a service wanting to provide both community and family mediation would need to fulfil two different sets of training and accreditation criteria.

The question of transferability of skills and organisational co-operation is already under discussion at a national level. The new Joint Mediation Forum, comprising MEDIATION UK, the family mediation organisations National Family Mediation and the Family Mediators Association, and the commercial mediation organisations Centre for Dispute Resolution (CEDR) and the ADR Group, has begun to meet to discuss the possibility of positive collaboration. In view of the points raised above, the first priority is to develop joint standards – which will also be expedited by the initiatives in the field of accreditation described in Chapter 11.

An important new development, as the number of community mediation services has grown, is the formation of the MEDIATION UK Community Mediation Network (alongside the Victim/Offender Mediation Network and the Schools Mediation Network). This network meets twice yearly and at the MEDIATION UK annual conference, and enables community mediation practitioners and co-ordinators to meet and share experiences. The meetings are well attended, with 30 to 40 people at each meeting, at a different venue each time. The programme is organised by different community mediation services in turn, and covers topics of interest, such as difficult cases, supervision of volunteer mediators, research, training, accreditation, funding and so on.

When practitioners come together to discuss such matters, questions arise and needs may be identified for further developments and sometimes new policy decisions. For instance, a need has been voiced for a 'Good Practice Guide' to follow on from other publications already produced. Groups of 30 to 40 can be rather unwieldy for decision-making, so there is a need for a smaller committee to take things forward, drawing on the accumulated wisdom in the field. This committee is about to be formed; both it and the network will need to be linked in with the MEDIATION UK decision-making structure.

Another parallel development is the emergence of regional networks and groups, bringing together those within easy reach of each other. These groups have grown in an *ad hoc* way to meet needs as they arise, and the groups are of different sizes; the smallest regional group being one county and the largest being the whole of Scotland! Where distances are small, and there is agreement over the needs and purposes, these groups have worked very well. However, some groups have folded due to increasing pressures on people's time.

Both these developments, the interest networks and the regional groups, have been the subject of a special project, funded by a charitable trust over the course of one year, to examine how they might be made more viable. The report and its recommendations were published in July 1997.[4] MEDIATION UK is committed to supporting both the regional and interest networks, as far as resources allow.

MEDIATION UK itself has been influenced by the huge expansion of community mediation. Following the circulation of the Department of the Environment booklet promoting mediation to local authorities, MEDIATION UK received a three-year grant (1995–98) from the Environmental Action Fund of the Department of the Environment, to promote the potential of mediation to resolve the escalating number of noise complaints. A condition of this grant was matched funding from other sources, which two large charitable trusts have together provided. As a result, MEDIATION UK has been able to consolidate its work for community mediation services, and draw up a strategic plan *MEDIATION UK into the Millennium* for the years 1997–2000.[5] This document outlines five priorities:

---

4   Liebmann, M, *The Development of Mediation Networks*, 1997, Bristol: MEDIATION UK.
5   MEDIATION UK, *MEDIATION UK into the Millennium*, 1997, Bristol: MEDIATION UK.

1   The promotion of mediation (and conflict resolution) services in the community as the principal option in handling disputes.

2   Ensuring everyone has access to mediation services in their local communities.

3   Ensuring a high standard of mediation.

4   Serving and representing the needs of its members.

5   Providing an efficient and effective organisation.

THE EUROPEAN DIMENSION

There have been several references in this book to American and Australian work in the community mediation field, but very little mention of other European countries. This is because there has been little development there, although this is now changing. By contrast, victim/offender mediation and schools conflict resolution and mediation are probably better developed in some European countries than in the UK. The European Conference in Peacemaking and Conflict Resolution (ECPCR), modelled on the US National Conference in Peacemaking and Conflict Resolution (NCPCR) and taking place in alternate years when NCPCR is not scheduled, has now taken place three times: in 1992 in Turkey, in 1994 in Spain and in 1996 in Bulgaria (with the next one planned for 1998 in Northern Ireland). These gatherings of up to 300 people have begun to make links across Europe between those with common interests in the field of mediation and conflict resolution.

Partly through ECPCR, but also through other meetings and conferences (for instance, on community safety), it has become clear that most European countries are currently looking to the UK for leadership in the practice of community mediation. There are far more practising community mediation services in the UK than anywhere else in Europe. Recently the director of MEDIATION UK has been asked to speak to groups or conferences in France, Belgium, the Netherlands and Germany, where there are the beginnings of community mediation. France and Belgium have community social workers who intervene in community disputes, from a social work perspective. Germany has some environmental mediation, which occasionally deals with housing issues, but is not free to disputants. Denmark has a Centre for Conflict Resolution which tries to resolve conflicts in communities. Italy has two initiatives in Milan and Turin with an emphasis on restorative justice and young people.

Although the UK has a language in common with North America and Australia, there are significant differences; and there are many factors in common between the UK and Europe. As the European Union becomes more of a reality, the UK will have a central role in helping a Europe-wide network of community mediation services into being. Perhaps this will even lead in time to a European model of community mediation?

MODELS OF MEDIATION AND FUNDING IMPLICATIONS

This book has described how most community mediation services in the UK operate, although there are many local variations. The most common model is still the independent community mediation service, probably because this is how community mediation started, and because it is seen as a good way of ensuring that mediation is seen as truly impartial. The availability of MEDIATION UK's *Guide to Starting a Community Mediation Service*[6] has probably also helped here.

As more local authorities decide that mediation is the way forward for them in handling neighbour disputes,[7] and many of them take the lead in starting them, some may wish to retain more direct control of the finances. These mediation services may then be part of the line management structure of the funding agency, often a local housing department. Some of these have multi-agency committees to ensure independence of operation, and all of them have a separate identity from the rest of the agency, eg separate premises, own headed notepaper, and so on. The few local authorities which employ in-house mediators at least make sure that the mediators do not have any other role in that agency.

Most local mediation services are now funded from a variety of sources.[8] The largest proportion of funding comes from local authorities, usually housing and environmental health departments, either in the form of a grant or increasingly in the form of a service level agreement or other contracted funding. Housing associations, which have taken over a considerable amount of social housing provision from local authorities, may also have contracts with local mediation services for referrals of disputes. Police in some areas may contribute to costs of mediation services, especially where they see the potential of community mediation as a crime prevention measure (see also section on research, pp 270–72). This funding from statutory agencies has done a great deal to achieve some stability and long-term viability for community mediation services, but it is rarely enough to cover the total budget. Local services still have to apply to charitable trusts and local businesses to have enough funds to keep going and meet all their

---

6   MEDIATION UK, *Guide to Starting a Community Mediation Service*, 1993, revised 1996, Bristol: MEDIATION UK.

7   Many local authorities are now using mediation as one (essential) element in an overall strategy.

8   For details see Dignan, J, Sorsby, A and Hibbert, J, *Neighbour Disputes: Comparing the Cost-effectiveness of Mediation and Alternative Approaches*, 1996, Sheffield: University of Sheffield.

commitments, especially where statutory agencies are only willing to fund certain kinds of work. Both businesses and charitable trusts are usually more interested in funding exciting new ventures than supporting core costs of existing services, so community mediation services tend to turn to these for help with new initiatives. The new National Lotteries Charities Board is rapidly acquiring a central role in funding community mediation services.

As has already been mentioned in Chapters 4 and 6, most community mediation services use trained volunteer mediators to do the actual mediation. However, one or two mediation services are trying out the use of paid sessional mediators – either because of frustration with volunteers who may not be available when needed, or inability to recruit volunteers, or because it is felt that community mediators should be paid, in the same way as family mediators usually are. It will be interesting to see whether community mediators continue to be volunteers, or whether payment becomes more usual. This would, of course, substantially change the spirit of community mediation.

Almost all community mediation services provide mediation free of charge to their clients, for reasons already stated in Chapter 4. Only one mediation service is known to be charging their mediation clients for the service – one of the few services which is trying out paid mediators. This mediation service covers a mixed area centred on a large university city, which has several wealthy districts – and some clients asked if they could pay! People on welfare benefits are not charged, and others are asked to pay on a sliding scale. It will be interesting to see if this is taken up by other services in the future, and if people are willing to pay for mediation for all kinds of neighbour disputes, or only those where a court case is the alternative (usually boundary disputes).[9] For many services based in poor inner city areas, it will probably never be worth even setting up the apparatus for collecting fees from mediation clients. It is also important that mediation services for certain disputes (such as noise) can be free at the point of delivery, because otherwise neighbours will continue to use the free statutory (and adversarial) complaints systems, with no encouragement to try another way.

STANDARDS AND ACCREDITATION

This has been discussed in detail in Chapter 11. As community mediation becomes more of a mainstream option, it is likely that accreditation – of services, mediators, training and trainers – will play a larger part. The benefits and drawbacks of this process have been listed (see pp 214–15), and it is too soon to say whether there will be a broad acceptance of accreditation, with the

9   See Chapter 1, p 9–10.

benefits it brings, or whether substantial numbers of community mediation services will see it as something which spoils the community ethos and therefore wish to distance themselves from it. It would be very unfortunate if such a difference of opinion developed into a 'two-tier system'. A lot may depend on the funding available to make accreditation accessible to community mediation services, and this is a political issue.

Given that the community mediation movement is very cohesive at the moment, it is hoped that opportunities for discussion and debate may help a positive view emerge. Certainly there will need to be a readiness for continuous evaluation of any steps taken – a recent first meeting of all those using or intending to use the MEDIATION UK *Handbook for the Training Programme in Community Mediation Skills*[10] gave rise to an animated discussion about jargon and the literacy problems of volunteers, who otherwise had all the personal qualities to be excellent mediators. There is a commitment from MEDIATION UK to update the *Handbook*, and other procedures too will need to be kept under review.

MEDIATION AND LEGAL ISSUES

An important point about mediation agreements is that they do not have any special legal status and are not legally binding (although they can be made binding if both parties wish). Mediation agreements are made and kept because it is in the interest of both parties to do so – one of the advantages of mediation is that agreements can be made without recourse to the law. Occasionally parties will make a formal contract to mediate before starting the process, but usually an informal agreement to do so is regarded as sufficient.

Given the advantages of informality, speed and ability to take both parties' interests into account, it makes obvious sense for mediation to replace legal solutions where possible. There is some evidence[11] that this is slightly more possible at the beginning of a dispute, when neighbours may still have a reasonable relationship with each other, and also at the end, when the dispute has 'run its course', and both sides are heartily sick of it and can see no good in continuing, especially if court costs are escalating out of hand.

There is also evidence from the Neighbour Dispute report[12] that those fairly intractable neighbour disputes which end up in court, with one party

---

10 MEDIATION UK, *Handbook for the Training Programme in Community Mediation Skills*, 1996, Bristol: MEDIATION UK.

11 Faulkes, Wendy, Plenary address, 'Community Mediation as a Crime Prevention Strategy', Forum for Initiatives in Reparation and Mediation Annual Conference, 2 July 1991.

12 Dignan *et al, op cit*, 1996.

being prosecuted by the local authority, tend to be very much more expensive than cases dealt with by mediation, raising the question whether mediation might have been successful at an earlier stage, if it had been tried. If so, the potential for cost savings could be considerable.

The increasing costs of civil litigation, and the length of time taken to deal with cases, have led to the Woolf Inquiry on *Access to Justice*. MEDIATION UK made a submission to this inquiry, and arranged for local mediation services to attend and speak at regional seminars. In the interim report published in April 1995, Lord Woolf highlighted the benefits of Alternative Dispute Resolution and especially mediation:[13]

> A number of organisations, including MEDIATION UK and schemes run by local authorities, provide mediation services which are designed primarily to resolve and defuse disputes between neighbours. These have made a considerable contribution to the resolution of disputes, resulting in a significant saving to the court system. Almost without exception the bodies who provide these mediation services are underfunded. This is not in the interest of their clients or of the court service. I recommend they are funded more appropriately. I would very much hope in any review of legal aid the need of bodies of this nature will be taken into account. In many situations, they provide the only way that the citizen can obtain access to justice, and in any event they may offer a better and less confrontational way of dealing with disputes between neighbours, when a continuing relationship is often important.

Following on from the Woolf Inquiry, the Lord Chancellor published a Green Paper on legal aid, *Legal Aid – Targeting Need*.[14] In this paper, the Lord Chancellor proposed that there should be block funding from legal aid for a variety of non-legal services. There is no reason why mediation should not be one of the services supported in this way, although this would require a change in the current law.[15] This would provide a possibility of funding local community mediation services to take cases which would otherwise to go to court.

The recent change of government (May 1997) means, however, that it is not certain that these proposals will be implemented. The new government has instituted a review of these proposed reforms of civil justice and legal aid, with a group appointed by the Lord Chancellor's Department and headed by Sir Peter Middleton. The Middleton Review is in progress as this book goes to press.

The general public seems to find the legal system unsatisfactory for similar reasons. A recent survey carried out by the National Consumer Council, on

---

13   Lord Woolf, *Inquiry into Civil Justice: Access to Justice*, 1995, IV, 21.

14   Lord Chancellor's Department, *Legal Aid – Targeting Need*, 1995, London: HMSO.

15   A change in the law has been made to enable family mediation to be available on legal aid, as part of the Family Law Act 1996.

Civil Law and the Public, showed that about three-quarters of those who had experienced a serious dispute agreed that the present legal system was too slow, too complicated, too easy to twist if you knew the rules, needed bringing up to date, and was off-putting for ordinary people.[16]

All those who had experienced a dispute were then given three alternative ways in which the case could be resolved and asked which they preferred. Only 8% preferred 'a full trial in court'. 23% opted for 'sitting round a table with an independent expert who makes the decision'. The largest majority, 53%, chose 'sitting round a table with an independent expert who helps you to reach an agreement between yourselves'. Those with recent experience of going to court made similar choices. Clearly the idea of mediation appeals to a growing number of people.

Although general developments are awaiting political action, the Lord Chancellor's Department has given its blessing to a mediation pilot scheme at the Central London County Court, and a mediation and arbitration project at the Patents County Court.[17] The Central London County Court scheme was launched in May 1996 for claims of monetary value between £3,000 and £10,000 (the next band above the informal small claims jurisdiction), and could well include some disputes from fields covered by community mediation services, as well as other more commercial disputes. Judge Neil Butter QC is overseeing the pilot scheme, in which each party pays £25 for the mediation session.

Mediators were recruited from commercial mediation organisations (the Centre for Dispute Resolution, the ADR Group, the Academy of Experts and the Chartered Institute of Arbitrators) and from MEDIATION UK, which in turn contacted the seven most established local services in London, resulting in 23 experienced community mediators coming forward. They received training in linking their experience to a more commercial environment, and a series of group meetings to discuss cases; the co-ordinator also made contact by telephone after each case.

By December 1996, 38 mediations had taken place, with 20 more in the pipeline, with a majority of cases reaching settlement at the mediation. Research and evaluation into effectiveness is being carried out by Professor Hazel Genn of London University, with a view to wider implementation of the scheme if it is judged successful. The report is expected later in 1997.

Nevertheless, there are some dangers in over-enthusiastic use of mediation. There is a fear that mediation will result in the least powerful party

---

16 Taylor Nelson AGB, *Civil Law and the Public*, 1995, London: National Consumer Council.

17 These paragraphs are based on: (1) Lord Chancellor's Department Press Office, 'Dispute Resolution – Pilot Mediation Scheme in London', press release 15 March 1996; (2) Burn, S, 'A Middle Course' (1997) Gazette 94/1, 8 January 1997; (3) Central London County Courts Pilot Mediation Scheme, Notes for Mediators and Clients; (4) MEDIATION UK letters and documents.

agreeing to the demands of the other party, because they 'fear the worst' outside the mediation setting. There is also anecdotal evidence from the US that mediation can be in danger of being used as 'cheap justice'. Poorer citizens may be diverted to mediation, because it is cheaper on the public purse, while citizens who can afford a lawyer have the choice whether to go to mediation or to go to law. There is also the point that compulsory mediation can result in parties just 'going through the motions' when they have been directed to mediation, rather than choosing it voluntarily. Most mediators feel that mediation has to be a voluntary process to stand a chance of working properly. There is still a great need for public education so that people can choose mediation appropriately.

In 1995 the Legal Action Group (LAG), a group working with lawyers and advisers to promote equal access to justice, undertook an investigation of mediation practice in the USA, commissioned a book, *Achieving Civil Justice: Appropriate Dispute Resolution for the 1990s*,[18] and held a high-profile conference and seminar (in November 1995) with speakers on mediation and ADR from both sides of the Atlantic. Many of the book's contributors were 'mediation enthusiasts' and indeed one of the book's purposes was to highlight the contribution of mediation – but also to ask some of the questions. Anne Grosskurth's chapter summarises these questions as being concerned with: power imbalances, the danger of 'two-tier justice', the danger of disguising responsibility (eg noise disputes where the real culprit is the landlord for not providing soundproofing), and ignoring rights.[19] All these points have been commented on in earlier chapters, as mediators need to be aware of them.

Many community justice centres in Australia, and some also in the USA, have found a useful compromise formula. The court may direct neighbours to attend a compulsory information session given by the mediation service, after which the parties may choose whether to go for mediation or to come back to the law court. In this way mediation is described by the people who will undertake it, while also giving parties the chance to ask questions and to check out the mediation service for themselves.

This approach is also being adopted in the UK for divorce mediation. Under the provisions of the Family Law Act 1996, those seeking divorce will be required to attend a compulsory information-giving session which outlines all their options, including mediation, before starting the divorce process. Wherever appropriate, mediation, rather than litigation, will be encouraged.[20]

---

18 Smith, R (ed), *Achieving Civil Justice: Appropriate Dispute Resolution for the 1990s*, London: Legal Action Group.

19 Grosskurth, A, 'Mediation: forming a view', in Smith, R (ed), *op cit*, pp 176–87.

20 Family Law Act 1996.

This may be an appropriate way forward for community mediation too, but it has to be remembered that, unlike divorce disputes, most neighbour disputes do not end up in court. There is a good case for leaving community mediation services in the community rather than attaching them to the court system. Lord Woolf opposed the institution of court-annexed ADR largely because independent mediation is already quite widely available.[21] Andrew Acland, in his book *Resolving Disputes without Going to Court*, also recommends dealing with as many disputes as possible in as informal a way as possible. He points out the biggest challenge facing us all: changing from an adversarial culture to a co-operative one, a change that is facilitated by learning about and practising mediation.[22]

RESEARCH

The current state of research into community and neighbour mediation has been described in Chapter 12, where the main focus was on the different approaches that have been developed. It also comments on the progress that has been made, and the issues that still need to be addressed. Early research into neighbour disputes[23] and two specific evaluative studies (by Grubb and OPUS)[24] were also described, in Chapter 2. The latter were focused on the nature and effectiveness of two particular community mediation services and the models of mediation they used, and did not focus on the nature of neighbour disputes. An Australian piece of research in 1991 showed, by comparing two districts where community mediation was available, with two matched districts without, that there was a lower incidence of neighbour violence where mediation was available.[25]

As someone who has in the past tried to raise funds for research in community mediation, it has surprised me how difficult it has been to persuade grant-makers of its importance. This contrasts with the situation in victim/offender mediation, where there are many more research studies, but far fewer actual services. Research results do not always lead to implementation, and lack of research does not seem to have stunted the

21 Woolf Report, para 18.30.

22 Acland, AF, *Resolving Disputes without Going to Court*, 1995, London: Century Business Books.

23 Tebay, S, Cumberbatch, G and Graham, N, *Disputes Between Neighbours*, 1986, Birmingham: University of Aston (Applied Psychology Department).

24 Quine, C, Hutton, J and Reed, B, *Community Mediation of Disputes between Neighbours*, 1990, London: The Grubb Institute. OPUS, *Newham Conflict & Change Project*, Evaluation Report, 1989, London: OPUS (An Organisation for Promoting Understanding in Society).

25 Faulkes, W, 'Mediation as a Crime Prevention Strategy' (1991), conference paper for Forum for Initiatives in Reparation and Mediation Annual Conference, July 1991.

burgeoning growth of community mediation. Nevertheless, research can be important, as the following example illustrates.

In 1993 the Housing Association Tenants Ombudsman Service (HATOS) decided, after consultation, to include a mediation service as part of their system for handling complaints, where informal processes had failed or were not appropriate.[26] The proposal stated:

> The Ombudsman will be responsible for overseeing an easily accessible mediation service. The Housing Corporation feels that this is a particularly important element in dealing with complaints. Tenants and landlords have to maintain a close and lasting relationship. It must therefore be preferable if disputes between them can be resolved by negotiation rather than third-party decisions which create winners and losers.[27]

and:

> For most cases which cannot be resolved straightforwardly, the Ombudsman will generally suggest mediation as the most satisfactory way of resolving the dispute.[28]

Invitations went out to tender to provide the pilot mediation service, and the contract was awarded to the ADR Group, a commercial mediation organisation with a panel of over 100 trained mediators nationwide. The ADR Group also proposed to co-operate with mediation services under the auspices of MEDIATION UK, in order to appoint suitable mediators for each case, bearing in mind ethnic and gender considerations, as well as appropriate experience.

This scheme was researched and evaluated over the first two years (November 1993 to October 1995). The research report (1996) showed that, in practice, mediation was not used as much as had been expected. Of the 738 cases resolved during this period, only 27 (4%) were resolved through mediation.[29] However, those cases resulted in markedly more positive feelings concerning the resulting tenant/housing association relationship.[30] As a result of this research, HATOS has refined procedures to enable earlier referrals to mediation, and also suggested better information about mediation for tenants, so that they can make a more informed choice. It is hoped that this

---

26 Housing Corporation, *Tenant Complaints: The Way Forward, A Public Consultation Document*, 1993, London: Housing Corporation, p 5.

27 Housing Corporation, *Resolving Housing Association Tenants' Complaints, Report on Consultation and Revised Proposals*, 1993, London: Housing Corporation, para 12(a).

28 *Ibid*, para 19.

29 Lickiss, R (with Giddings, P, Gregory, R and Karn, V), *Setting up the Housing Association Tenants' Ombudsman Service: The Debate and the Outcome*, Research Report 2, 1996, London: Housing Association Tenants' Ombudsman Service.

30 USER Research Ltd, *Feedback Research Study: The Handling of Complaints: Complainants' and Housing Associations' Views*, Research Report 3, 1996, London: Housing Association Tenants Ombudsman Service.

will increase the take-up of mediation and lead to increased satisfaction concerning complaints.[31]

The most substantial piece of research undertaken in the UK on neighbour disputes has already been described in Chapter 12. As part of this research, Jim Dignan and his two colleagues undertook a survey of the work of existing mediation services, devised a standard data-collection system (see Appendix to Chapter 4), provided an overview of the work of local authority housing and environmental health services relating to neighbour disputes, and worked with a small number of case studies to compare costs of mediation services with other ways of handling neighbour disputes.[32]

The research also shows that there is greater scope for the use of mediation, especially to help prevent some of the more intractable cases escalating. This may offer scope for significant savings. However, there was no time in this research for testing whether mediation was perceived as a *better* as well as a cheaper method of handling neighbour disputes. One of the main reasons for doing the cost-effectiveness research was the mood of financial stringency pervading the public sector in the mid 1990s – it was thought this would be the only way of persuading government to look seriously at mediation. A couple of years further on, and with this piece of research completed, the 'missing piece' is research on client satisfaction with mediation – it is no use having something that is 'cheaper' if no one finds it useful!

This is the subject of the next piece of research which Jim Dignan and his colleagues hope to undertake. It will have three main aims: to undertake a comparative consumer survey on the outcomes of different processes, including mediation, for dealing with disputes; to assess the durability of these outcomes; and to undertake a cost-benefit analysis on the data, using methods developed in the previous research, in order to match up costs and benefits.

CONCLUSION

Community and neighbour mediation in the UK has made great strides over the last 10 years, and this looks set to continue. We may even be looking towards a situation when most citizens have access to a mediation service in their local community, or even complete coverage. As mediation becomes a mainstream option, questions of standards, training and accreditation need careful consideration, and further research into mediation is a priority.

---

31 Lickiss, R, *op cit*.
32 Dignan *et al*, *op cit*.

The relationship of mediation services to the state, both at local and national level, will be a crucial issue. Already local authorities are taking the lead in promoting mediation, and providing funding for it; and accreditation as quality assurance is becoming a passport to funding. If mediation is funded by the state, does it become an agent of the state, and is this compatible with grass-roots involvement? On the other hand, totally independent mediation would have a very small funding base. Is the choice one between a flexible, innovative style of mediation, with erratic, private or no funding, and a mainstream, less innovative but financially assured service?

Perhaps our task is to learn from these dilemmas and some of the pitfalls encountered by established mediation services elsewhere, and aim to prevent the 'routinisation' of mediation into a cheap and substandard form of justice. Even if the state is paying the bill, there is still room to retain the 'transformation' ideals of the community mediation movement, and to use mediation to help people gain a greater understanding of each other.

There are many new applications of mediation and many more to be tried – perhaps community mediation services will be the ones to provide the base for these. Resources will always be an issue, but with more and more people involved in mediation, it is to be hoped that its provision will become 'common sense'. In the midst of the intense work needed for its development, we must keep at the forefront of our thinking, that we are talking about ways in which mediation can help neighbours to communicate with each other better, and be empowered to lead happier lives alongside each other.

COMMUNITY MEDIATION SERVICES IN THE UK

This list is alphabetical by town or district within the geographical regions of England, Northern Ireland, Republic of Ireland, Scotland and Wales. London services are listed separately. This list was correct in November 1997.

Information supplied by MEDIATION UK, Alexander House, Telephone Avenue, Bristol, BS1 4BS. Tel: 0117 904 6661, Fax: 0117 904 3331, Email: mediationuk@cix.compulink.co.uk They can be contacted for up to date information.

Ashford Neighbour Conciliation Service

Room 11, Wellington House
14 Church Road
Ashford, Kent TN23 1RE
Telephone 01233 663488

Babergh District Council Mediation Service

Hadleigh
Ipswich
Suffolk IP7 6SJ
Telephone 01473 825750

Northern Devon Community Mediation

Oakenbury
Silford Cross
Bideford
Devon EX39 3BT
Telephone 01237 475280

Bliss Mediation

Eric Tolhurst Centre,
3–13 Quay Road
Blyth,
Tyne & Wear, NE24 2AS
Telephone 01670 540979 Fax 01670 540933

Bolton Neighbour Dispute Service

Adelaide House
Adelaide Street
Bolton BL3 3NY
Telephone 01204 660141 Fax 01204 657210

Bracknell Forest Neighbourhood Mediation Service

PO Box 7810
Crowthorne
Berkshire RG45 6FA
Telephone 01344 772220 Fax: 01344 772048

Bradford Mediation Centre

Ground Floor, City Hall
Bradford
West Yorkshire BD1 1HY
Telephone 01274 751565 Fax 01274 741487

Breckland Neighbour Mediation Service

35 St Nicholas Street
Thetford
Norfolk IP24 1BE
Telephone 01842 764039

Brighton and Hove Mediation Service

c/o 26 Ashburnham Drive
Coldean, Brighton
East Sussex BN1 9AX
Telephone 01273 700812

Bristol Mediation

Alexander House, Telephone Avenue
Bristol BS1 4BS
Telephone 0117 904 3321

Cambridge & District Community Mediation Service

Llandaff Chambers
2 Regent Street
Cambridge CB2 1AX
Telephone 01223 302514

Mediation West Cornwall

PO Box 95
Truro
Cornwall TR3 7YG
Telephone 01736 757872

The Community Safety Mediation Project

4 Honiley Way, Wood End
Coventry
West Midlands CV2 1SN
Telephone 01203 602650

Coventry Mediation Partnership

31 Primrose Hill Street
Hillfields, Coventry CV1 5LY
Telephone 01203 227176

Lin Cronin Mediation (Charges for service)

Sherwood, 35 Berks Hill
Chorleywood
Hertfordshire WD3 5AJ
Telephone 01923 283427

Derby Mediation Service

87 Pear Tree Road
Derby DE23 6QB
Telephone 01332 290918

Mid-Devon Mediation

Langford Bridge House
Newton St Cyres, Exeter
Devon EX5 5AQ
Telephone 01392 851459

South Hams Mediation Scheme

Ridgeways, 2 Lower Warren Road
Kingsbridge
Devon TQ7 1LF
Telephone 01548 853569

Dewsbury & District Community Mediation Service

Field House, 15 Wellington Road
Dewsbury
West Yorkshire WF13 1HF
Telephone and fax 01924 438588

Mediation Dorset

5 Weymouth Avenue, Dorchester
Dorset DT1 1RQ
Telephone and fax 01305 257717

Dudley Mediation Network

Flat 1, St Thomas's Vicarage
King Street, Dudley
West Midlands DY2 8QB
Telephone 01384 238888

Community Mediation Service

100 Garibaldi Street, Grimsby
N E Lincolnshire DN32 7DU
Telephone and fax 01472 251054

Guildford Community Mediation Service

P O Box 747
Guildford
Surrey GU1 2XD
Telephone 01483 301010

Hastings & St Leonards Mediation Service

24 Cornwallis Terrace
Hastings
East Sussex TN34 1EB
Telephone 01424 446808

Herefordshire Neighbourhood Mediation Service

c/o Hereford City Council
Garrick House, Widemarsh Street
Hereford HR4 9EU
Telephone 01432 364692 Fax 01432 353262

New Forest Mediation

c/o New Forest Council Community Service
76a Brookley Road, Brockenhurst
Hampshire SO42 7RA
Telephone 01590 623700 Fax 01590 623960

West Kent Independent Mediation Service

16 High Street
Swanley
Kent BR8 8BG
Telephone 01322 615774

Leeds Community Mediation Service

Oxford Place Centre
Leeds
West Yorkshire LS1 3AX
Telephone 0113 242 4110

Leicester Mediation Service

Unit 7, Royal Arcade
High Street, Leicester
Leicestershire LE1 5YN
Telephone 0116 253 2900 Fax 0116 253 2911

Liverpool Mediation Service

Room 414, Tower Building
22 Water Street
Liverpool L3 1AB
Telephone 0151 227 1374 Fax 0151 227 4014

Luton Mediation

10 Gordon Street
Luton LU1 2QP
Telephone and fax 01582 411822

Maidstone Mediation Scheme

Community Support Centre
Marsham Street
Maidstone, Kent ME14 1EW
Telephone 01622 692843

Mediation Manchester

Room 207 & 208, Gainsborough House
109 Portland Street
Manchester M1 6DN
Telephone 0161 237 3434 Fax 0161 237 2356

Moss Side & Hulme Mediation Service

Flat 204, 41 Old Birley Street
Hulme, Manchester M15 5RF
Telephone 0161 227 9068

Mansfield Tenant Mediation Service

Civic Centre, Chesterfield Road South
Mansfield
Nottinghamshire NG19 7BU
Telephone 01623 656656 ext 3417 Fax 01623 720197

Medway & Gillingham Mediation

Room 6, First Floor
St Bartholomew's Hospital
New Road
Rochester, Kent ME1 1DS
Telephone 01634 832285

Milton Keynes Neighbour Dispute Mediation Service

379 Acorn House
Midsummer Boulevard
Central Milton Keynes MK9 3HP
Telephone 01908 200828

Mole Valley Mediation Service

22 Monks Green, Fetcham
Leatherhead
Surrey KT22 9TW
Telephone 01372 375245

Castle Morpeth Mediation

Tower Buildings
9 Oldgate
Morpeth
Northumberland NE61 1PY
Telephone 01670 510259

Newark & Sherwood District Council

Kelham Hall, Kelham
Nr Newark
Nottinghamshire NG23 5QX
Telephone 01636 605111 ext 562

Resolve (Newbury & District Mediation Service)

PO Box 2503
Reading
Berkshire RG1 5XG
Telephone 0118 961 0464

New Town & South Aston Mediation Scheme

Safety Shop
Units 7–9 Wheeler Street Shopping Precinct
New Town
Birmingham B19 2ER
Telephone 0121 523 0188 Fax 0121 523 0236

Norwich & District Legal Services

The Advice Arcade
4 Guildhall Hill
Norwich
Norfolk NR2 1JH
Telephone 01603 661779 Fax 01603 616166

Mediation Norwich

Queens House, Queens Road
Norwich NR1 3PL
Telephone 01603 629421 Fax 01603 620181

Oxford Community Mediation

75 London Road, Headington
Oxford OX3 9BB
Telephone 01865 742439 Fax 01865 742205

Plymouth Mediation

St Peter's Centre, 18 Hastings Street
Plymouth
Devon PL1 5BA
Telephone 01752 671078

Portsmouth Mediation Service

c/p 3rd Floor, Civic Offices
Guildhall Square, Portsmouth PO1 2AL
Telephone 01705 841303

Preston Area Neighbour Dispute Action (PANDA)

PO Box 10, Birley Street
Preston PR1 2RL
Telephone 01772 558978 Fax 01772 906446

Reigate & Banstead Community Mediation Service

PO Box 187, Reigate
Surrey RH2 0FT
Telephone 01737 248559

Ridgehill Housing Association Mediation

12 Elstree Way
Borehamwood, Herts WD6 1JE
Telephone 0181 235 7000 Fax 0181 235 7290

Rochdale Mediation Service

Newbold Housing Office
Whitley Road, Newbold
Rochdale OL16 5HE
Telephone 01706 867004 Fax 01706 867002

Rugby Mediation Service

Room 41, The Retreat
Newbold Road
Rugby CV 21 2LN
Telephone 01788 533575

Sandwell Mediation Service

79 Birmingham Road
West Bromwich
West Midlands B70 6PX
Telephone 0121 525 4659 Fax: 0121 525 4672

Mediation Sheffield (MESH)

1 Barkers Pool
Sheffield
South Yorkshire S1 1EN
Telephone 0114 275 8791

Sneinton & St Anns Neighbourhood Mediation Service

27–31 Carlton Road
Nottingham NG3 2DG
Telephone 0115 958 9445 Fax 0115 924 3417

Mediation Somerset

Victoria House, Victoria Street
Taunton, Somerset TA1 3FA
Telephone 01823 352210

St Edmundsbury Area Mediation Service (SEAMS)

77b St Johns Street
Bury St Edmunds
Suffolk IP33 1SQ
Telephone 01284 762310 Fax 01284 700676

St Helens Mediation Dispute Service (MEND)

Ashtons Green, Ashtons Green Drive
Parr, St Helens WA9 2AP
Telephone 01744 451545

Sunderland Mediation Service

53 Blackwood Road
Town End Farm, Sunderland SR5 4PT
Telephone 0191 536 5479 Fax 0191 536 6564

Swale Mediation Service

Sanders House, 153 London Road
Sittingbourne
Kent ME10 1PA
Telephone 01795 410817

Walsall Mediation Scheme

1 Butts Street, Butts
Walsall
West Midlands WS4 2BJ
Telephone 01922 37713

MINT – Mediation in North Tyneside

St Luke's Church House
Station Road/Hugh Street
Wallsend
Tyne & Wear NE28 6RL
Telephone 0191 200 7392 Fax 0191 200 7389

Warrington Mediation Service

26 Cairo Street, Warrington
Cheshire WA1 1EH
Telephone and fax 01925 575303

Waverley Community Mediation Service

Scotsgrove, Gonghill Drive
Farnham, Surrey G10 3HG
Telephone 01252 794684

Whitstable Mediation

(also covers Herne Bay & Canterbury)
1 Tankerton Road
Whitstable
Kent CT5 2AB
Telephone and fax 01227 771283

Wolverhampton Neighbourhood Mediation Service

282 Long Ley, Heath Town
Wolverhampton
West Midlands WV10 0HS
Telephone 01902 352322

Resolve Mediation Service

Units 7 & 8 Mobet Building
40 Peart Road, Derwent Howe,
Workington, Cumbria CA14 3YT
Telephone 01900 603229

Worthing & District Mediation Service

Anchor Lodge, Latimer Road
Worthing, West Sussex BN11 5EP
Telephone 01903 260360

Face to Face – Neighbourhood Mediation in York

Yearsley House, Huntington Road
York
North Yorkshire YO3 9DU
Telephone 01904 555200 Fax 01904 555209

UNITE

Offers a service in the following areas:

- Middlesbrough Telephone 01642 311633
- Redcar & Cleveland
- Darlington Telephone 01325 350318
- Hartlepool

Southlands Centre, Ormesby Road

Middlesbrough TS3 OHG

Telephone 01642 311633

LONDON

Bromley Neighbour Mediation Service

Room 14, The Burnhill Business Centre

50 Burnhill Road

Beckenham, Kent BR3 3LA

Telephone 0181 249 6041/2 Fax 0181 249 6006

Camden Mediation Service

11–17 The Marr, Camden Street

London NW1 0HE

Telephone 0171 383 0733 Fax 0171 383 7110

Ealing Neighbour Mediation Service

2 The Green, Ealing

London W5 5DA

Telephone 0181 579 8164 Fax 0181 566 5581

Greenwich Mediation

Valley Mediation Centre

1A Gallon Close, Charlton

London SE7 8SZ

Telephone and fax 0181 858 3014

Hackney Mediation Service

205 Morning Lane
London E9 6JX
Telephone 0181 525 4794 Fax 0181 533 1797

Hammersmith & Fulham (CALM)

Bishop Creighton House
378 Lillie Road, Fulham
London SW6 7PH
Telephone 0171 386 9775 Fax 0171 385 1377

Haringey Mediation Service

Selby Centre, Selby Road
London N17 8JL
Telephone 0181 880 3994

Hounslow Mediation Service

Suite 15, Thanet House
191–195 High Street, Brentford
London TW8 8LB
Telephone 0181 568 5522 Fax 0181 568 5566

Community Action Project

21–22 Peel Precinct, Kilburn (South)
London NW6 5BS
Telephone 0171 372 6544

Kingston Friends Workshop Group

Quaker Meeting House, 78 Eden Street
Kingston upon Thames
Surrey KT1 1DJ
Telephone 0181 547 1197

LAMP (Lewisham Action for Mediation Project)

c/o Evelyn Neighbourhood Office
8 Kingfisher Square (Off Clyde Street)
Deptford
London SE8 5TW
Telephone 0181 691 0733

Lambeth Mediation Service

1 Barrhill Road
London
London SW2 4RJ
Telephone 0181 678 6046

Newham Conflict & Change Project

2a Streatfield Avenue
East Ham
London E6 2LA
Telephone 0181 552 2050

Southwark Mediation Centre

92 Camberwell Road
London SE5 0EG
Telephone 0171 708 4959 Fax 0171 708 5568

Tower Hamlets Mediation Service

The Toby Club, Vawdrey Close
Cleveland Way
London E1 4UA
Telephone 0171 702 8305

Waltham Forest Neighbour Mediation Service

Alpha Business Centre, 60 South Grove
Walthamstow
London E17 7NX
Telephone 0181 509 2320

Wandsworth Independent Mediation Service

c/o WPCC
PO Box 118
London SW18 2PF
Telephone 0181 871 6010

NORTHERN IRELAND

Mediation Network (N Ireland)

74 Dublin Road
Belfast, Northern Ireland BT2 7HP
Telephone 01232 438614

REPUBLIC OF IRELAND

Conflict Resolution Services

95 Stillorgan Wood
Stillorgan
Co Dublin, Republic of Ireland
Telephone and fax 00 35312 884190

SCOTLAND

Community Mediation Dundee

49 Meadowside
Dundee
Scotland DD1 1EQ
Telephone 01382 206406

Edinburgh Community Mediation Project

27 York Place
Edinburgh
Scotland EH1 3HP
Telephone 0131 557 2101

Fife Community Mediation

24 Hill Street
Kirkaldy
Fife, Scotland KY1 1HX
Telephone 01592 597063 Fax 01592 593133

Livingston & District Community Mediation Service

c/o St Kenneth's Community Resource Centre
Ogilvie House, Sinclair Way
Knightsridge, Livingston
Scotland EH54 8HL
Telephone 01506 435118

WALES

Cardiff Mediation

Friends Meeting House
43 Charles Street
Cardiff CF1 4EB
Telephone 01222 382021 Fax 01222 390421

Cyfryngu yn y Canolbarth (Mediation Mid Wales)

Sefton House, Middleton Street
Llandrindod Wells
Powys, Wales LD1 5DG
Telephone 01597 825123

Monmouthshire Mediation

Charter Housing Association
11 Devon Place, Newport
Gwent NP9 4NP
Telephone 01633 212375 Fax 01633 258509

Tawe Afan Nedd (TAN) Mediation Service

20 Craddock Street
Swansea SA1 3AT
Telephone 01792 648916

MEDIATION UK AND ITS MEMBER SERVICES

MEDIATION UK is a network of projects, organisations and individuals interested in mediation and other forms of constructive conflict resolution. It is a registered charity supported by grants and donations. MEDIATION UK is the only umbrella organisation for all initiatives and individuals interested in conflict resolution in the UK.

Currently, in July 1997, it has a membership of 489, of which 178 are organisations and 311 are individuals. One hundred and thirty-five of the organisations are mediation services:

Community/neighbour mediation	97
Victim/offender mediation	30
Conflict resolution work in schools	25

This adds up to more than 135 because some services do more than one kind of work.

MEDIATION – A DEFINITION

Mediation is a process whereby an impartial third party helps two disputing parties to sort out their disagreement. The parties, not the mediator, decide the terms of the agreement.

COMMUNITY MEDIATION SERVICES

The fastest growing area of work is in community and neighbour mediation. The community mediation services are spread throughout the UK.

Almost all use trained volunteers to do the mediation, and volunteers work in pairs, for safety and for maximum effect and learning. Most services have a paid co-ordinator, but a few run entirely on volunteers. Some cover large districts while others concentrate in a more proactive way on small troublesome housing estates.

How a community mediation service operates

Most community mediation services take referrals from community agencies and disputants themselves. Mediators visit the first party (who has requested help) and then if appropriate, contact the second party, and visit if welcomed. If both parties wish, the case proceeds to mediation. Sometimes just listening to the parties helps them to solve their dispute on their own. Of the 20% that result in face-to-face mediation, about 90% result in agreements which hold over several months. Many agreements are also reached by 'shuttle mediation', with mediators acting as go-betweens for parties who do not actually meet. The mediators often follow up both parties after three months or so.

The most common complaints from neighbours are about noise (60%). The noise can be from music, hi-fi, DIY, dogs, children, TV, talking or household appliances. Other disputes concern boundaries, children, rubbish, harassment, abuse and other annoyances.

SCHOOLS WORK

Some member projects specialise in schools work, and some community mediation services develop a 'schools group'. They go into schools and teach children how to resolve conflict in non-violent ways. Several of these projects are now also training children to be peer mediators for playground quarrels. There is increasing interest in this work, especially in its potential to reduce bullying.

VICTIM/OFFENDER WORK

These projects bring victims and offenders together to discuss the criminal offence that has occurred, to help mutual understanding and see if appropriate reparation can take place, eg paying the costs of damage, mending a wall, and/or an apology. These services may operate at the pre-court, court or post-sentence stage.

OTHER PROJECTS

There are many other interesting member projects, such as these developing conflict resolution through drama, or doing prejudice reduction work. They are all concerned with helping people to resolve conflicts in a constructive way.

For further information contact:

MEDIATION UK
Alexander House
Telephone Avenue
Bristol BS1 4BS

Tel: 0117 904 6661
Fax: 0117 904 3331
Email: mediationuk@cix.compulink.co.uk

NOTES ON CONTRIBUTORS

Gavin R Beckett began his research on conflict transformation whilst reading Social and Political Sciences at Cambridge University. He graduated from Bradford University's Department of Peace Studies in 1997 with a PhD thesis that explored the theory and practice of conflict transformation in Croatia. He trained as a community mediator with Cambridge and District Mediation Service in 1993, and as a victim/offender mediator with the Bradford Mediation and Reparation Service in 1994, with whom he worked as a sessionally paid mediator. He trained community mediators for the Bradford Community Mediation Service in 1995 and worked for them as a volunteer mediator. Since 1996 he has been a volunteer mediator with Bristol Mediation Service. Gavin has been a member of MEDIATION UK since 1992 and has worked with them on a number of projects, including the 1994 *Directory of Mediation and Conflict Resolution Services* and the *Training Manual in Community Mediation Skills*. He is currently a member of the MEDIATION UK Accreditation Committee and the Bristol Mediation Development Group. Since December 1996 he has been working as a housing officer for Bristol City Council.

May Curtis has had a career in education, training and staff development, both in local government and the voluntary sector. She is the author of a number of 'in-house' guides and pamphlets including: 'Developing Training Programmes'; 'Using Standards in Management Development'; and a manual for the training of sessional youth workers. May has had extensive experience of steering accreditation and endorsement processes, establishing quality assurance procedures for assessment, and writing occupational standards. She has served on a national panel for the endorsement of Regional Accrediting Bodies for youth and community training and is the external moderator for professional placements on the degree programme at St Mark and St John College, Exeter University. She works as an independent consultant and is currently MEDIATION UK's Accreditation Co-ordinator.

Jim Dignan is a senior lecturer in law at Sheffield University where he teaches courses on penology, criminology and legal systems. He has co-authored a book on the English Penal System (published by Sage) and is currently working on a book on comparative penology and another looking at the future of the criminal justice system beyond the millennium. Between 1987 and 1990 he evaluated the Kettering Adult Reparation Bureau which was the first English victim/offender scheme dealing exclusively with adult offenders, and since then he has written various pieces on the subject of restorative justice. He has recently completed the first systematic British evaluation of the cost-effectiveness of mediation compared with more conventional approaches in relation to neighbour disputes and maintains an active involvement in this field of research.

Marian Liebmann trained as a teacher, social worker and art therapist. She has worked in education, social work and the criminal justice system, and has been involved in community, victim/offender and schools mediation. She was a member of the group that worked on setting up Bristol Mediation from 1987 until 1991. From 1991 to 1995, she was the Director of MEDIATION UK, and now works part-time as Projects Adviser for MEDIATION UK. She convened the working groups that produced the *Training Manual in Community Mediation Skills* and the *Community Mediation Video*. She has written/edited several books in the fields of art therapy, mediation and conflict resolution and contributed to many others. She has a special interest in arts approaches to conflict and runs workshops in this area.

John C Patrick is a freelance trainer and training adviser to the Milton Keynes Neighbour Dispute Mediation Service. A former senior probation officer, he has been working as a freelance trainer since 1992 and has wide experience of training in various settings. He was involved in the setting up of the Milton Keynes Neighbour Dispute Mediation Service. He was a member of the groups which produced the MEDIATION UK *Training Manual in Community Mediation Skills*, and the *Community Mediation Video*. He is currently a member of a working party on the development of MEDIATION UK's training policy. He has considerable experience of mediation in the divorce court as well as in neighbour disputes.

Marion Wells is a community mediator and trainer. She chaired Bristol Mediation for five years and is currently its vice-chair. She was part of the working group that produced the *Community Mediation Video*. She convenes MEDIATION UK's Accreditation Committee and helped to get national recognition through the National Open College Network of a training programme based on MEDIATION UK's *Training Manual in Community Mediation Skills*. She also works as a tutor for the National Association of Citizens Advice Bureaux.

FURTHER READING

Acland, AF, *A Sudden Outbreak of Common Sense, Managing Conflict Through Mediation*, 1990, London: Hutchinson Business Books

Acland, AF, *Resolving Disputes without Going to Court*, 1995, London: Century Business Books

Augsburger, D, *Conflict Mediation Across Cultures*, 1992, Louisville, Kentucky: Westminster/John Knox Press

Beer, JE, *The Mediator's Handbook*, 1997, Philadelphia, US: Friends Suburban Project. Available from Jon Carpenter Publishing, The Spendlove Centre, Charlbury, Oxfordshire

Bines, W, Kemp P, Please, N and Radley, R, *Managing Social Housing*, 1993, London: HMSO

Bristol Mediation, *Good Practice Guidelines for Mediators*, first published 1994, updated regularly, Bristol: Bristol Mediation

Bush, RAB and Folger, JP, *The Promise of Mediation, Responding to Conflict Through Empowerment and Recognition*, 1994, San Francisco: Jossey Bass

Chartered Institute of Housing, 'Neighbour Nuisance: Ending the Nightmare' (1995) *Good Practice Briefing* Issue 3, December, Coventry: Chartered Institute of Housing

Cornelius, C and Faire, S, *Everyone Can Win*, 1989, Sydney: Simon and Schuster

Crawley, J, *Neighbours, Nuisance and Mediation: A Study for Hackney Housing*, 1994, from Plus Training, Lane Farm, Heydon Lane, Heydon, Royston, Hertfordshire SG8 8TL

Department of the Environment, *Bothered by Noise? What you can do about it. A Guide to Noise Complaints Procedure*, 1994, Department of the Environment

Department of the Environment, *Mediation: Benefits and Practice – Information for those considering mediation as a way of resolving community disputes*, 1994, Department of the Environment

Dignan, J, *Community Mediation Service General Survey 1995*, 1995, Sheffield: University of Sheffield. Available from MEDIATION UK

Dignan, J, Sorsby, A, and Hibbert J, *Neighbour Disputes: Comparing the Cost Effectiveness of Mediation and Alternative Approaches*, 1996, Sheffield: Centre for Criminological and Legal Research, University of Sheffield. Available from MEDIATION UK

Eldridge, J, Madigan, R and Daglian, S, *Neighbour Disputes: The Response of Glasgow's Housing Department to Tenants' Complaints*, 1982, Glasgow: Sociology Department, University of Glasgow

Farrant, S et al, *Managing Neighbour Complaints in Social Housing: A Handbook for Practitioners*, 1993, Aldbourne: Aldbourne Associates

Faulkes, W, *Mediation as a Crime Prevention Strategy. Conference Paper 1991*, 1991, Bristol: MEDIATION UK

Feeley, MM (ed), *Neighbourhood Justice: Assessment of an Emerging Idea*, 1982, New York: Longman

Ferguson, A, *Housing and Anti-Social Behaviour – The Way Ahead*, 1994, Coventry: Chartered Institute of Housing

Hinton, A, *Factors in Neighbour Disputes. Conference Paper 1993*, 1993, Bristol: MEDIATION UK

Hughes, D, *Environmental Law*, 1992, London: Butterworth

Institute of Environmental Health Officers, *Environmental Health Statistics 1995/96*, 1997, London: IEHO

Karn, V, Lickiss, R, Hughes, D and Crawley, J, *Neighbour Disputes: Responses by Social Landlords*, 1993, Coventry: Institute of Housing

Kemp, C, Norris, C and Fielding, NG, *Negotiating Nothing: Police Decision-making in Disputes*, 1992, Aldershot: Avebury

Lederach, JP, *Preparing for Peace: Conflict Transformation Across Cultures*, 1995, Syracuse: Syracuse University Press

Legg, H, *Creating a Climate of Trust: Time to Listen, Bristol Mediation Southmead Project 1991–95 Report*, 1997, Bristol: Bristol Mediation

Lickiss, R, Giddings, P, Gregory, R and Karn, V, *Setting up the Housing Association Tenants Ombudsman Service: The Debate and the Outcome*, 1996, Research Report 2, London: HATOS

Lord Chancellor's Department, *Resolving Disputes Without Going to Court*, 1995, London: Lord Chancellor's Department. Scottish and Welsh versions, 1996, available from Scottish and Welsh Offices respectively

Lord Chancellor's Department, *Legal Aid – Targeting Need*, 1995, London: HMSO

McCarthy, P, Simpson, B, Hill, M, Walker, J and Carlyon, J, *Grievances, Complaints and Local Government*, 1992, Avebury: Aldershot

Mackay, RE and Moody, SR, with Walker, F, *Neighbour Disputes in the Criminal Justice System*, 1994, Edinburgh: Scottish Office Central Research Unit. Available from HMSO

Mackay, RE and Moody, SR, 'Diversion of Neighbourhood Disputes to Community Mediation' (1996) 35 *Howard Journal of Criminal Justice* 4 November

Marshall, T, *Reparation, Conciliation and Mediation*, 1984, Home Office Research and Planning Unit, Paper 27, London: HMSO

Marshall, T and Walpole, M, *Bringing People Together: Mediation and Reparation Projects in Great Britain*, 1985, Home Office Research Planning Unit, Paper 33, London: HMSO

Marshall, T, *Community Disorders and Policing*, 1992, London: Whiting and Birch. Also available from Mediation UK

Matthews, R, *Informal Justice*, 1988, London: Sage

Michel, P, *The Noisy Neighbour Survival Guide*

Moody, SR and Mackay, RE, *Greens Guide to Alternative Dispute Resolution in Scotland*, 1995, Edinburgh: W Green/Sweet & Maxwell

Moore, C, *The Mediation Process: Practical Strategies for Resolving Conflict*, 1986, San Francisco: Jossey Bass

National Consumer Council, *Civil Law and The Public*, 1995, London: National Consumer Council

Neighbour Noise Working Party, *Review of the Effectiveness of Neighbour Noise Controls*, 1995, London: DoE, Welsh Office, Scottish Office

OPUS, *Newham Conflict & Change Project, Evaluation Report*, 1989, London: OPUS

Opinion Research Business, *Good Neighbours Survey*, 1995, Perth: General Accident

Quine, C, Hutton, J and Reed, B, *Community Mediation of Disputes Between Neighbours, Report of an Evaluation Study on the work of Southwark Mediation Centre 1987–89*, 1990, London: The Grubb Institute

Scott, S (ed), *Neighbour Disputes – Is There An Answer?*, 1991, Edinburgh: TPAS Scotland

Scottish Office Environment Department, *Anti-Social Behaviour on Housing Estates: Consultation Paper on Probationary Tenancies*, 1995, Edinburgh: Scottish Office

Simpson, R, *Promise and Pragmatism: Community Mediation into the Nineties. Conference Paper 1992*, 1992, Bristol: MEDIATION UK.

Smith, R (ed), *Achieving Civil Justice: Appropriate Dispute Resolution for the 1990s*, 1996, London: Legal Action Group

Taylor, M, Russell, F and Ball R, *Good Practice in Housing Management: Literature Review*, 1992, Edinburgh: Scottish Office

Tebay, S, Cumberbatch, G and Graham, N, *Disputes between Neighbours*, 1986, Birmingham: Aston University

The Right Honourable Lord Woolf, *Access to Justice*. Interim and Final Reports to the Lord Chancellor on the civil justice system in England and Wales, 1995 and 1996, London: Woolf Inquiry Team

USER Research Ltd, *Feedback Research Study: The Handling of Complaints: Complainants' and Housing Associations' Views*, Research Report 3, 1996, London: Housing Association Tenants Ombudsman Service

Also available from MEDIATION UK:

TB2, *Accreditation Pack*, including MEDIATION UK Practice Standards, £10.00

CL3, *Boundary Disputes*, £1.00

CL7, *Community Mediation Services List*, £1.00

CL8, *Community Mediation Resources List*, £1.00

TV1, *Community Mediation Video, Part 1 Mediation in the Community, Part 2 Training in Communtity Mediation Skills*, £46.50, £20.00 discount for members

CL5, *Dealing Directly with Your Neighbours*, £1.00

GB1, *Directory of Mediation and Conflict Resolution Services 1996*, complete list of services in the UK, £10.00

CB1, *Guide to Starting a Community Mediation Service*, £12.00

TB4, *Handbook for the Training Programme in Community Mediation Skills*, £17.00 (£3.00 discount for members)

CL2, *How to Start a Community Mediation Service* (leaflet) £1.00

TB1, *MEDIATION UK Practice Standards*, £2.50

CL6, *Neighbours' Quarrels. Broadsheet prepared for Channel Four Television*, £2.00

CL4, *Noise from Neighbours*, £1.00

TB3, *Training Manual in Community Mediation Skills*, £44.50 (£10 discount for members)

CL1, *What is Mediation?* (leaflet) £1.00.

GL2, *Mediation Takes a FIRM Hold* (leaflet) History of first 10 years, £1.00

INDEX